DON'T GO AWAY MAD

and Two Other Plays

WILLIAM SAROYAN

Don't Go Away Mad

AND TWO OTHER PLAYS

Sam Ego's House
A Decent Birth, A Happy Funeral

HARCOURT, BRACE AND COMPANY · NEW YORK

first edition

For my son Aram

Contents

Introduction

THE LURE of the theatre appears to have frequently bothered writers, for it is scarcely possible to read a biography of one and not discover that he had hopes of writing a play, or that he was trying to write one, or that he had written one but could not find a producer for it, or that he had written one, had had it produced and had watched it die on the stage opening night.

I am thinking of writers who enjoyed fame: Charles Dickens, Henry James, Mark Twain, to name a few. These men were probably not after more fame. They probably had all they could abide. If they were after money, they were certainly not after it as earnestly as they were after something else.

What was this other thing they were after? My guess is that it was a longing to satisfy the need to escape from the isolation of the writer who writes solely for the printed page—to escape from themselves, to step out of the study onto the stage. Generally speaking, this isolation is deeply cherished, and yet sooner or later even the most retiring writer wants a holiday from it. And the best way to have such a holiday has often seemed to be to write a play and see it performed, to be in the theatre among the people.

Were they also after something else? Were they after, for instance, a child-like pleasure, the pleasure of watching other children do as one has instructed them to do? Were they after the founding of a church, the church which every playwright creates when a play he has written is produced?—one man's own church which at its best has a very short and harmless life, and yet is needed again and again by the enormous numbers of people who are faithful to the theatre?

Were they after an excuse to meet actresses? Were they

thinking along lines of fun as well as along the more readily admissible lines?—to achieve through playwriting, for instance, a more acceptable belief in one's understanding of reality? To expand, to set free, the reality one created and by which one began to find one's self held prisoner? The good poet, the expert novelist, even the exact philosopher must often glance at his work and wonder, "Yes, all well and good, but where's the blood, tissue and breathing of it right *now?*" To see the art *happening* rather than only to know that it had been made to happen.

In any case, whatever they were after, they didn't often find it. Either they were discouraged and did not finish their plays or they were discouraged after the production of a play which did not impress very many people.

Or is it this? Is it inevitable for everybody to be theatrical, each in his own way, even when the means of being theatrical is anti-theatricalness? Could anyone be more theatrical, for instance, than the shy man? Isn't shyness even more attention-drawing than boldness? Sleep and death would appear to be the only truly untheatrical forms of human behavior, but even these forms are not altogether exempt, for there is a whole tradition of dying and saying something original at the last minute. I can't remember just now what any of the great men are supposed to have said just before they died, but I found and read a list of perhaps three or four hundred of these sayings in an old almanac when I was eleven or twelve; and I do remember that I couldn't wait to die so I could have my chance. For awhile I thought of saying, "Well, what the hell, I did my best." Then when I was seventeen or eighteen I had it, "That's it, boys." Or, "O.K., take it away." For a time, it was the four-letter word which is so right for so much in our culture but which everybody is afraid to use in polite literature.

At any rate, it would appear to be true that whoever does not give over to dying immediately, by that very fact demonstrates a certain theatricality, for survival itself is theatrical, and no one need be surprised that staying alive is basically a matter of acting. How could it be anything else?

Watch the people you see in newsreels, the big people, the stars, so to speak: the politicians, the ecclesiastics, the rich men, the lucky nonentities who've just won fifty thousand dollars, the labor leaders, the industrialists, the cops, the criminals, the athletes, anybody the newsreels happen to notice. You will notice that they are all acting. It is the style nowadays for inept acting—or non-acting acting—to seem more appealing than artful acting or acting acting, which in the theatre is called hambone. But the biggest ham of all is the one who affects non-acting acting. The minute he opens his mouth he is beat, he is exposed, and even if it turns out that he actually appears to believe he is sincere, it does him little good.

Is there, then, no behavior that is not theatrical? I believe there is no such behavior; it is simply that the acting of some people is more tolerable than that of others. The nearest thing to pure or non-ham behavior is the behavior of people under stress of extreme emotion, and the only reason such behavior is non-ham is that it is impersonal, animal and pathetic, even when it turns out that what has been done may be placed in the category of the heroic. It is not natural for man to do heroic things, but it is natural for him sometimes to get excited and to behave helplessly. A lot of people go out of their way to be nice, to do kind things for other people, or to perform deeds of daring and danger, but these people are amateurs. Human beings don't know enough about themselves, or don't amount to enough, to act truly great, truly natural, or truly artful.

Is there, then, anything the matter with ordinary acting? There is. It is ordinary. It has no style. We know it is not possible for any man to be altogether whole, so the only thing that can save him is style.

We are concerned now with the theatre within the theatre: the small theatre. That is, the building with the stage and auditorium brought alive with people come at a given time to see something someone has written and others have designed into a dramatic flow of anywhere from ninety minutes to a hundred and eighty. The make-believe of the contemporaneous multitudes which inhabit the world has provided a playwright with anywhere from two to two hundred characters, and this make-believe is worked upon and put into a time-frame of another kind of make-believe. The result is a play. In America the running time—with one or more recess periods included—is generally from 8:30 to 11 P.M., a matter of only two and a half hours. The play has a beginning and an end, which the faithful are comforted by: start and stop: get involved and get out of it: go to the theatre, see the play, get up and go home, and before morning act out three plays of your own: three plays generally composed of two parts boredom, one part sleep.

The professional actor is a real problem, and has a real problem: the problem of having twice as much confusion to deal with as the non-professional actor, or the human being who gets his bread and lore out of being his own hero. But the fact that a good many professional actors have become national and sometimes international figures—enjoying fame of a romantic or even intellectual order—suggests that a devotion to acting alone can bring about startling results. It is not inconceivable that in time the most important positions in the world will be cast from the ranks of professional actors, as small parts are now cast.

Actors require audiences, but in the nature of things it is not possible for an audience not to exist for everybody, for there is little difference between performing for the everlasting witness and performing for one's self. It is in fact much the same thing. In short, we are watched, and being watched we are helpless not to perform in one manner or another. We are watched by the witness, we are watched by other human beings whom we in turn watch, we are watched by those we know or by strangers, and we are watched by ourselves.

The autobiography, or the autobiographical note, written or spoken, is acting. Praying is. Being humble is. Trying to behave decently is. The writing of poetry is acting, and poetry itself is drama. A poem, I mean to say, is theatre, it is a play. And so it is with a short story, an essay, or a novel. The intent is always the same: to entertain or astonish or impress the witness, one's self and one's kind. By which I mean to say that it is perfectly understandable that writers who achieve success in one form of writing wish to achieve success in writing for the theatre, also.

From the little I know about the theatre I cannot easily understand the failure of a man who was such a skilful and self-conscious actor—Mark Twain. The failure of Henry James on the other hand is not difficult to understand, for his acting was interior and he was fearful of stepping out in any sense. Delicate thinking, an earnest and cautious sensibility in action, may some day be possible to communicate dramatically to an audience from the stage of a theatre, but it isn't being done just now.

Still, I have always believed, and still believe, that anything can be put across effectively—no, *irresistibly*—on a stage.

In my opinion when all is said and done it is the witness, the audience, which makes the play. It is the audience which performs the play and not the other way around, or at any rate not solely the other way around. And of course there are plays which are good or great, and plays which are not; but while a good or great play is one which many people find it possible to perform, there are also many more plays which many more people find it possible to perform which are neither good nor great; and in this exists much of the mischief of the small theatre as well as of the large one.

The condition of a given audience determines whether or not it will be able to perform a given play. When part of the condition of an audience, for instance, is that it believes it is afraid of a political or economic system, such as Capitalism, and a perfectly good play about the problem of trying to get a little nearer to the truth, and also about human beings who believe they are Capitalists, is presented to such an audience, the play itself may very well be theatrically effective and morally sound and satisfying and still go unperformed by that audience.

Now, a playwright, even without giving the matter very much thought, will not generally find himself working hard to write a play which he is quite sure *his* audience will not be happy to perform for him. But there are playwrights, there are men, there are actors who either resist the dictatorship of their audience or insist upon trying to liberate their audience from its prejudices. Such a playwright may be mistaken about the importance of what he is about, but as it is never a mistake to believe there is always more to know about everything and that it is desirable to go after this additional truth, this does not matter.

It would do no harm for those actors who perform by means of creative language—all men who think creatively—to deny themselves the pleasure and honor of writing for one year out of every three in order to work with men of science; and for men with whom realistic thinking has been continuous for years—scientists and the better philosophers—to move over for one year out of three into the realm of creative thinking. For while specialization is inevitable and desirable, it is also desirable for one kind of thinking and expression to overlap and be blended with another kind; and in the end for *all* kinds to become one kind: the kind which will tend to give meaning, comfort, confidence, health, zest and perhaps even dignity to a maximum number of human beings. Of course every man is forever entitled to resist anything he chooses to resist.

The grand uselessness of man is well-known to men who think in grand terms. In a predictable amount of time this earth will burn out and be finished forever, and with it will go man and his small achievement. This circumstance has comforted famous men in their old age, or when they have been on the brink of failure, death, or belittlement; and it has startled and annoyed small men who feel the need to believe that everything about them goes on forever. It would appear, however, that both the comfort and the amazement are irrelevant, for if all men had only another year to live that would not alter the problem of living in any important way, and writers do not write in order to be remembered longer than farmers, scientists do not search after truth all their lives in order to be famous ten years or ten hundred after they have died: they write and they search because that is the way for them to spend their time while they are alive, because that helps them to enjoy or tolerate themselves and others while they are alive, because writing and searching is for them *living*. And there can never be any argument against putting the accident of presence on this earth to use by staying here as long as it makes sense, or as long as anybody wishes to discover if it cannot be fun. There can be no argument against staying alive for its own poor sake.

The lure of the theatre, the lure of living, the lure of truth, the lure of fun has bothered this writer all his life—the lure of love, of fame, of money, of importance—for I was always theatrical, and wherever I happened to be there also was the theatre, and I could not resist it.

Here in this book are three more of my plays. As always, I am every character in every play. I am, that is, until the plays are produced and amateur or professional actors take over the various roles and each character in each play becomes the creation of an actor on a stage, and the creation of actors in the audience. That is how it is. It is not any other way than that, and not with myself alone, but with all of us. That is the story.

Or rather I was for awhile every character in every play. Slowness and poverty of all kinds and in all dimensions have always been my enemies: boredom and miserliness, ineptitude and caution. Hence, my profession, writing. I am sometimes asked, "Why do you write?" God help me, I write to show off. But writing is still for me the best and most honorable profession of all. There are times, however, when I am not able to show off. At such times I'll be damned if I know why I write. Maybe it's because I hate to believe I'm sick or half-dead; because I want to get better; because writing is my therapy.

In short, since I must act whether I will or no, I prefer to act alive, I prefer to believe that that is the proper way for me to act.

I long ago became resigned to the truth that my thinking is unskilled, haphazard and swift. Still, I've got to take my thinking as I find it and go about my business. If I think with my feet, as I probably do, it's better than no thinking at all, and I won't go out of my way to belittle such thinking. I have always done the best I have known how to do, and do not feel I need to apologize for what I have done.

My intention here is to give anybody who happens to be interested three of my plays to read.

Plays as such do not make easy reading. They are certainly not as easy to read as novels. For one thing, the reader is asked to keep track of the action on the stage by reading directions which are generally printed in italics, and this can become a chore instead of a pleasure. Still, I believe plays by certain playwrights—myself included—are as much for reading as for beholding in action on a stage. And I believe there is the same kind of pleasure in the reading of these three plays as in the reading of anything of mine. If you can abide my writing at all, you will probably not have too difficult a time with these plays, and may Heaven reward you for your patience.

San Francisco, August 31, 1949

DON'T GO AWAY MAD

A Play in Two Acts
and Four Scenes

PREFACE

IN NOVEMBER of 1947 my son Aram, then four years old, invented a character whom he called Poseyo, about whom he said he was going to write a play. Several days later he reported that he had not had very good luck in the writing of the play and asked if I would write it for him. We lived at that time in San Francisco on a street called Taraval in a house meant to contain two small families in two small flats, with a common yard, staircase, and basement, but I had bought the house for my family alone, and used the upper flat as my workroom. I told my son that I would be glad to write his play for him and went upstairs to do so. The play was written in an hour or so.

After dinner that night I read the play to him and he said that it was not what he had had in mind. He had had in mind a real play, a long play, the kind that I myself, as he had heard, sometimes wrote. I told him that I had not known that that was the kind of play he had had in mind and that I would see what I could do about it.

The next day I started the whole thing over again, expecting to write a full-length play in certainly not more than six or seven days, but one day went along to another, I added a little to the play each day, there were interruptions of the sort usual in families, but at last after about a month the play was finished, and I told him so. He asked to have a look at it, so I took him upstairs and showed him the manuscript. It didn't look like very much. It was seventy or eighty sheets of paper covered with typing and corrections in pen and ink. He examined some of the sheets, then said, "Let's go to the ocean and walk." He was bored to death.

That was the first version of the play. I sent the play off to be typed and when it came back I went over it and saw that

3

it needed more work. There was a second version, a third, a fourth, and finally a fifth and final version. The play was originally called *The Incurables*. Then it was called *Golden Gate and Alcatraz*. Finally *Don't Go Away Mad*.

I feel that my son wrote it, for I know I would never have done so had he not invented Poseyo, had he not asked me to write a play about Poseyo for him, and had he not rejected the play I wrote in one hour. I wrote the play for him because I love him and because I wanted to know if I could take a character who was nothing more than a name invented by a small boy and turn it into a play. But Poseyo was a jolly man to my son, and whenever he spoke of him it was with laughter in his voice and jumping in his body. That is, he laughed and danced whenever he remembered his friend. I believe I began to write the play intending to capture some of that joy, but the result was something else again, as the reader will see. My son is a serious man, and like such men he is full of laughter. It is the best laughter one will ever hear in this world, being simultaneously heartrefreshing and heartbreaking. Perhaps that is why the play turned out the way it did, though who will ever know why anything turns out the way it does? Who will ever know that with accuracy?

The remark "Don't go away mad" came back to memory while I was revising the second version of the play, and it amused me so much and seemed so apt for a play with such a bleak theme, that I could not resist flooding the entire play with the conceit and nonchalance of the remark. There was a girl twenty years ago in San Francisco whom I adored because I didn't believe anybody had ever before been so beautiful, but one evening when I called on her I found her jitterbugging all over the parlor with an automobile mechanic I had never before known existed. He was not a poet, I mean to say. I was deeply hurt and was not able to conceal it, for after a moment when I turned to go—I hadn't sat—the girl laughed gaily, "Don't go away mad!"

But the damage was done, I was mad, and that's how I went away. She didn't marry the mechanic either, as it turned out, however; she married a jeweler with a thin moustache, and

the next time I saw her, two years later, she was walking through
the slums with him, pushing a baby carriage, and I was aston-
ished to notice that she was short, fat, and nothing at all like
the most beautiful woman in the world I had believed her to
be. Hence, I was grateful to her for having thrown the remark
after me, for had she not done so, I believe I would have gone
back to see if I could argue her into not throwing her life away
on a mechanic, and had I done so I might have been successful
and had her all to myself.

My plays are criticised by the better critics, or at any rate
by the ones who seem most to cherish truth and the theatre,
for two things: carelessness and an air of optimism which seems
false to them. Mr. Eric Bentley has noticed in *The Playwright
as Thinker* both of these faults. Have I an answer for the
critic? I have, but first of all I must say that the charges appear to be justified; and I must remark that when the charges
became known to me I found it impossible not to examine my
work carefully and not to feel that I must henceforth seek to
improve, for I felt this critic was intelligent and sound, and
therefore could not be ignored. It is in order, that is to say,
for a creative writer to learn from a critical writer; it is in fact
in order for him to seek to learn from anybody; but one has to
select carefully the criticism to take seriously and by which
perhaps to achieve improvement.

My work *is* often careless. I believe in carelessness. An altogether careful dramatic literature would soon be tiresome, I
think. A careless play which fails may nevertheless succeed in
liberating playwrighting a little for other playwrights. Now, the
carelessness that I am thinking of may not be the carelessness
Mr. Bentley had in mind. I am thinking of an interior carelessness, not a technical carelessness. By interior I mean creative:
that is to say, the carelessness which would appear to be more
nearly natural than carefulness. I am thinking, in short, of a
deliberate carelessness. Let me see if I can illustrate what I
mean by this carelessness. A man says to a woman, "I love
you." That is carefulness. Or he says, "For all I know, I love
you." That is carelessness. As lines to be said in a play one is
certainly as good as the other. In context one is as valid and as

accurate as the other, but the careful line, though dramatically more convenient for the playwright, is actually the more irresponsible of the two. To go on, a man who seems to be in love with a woman says to her, "Let me make you happy." That is carefulness. Or he says, "Let's walk to 45th Street, to the Caramel Corn place, and breathe the smell a few minutes." That's carelessness, but in my opinion the careful line means nothing and the careless one means drama. But these illustrations prove nothing.

My writing is careless because it is my writing, and that's the end of it. If and when my writing stops being careless, then it will no longer be careless, that's all. In short, to put it carelessly, one cannot ask an Armenian to be an Englishman.

There is probably a better case for the charge of false optimism, but at the same time I am afraid my accounting for the existence of this embarrassing element in my work is going to be even less satisfactory than my accounting for the carelessness.

First of all, as I have already said, when the chips are down, as the saying is, every man in the world, including a playwright, is helpless, and he does what he must, what he can't help doing. If it turns out that he does something shabby, well, that's the truth and the man had better become resigned to it, for how shabby should any of us ever permit ourselves to get? Refusal to accept the truth—if we've gotten hold of it and we're sure we have and we're sure it *is* the truth—is perhaps the shabbiest behavior of all, and without a doubt the most common, the most universal, the most pathetic, and in some cases the most magnificent. This refusal to accept the truth is in fact, as almost everybody knows, the basis of tragedy, in slow life as in swift art.

I believe the word optimism is out of order as an identification of what it is in my work with which Mr. Bentley finds fault. But whatever the accurate word is for it, I am willing to go along for a moment with the theory that it is false.

The reader must understand that what we are after here is a clear, honest and decent *way-of-seeking-the-truth* because we believe that nothing is more important than to achieve this way of seeking the truth. The truth is damned elusive and almost impossible to pin down, except by blockheads, and I shall not pretend that we shall pin it down here. I may permit myself to believe only that perhaps a decent way of seeking it, of getting a little nearer to it, may be achieved.

To begin with, then, let me accept that my work frequently contains a false optimism. In other words, people and events turn out better than they appear to have a right to do, or even the capacity to do. Out of ignorance and desperation, poverty and pain, for instance, emerges intelligence and grace, humor and resignation, decency and integrity.

Why? the critic wants to know. Who says so? If you subtract, in other words, thirty-nine from forty, how do you get a hundred?

Well, it is here that I am helpless. I don't know why or how, precisely, this sort of thing happens, but I do know that it does happen, and that I feel it is right for it to happen, although I know I am seldom equal to the job of making it seem *unquestionably* right—which is a matter of skill.

To sum up, and to move along, I don't seem to be able to help it. The facts and figures are against the results I get, but I know I am not kidding and I know there is an effective and acceptable way to get the results I get, and that it is right for me to seek to find this way, and that the results are not wrong, the way I got them was wrong.

In the first version of *Don't Go Away Mad*, for instance, the stage was littered at the end with the dead. There were planned murders and accidental murders. Being an allegory, I thought that this was accurate. But when I read the play carefully it seemed to me that this was accurate as arithmetic alone, and false as art.

Despair overwhelms everybody, but for how long? If it is for an instant now and then, if it is for years now and then, for centuries now and then, the fact remains that despair is never by itself *all* of the story whether in an individual or in an entire people; despair may dominate, it may qualify and color everything else, but everything else is also always there; and it would be inaccurate, though it would make for easier playwrighting, to pretend that this were not so.

All life ends in death—this is basic; but is it any less basic that death is known only by hearsay and that art is receivable only by those who are not yet dead, and that as long as men are not yet dead the problem of how to live in order to become resigned to dying is the basic problem? Therefore, I rewrote the ending of the play. There was pessimism in the original ending, but this too was false.

The trouble is that I know what Mr. Bentley means by false optimism—if he actually said such a thing, if I myself have not condensed what he said and put it into these words. I know what he means, and I know the existence of it in my work is a serious fault. I seem to insist that people are good, that living is good, that decency is right, that good is not only achievable but inevitable—and there does not appear to be any justification for this. At least, not in the terms of my own work. In short, the idea is all right but I don't know how to put it over. This is criticism that I accept, for I know I have failed to put it over. It's worth putting over, it's worth trying to put over, it's necessary for me to try to put it over, but I just haven't learned how to do it yet. How to do it and still achieve right art, proper art, purposeful art, good art, meaningful art, helpful art, irresistible art—that is what I hope to learn.

The subject of *Don't Go Away Mad* is the human creature. The play is an examination of who he *thinks* he is, what he thinks he's about, how he thinks he is to achieve what he thinks he is about, and finally how I think he actually achieves or fails to achieve what he thinks he is about. The play fails, but it is a good try. I think it fails because it is not yet in our natures to succeed except in the easiest kind of tasks; but the reader must understand that I regard as failures the finest works in literature, and even in science. There is not in fact any such thing as success, there cannot be, and what's more there need not be. There can only be essay and effort, great failure or small failure. The cult of success has always plagued the American. Measurement and comparison (of the irrelevant) has always preoccupied him. No other cult or preoccupation could possibly put an entire people into greater spiritual ill-health or assure them of a more terrible ultimate disillusionment and collapse. We are not different, we are not better, we are not superior. We are in fact ignorant, and our thinking is obsolete. It has not moved forward from the Declaration of Independence, which certainly could not have been intended to be a halt to thinking, a penitentiary for it, but was obviously meant to be the first declaration of its kind, to be amended, extended, and succeeded by as many more declarations as new circumstances (unforeseeable at that time) happened to arise. There is no such thing as the old time religion, for there is no such thing as the old time. There is always the present world, the present time, the present people, and the present problems; and it is a sorry creature which insists upon thinking with the intelligence of the dead. The relative best in thinking is entitled to stand as such only as long as it is not surpassed, but if it is not surpassed in centuries this does not mean that it is unsurpassable. It means that trying has been inhibited, and that it must become uninhibited.

In the play, Greedy Reed discovers the dictionary (language) and looks upon a thorough examination of it as the sole means of his (man's) salvation, rejecting the Bible (religious dogma) as well as his fear of and hatred for those whose skin is not colored (mores). But the struggle is difficult, the reader of the dictionary dies, Greedy Reed believes this is his betrayal by God and by man, he embraces the bitter mores again, renounces the hope of salvation, falls back into a behavior of disintegration, plans a crime, and then (and this is perhaps the most important element in the play) leaps upon and re-embraces the hope of salvation which reaches him by means of another man's crime, a murder for revenge; he conspires to conceal the crime, exults in its having been committed, takes pride in having survived the murdered man, is full of admiration and affection for the murderer, and believes implicitly in the rightness of the means to the end.

I don't know how it is with other readers, but almost everything I have ever read with pleasure, almost everything I have read that has seemed worth reading has tended to put me to sleep. I know that it is a cliché of book-reviewers to say that a book has kept them up all night, and I suppose it has, though I can't imagine why it should. The cliché is meant to be a compliment, but to me it sounds like an insult. Any book that does not tend to put me to sleep I put aside immediately, for I know all about it. I don't know all about the book that tends to put me to sleep. I enjoy spending time with it, allowing it to put my mind to rest, to become refreshed in the book's own dreaming. This would suggest that sleep is even more important than we already know it is; for it must be nearer than we suspect to creation, and if the ultimate end of creation is to make for wholeness, here is sleep and creation working to that end together. For we know the whole man sleeps peacefully, the broken man by leaps and bounds, starts and stops; and so it must also be with creation. If the created has wholeness it will be out of sleep and it will encourage sleep. I think a reading of all or part of *Don't Go Away Mad* will tend to put anybody to sleep. I certainly hope it will.

THE CHARACTERS

GREEDY REED

GEORGIE PORGIE

BRICK

POSEYO

ANDY BOY

BUSTER

MOPPER

DR. STARK

DR. BOHAN

DAY NURSE

NIGHT NURSE

THE SCENE

The Sun Room at the end of Ward Three in the City Hospital
of San Francisco.

THE TIME

November, 1947.

ACT ONE

Scene I

There is very little light in the Sun Room at the end of Ward Three in the City Hospital at the top of Legion of Honor Hill in San Francisco. The curved far wall of the modern room is plate-glass from floor to ceiling. The floor is bright yellow linoleum, and the walls are painted in thick orange and white stripes, some vertical, some horizontal. It is a wet, foggy morning in November, and every now and then the nearby foghorns are heard moaning. When the sun comes out and the fog clears the view from the plate-glass window will be good to see. Far down the hill, spanning the waters of the channel, will be the slim handsome Golden Gate Bridge, upon the waters will be Alcatraz Island, across the waters will be the steep green hills of Marin County, and over them will be the sky. Thus the room gives the impression of being a small part of something large in high flight.

The room's furnishings are good but depressing, for one senses that they are public property: two folding tables for cards or sitting and talking; a red-leather davenport and chair; a half dozen folding chairs; and shelves containing books, magazines and games. In a corner is a spinet piano, painted white. Near the piano is a blonde-wood combination radio-phonograph, and beside the machine is a small gray table cluttered with phonograph records.

The ward janitor, called MOPPER, is almost finished mopping. He is one of those enormous, simple souls who are always doing the dirty work at public hospitals, jails, poorhouses, and asylums. Almost a freak, he is an old man who never grew out of childhood. One shoulder is lower than

13

the other, something seems to be the matter with one leg, his whole body seems to be off balance, and he seems to be asking himself questions all the time. His voice is high-pitched, like a boy's, and the upper part of his body weaves a rhythm when he is excited or troubled.

A small man of sixty-five or so, a Greek who is called POSEYO, whistles Mozart softly as he searches through the records on the table beside the phonograph. Over his gray pajamas he wears the long white robe of the hospital and looks as if he had been costumed by an amateur play-producer to represent the angel in a Sunday School pageant. His enormous black moustache and his deep voice do not help the impression very much, however. He puts a twelve-inch record on the machine, draws up a folding chair, opens it, and sits down to listen.

MOPPER stops work to listen, too. He listens ten seconds or so, his freak's face bewildered by what he hears, his body weaving a rhythm. Then he goes back to work, stopping every now and then to listen some more. At last he takes his bucket and mop and leaves quietly.

The record is Victor Red Seal No. 16086-A, Mozart's Concerto in C Major, 2d Movement, Andante, Artur Schnabel at the piano with the London Symphony Orchestra, conducted by Malcolm Sargent, but POSEYO has moved the volume dial up so little that some of the music can scarcely be heard, and none of it is ever loud enough to seem a breaking of silence. The music seems in fact to be silence itself. When the record ends, POSEYO goes to the window to look out into the fog, and the machine automatically starts the record again.

Now, a very black Negro in his early forties who calls himself GREEDY REED comes into the room slowly, looks around, and very quietly slides the big glass door shut behind him. He is puffing at a freshly-lit cigar. He listens to the music a moment, looking from the machine to the man, then carefully sits himself down on the small stool in front of the piano, sets his cigar on the piano, and tries to pick out a soft accompaniment to the music. Suddenly he assaults the instrument with all his might, making an astounding racket of piano gibberish, as POSEYO turns to watch and listen, and MOPPER comes back in to see what all the noise is about, and then steps out. GREEDY REED ends his solo with a flourish, whereupon the sombre music of the phonograph is heard again. He stands, steps away from the piano, bows as if to an audience, kisses the palms of both hands loudly and flings them out in front of him, walks off smartly as if in concert exit, comes back shyly, bowing and throwing kisses, falls on his knees, touches the floor with his head several times, and then gets up wearily and settles down on the piano-stool to catch his breath. When he is breathing easily again he takes up his cigar and swings around slowly to face POSEYO.

GREEDY. You know what I hear about you, Poseyo? You know what I hear the men in the ward say about you just now, sitting in bed eating breakfast?

POSEYO. What?

GREEDY. Man, I hear Brick and Georgie Porgie say you ain't no good. That's exactly what I hear them say. Now, why they say that about a little man like you, no bigger than a small boy and always nice? Why they say you *ain't* nice, Poseyo?

POSEYO. Why?

GREEDY. Because you hate everybody, Georgie Porgie say. You hear me, Poseyo? *Hate.* Now, why he say that about *you?* I know you don't hate *me.* Who you hate, then?

POSEYO. Who?

GREEDY. Nobody, that's who. If you hate somebody, why you give me your whole breakfast this morning, except the orange juice? Why you give me your whole supper last night, except the tapioca pudding? Why you invite me, the only colored man in the ward, to take the bed next to your bed when I come here three days ago? If you hate, Poseyo, why you talk to me like a father all night that first night?

POSEYO. I don't know.

GREEDY. Who give me a whole dollar the next day for cigars? You did, Poseyo! Man, I been living this life forty-four years and I never see a man like you before. Here you are, the nicest man of all. Here you are with the dying men, and they talking behind your back. That ain't right! I *know* you don't hate nobody!

POSEYO. I don't know.

GREEDY. Go on, man, you never hate nobody in your whole life. You ain't got no hate in your whole nature. I've done a lot of hating in my forty-four years, but *you* can't pass for no hater. You know what's the matter with Georgie Porgie and Brick?

POSEYO. What?

GREEDY. They're *jealous*, that's what!

POSEYO. No. They just sick.

GREEDY. No, they're *jealous* because a little bit of a man like you who's nice to everybody is going to be alive when *they're* dead.

POSEYO. (*Shaking his head*) No. You make mistake.

GREEDY. Mistake? Didn't Jasper die last night who was bragging in bed yesterday morning how he was going to be here all through the next big war and depression? Didn't the Doctors come to his bed after lunch, talk to him, put him on the wagon, wheel him away? Didn't he go and never come back? Well, who told you to your face he'd be here long after you were cold and dead? Jasper told you, that's who! He was sick all right, but he was jealous, too, just like all the others. Man, to hear *them* talk, it's your fault Jasper kick the bucket. They're *mad* at you now, Poseyo. I see tears in the eyes of Brick because the leader of the choir ain't going to be around no more to make him feel good with his smart-aleck bragging, but you ain't going to see no tears in my eyes for the leader of the choir. No, sir! (*Pause, softly*) I got a whole choir of my own to lead.

POSEYO. I don't know. Jasper want to live.

GREEDY. Is that the way to live? Laughing and bragging and ganging up with your own kind because you're so scared and jealous? (*He falls silent a moment, as the sun begins to shine into the room*) Man, you saw me make a fool of myself here at this little piano a minute ago, all alone in this lonesome place. You saw me cutting up like a boy with a pie. Is that the way to live? Sure Jasper want to live. Sure Georgie Porgie and Brick and all the others out there who don't even get out of bed no more want to live, but is that the way to do it? Laughing and bragging, ganging up, singing in the hate choir, talking behind your back because you been here three months and they ain't, and never will be? Hating you because they're afraid to die, and you ain't? Every one of them sick and jealous? (*Pause*) I got something to tell you, Poseyo. (*He falls silent again. He looks* POSEYO *straight in the eye*) I'm jealous, too.

POSEYO. Oh?

GREEDY. Yeah, that's right! You got a right to be surprised, but it's true. I am jealous. Jealous and scared to death. I'm jealous of the three months you been here, Poseyo, and I'm scared to death of this whole dying business. Man, I didn't think about dying one time in my whole life until I come here, and now that's all I think about. Where will I be three months from now? Will I be walking down Lenox Avenue in New York in a brand-new gabardine suit? No. Will I be sitting in the ball park eating peanuts and drinking beer? No. That's too much to ask for, and I got sense enough to know it. I know there ain't no more good times like that for me. I'm here now. Well, will I be here three months from now? Will I be in this nice room, listening to this nice music, looking down the hill at the Golden Gate Bridge and Alcatraz Island, smoking this nice cigar? How about that, Poseyo? You made it, and I want to make it, too, but I'm scared to death I won't make it. I swear to God I did all that ornery stuff to get on your nerves, Poseyo, and make you go back to bed and die, so I could feel better about the short time I got left. I wanted to get your goat, Poseyo. I wanted to spoil your morning peace in this nice room. I wanted to spoil the nice music you was listening to. I wanted to spoil the whole day for you, and the rest of your life—me, Greedy Reed, the man you been so nice to.

POSEYO. That's all right.

GREEDY. There! You see? You don't even hate a man who wants you to die, so he can feel a little better about the short time he got left. Is that the way to live?

POSEYO. That's all right.

GREEDY. No, that's no way to live. That's the way of a man who's scared, a man like *me*—big like this for no good reason, black the way I am for no good reason, cheap and stingy and mean for no good reason, hating all the time for no good—well, I can't say I *hate* for no good reason. I'd be a liar to say *that*. I never did a right thing in my whole life, I guess, but I know I got good reasons to hate. I guess I got just about the best reasons in the world to hate. Well, here I am, going to die. Here I am, *still* hating and *still* wanting to get even on somebody—so who do I pick? You, Poseyo, the best man I ever saw. Is that the way to live? You don't look at me the way I been looked at all my life, *every* day of my life, and me always wanting to be liked, trying my best to be friendly and polite. Afraid I'll turn myself loose and let the murder go free if I *ain't* friendly and polite all the time, if I let *my* eyes look at them the way *their* eyes look at me. I know that ain't the way to live, but what other way can *I* live, black this way? (*Pause*) I could have been a white man in another life, but here I am black as ever and scared to death I'll be dead before I get a chance to get even. Man, I *got* to get even. I got to get even on *somebody*. (*Softly*) I wish to God I was in Africa, a place I never saw. I wish to God I never saw *America* instead—to make me feel so wrong, so out of place, and then put me here on top of everything else. I wish to God I was born in the jungle with decent animals for enemies instead of crazy men. I wish to God the tiger take my hide instead of disease. (*He sighs*) You're the only man I ever tell the truth to in my whole life, Poseyo. I know you don't hate nobody, but you might as well know I *do*. I hate everybody, even you! I even hate you for being the best man I ever saw. What right you got to be a good man in this crooked life?

I give you fair warning, I going to kill somebody before I die, so if you want to be safe, go ahead and tell the hospital and let them put me where I be alone. I been alone all my life anyway. (*Pause; softly*) I see Georgie Porgie and Brick getting out of bed now, getting ready to come out here and be in the sun, so go ahead and tell them if you want to be safe.

POSEYO. I no tell.

GREEDY. Why not?

POSEYO. I take chance.

GREEDY. Don't you believe me?

POSEYO. I believe.

GREEDY. Then why you let me go? Why you let the murder go free?

POSEYO. In this place every man know his own sickness. Every man talk. I don't know. I listen to music.

GREEDY. You know, Poseyo, I believe you know something? I believe you keeping something back? (*His face brightening with the pose of friendship*) Here they come now.

GEORGIE PORGIE, a heavy-set, red-headed man in his late forties with his left eye and part of his face covered, comes in, followed by BRICK, a man in his late thirties.

GREEDY. Well, it's about time you boys got out of bed. Seem like I been hanging around here a whole hour wasting my time listening to Poseyo's music.

GEORGIE. That's Mozart. (*He pronounces the name correctly.*)

GREEDY. Oh, I don't say it ain't Mozart all right, Georgie Porgie. It's Mozart through and through, no doubt about that. Mozart over and over again telling Poseyo something. (*Taking an open deck of cards off a shelf and riffling them*) Old Mozart, he don't tell Greedy Reed nothing. Brick, you feel like a little game of casino this nice morning?

BRICK. (*Wandering to the window*) I'm too damn tired to play cards—too tired, too tired.

GREEDY. (*Watching him*) How come you too tired to play cards so early in the morning, man?

BRICK. Too damn tired. Too tired to *talk*, even. Too tired to listen.

GREEDY. You wasn't too tired to eat your breakfast. You wasn't too tired to talk *a little while ago*.

BRICK. So damn sick and tired I can barely stand here and look down at Alcatraz. Sick and tired of looking down at Alcatraz. Sick and tired of Poseyo's music.

GREEDY. You may be sick and tired of Poseyo's music, but you wasn't too sick and tired a little while ago to cry about your friend who kick the bucket last night. (BRICK *turns and stares at* GREEDY REED'S *feet.* GREEDY *riffles the cards until* BRICK *turns away*) How about you, Georgie Porgie? You want to pass a little time playing casino?

GEORGIE. I promised old Doc Stark I'd take things easy. I *ain't* sick and tired of anything, so I'm going to keep my promise. Games make me nervous. I'll just sit here and read this comic book about Joe Palooka.

GREEDY. Yeah, you take good care of yourself now. You keep your promise to old Doc Stark. I just thought maybe you could take things easy playing a little casino.

GEORGIE. (*Looking into the comic book*) No, I get nervous when I play games.

GREEDY REED watches GEORGIE PORGIE turn the pages of the book, turns to BRICK, whose back is turned, then glances at POSEYO as ANDY BOY, a Chinese boy of twenty-five or so, comes in.

GREEDY. Andy Boy, I'm glad to see you out of bed! I know you ain't going to refuse no invitation to sit down and play a little casino.

ANDY. (*Weakly*) I don't know how to play *casino*, but I'll play you a little gin rummy.

GREEDY. (*Helping him*) Well, all right, sit right down here and make yourself comfortable. Casino or gin rummy, it's all the same to me, but you keep score because I don't know how.

ANDY BOY sits down. GREEDY REED shuffles the cards and deals. NOBODY speaks for a moment, but GEORGIE PORGIE laughs as he looks at pictures of Joe Palooka, and GREEDY REED looks over at him.

BRICK. Know anybody who ever did time at Alcatraz, Georgie Porgie?

GEORGIE. Did what where?

BRICK. Anybody around here know anybody who ever did time at Alcatraz?

GREEDY. If you talking to me, the name's Greedy Reed. I give the name to myself because I been so hungry all my life. Anybody do time at Alcatraz, *still* doing time at Alcatraz. Time and time again. Part-time, full-time, over-time.

ANDY BOY. Gin!

GREEDY. Gin already, Andy Boy? Man, you catch me with a whole handful. Listen to me count. Ten, twenty, thirty, forty, forty-nine, fifty-seven, sixty-four, seventy-one, and this little old lousy ace of hearts, seventy-two. Seventy-two plus twenty for gin, ninety-two. (*He turns to* BRICK, *whose back is still turned*) Is that right?

ANDY BOY. Ninety-two all right. That's the most I ever caught anybody with. (*He writes on the score card, shuffles and deals.*)

BRICK. I feel sorry for those guys on Alcatraz looking at San Francisco every day.

GEORGIE. Looking at San Francisco's not as bad as looking at the Golden Gate Bridge.

BRICK. What's so bad about looking at the Golden Gate Bridge?

GEORGIE. The ideas you get.

BRICK. What ideas?

GEORGIE. What do you think you'd like to do when you see a bridge? You think you'd like to cross it. Well, if you're on the Rock, you know you'll *never* be able to cross the bridge.

BRICK. You make me laugh.

GEORGIE. I don't *hear* you laughing. I been laughing about Joe Palooka ever since I sat down. I don't hear *you* laughing, though.

BRICK. I suppose you can cross the bridge?

GEORGIE. I know damn well I can cross the bridge any time I feel like it.

BRICK. Ah, you're always talking big. Sure you can cross the bridge—once!

GEORGIE. Me and everybody else, too.—Once!

BRICK. Everybody else don't have to think about crossing it in the same kind of hurry that you do.

GEORGIE. I'm satisfied. I ain't kicking. I'm not going to cross the bridge until I feel like it. I don't feel like it just now because I know I *can* cross it any old time I feel like it. I know I'm free. The boys on the Rock know they're not free.

BRICK. Yeah, and I don't want to hear any more about it. You're just naturally *cheerful*, that's all.

GEORGIE. (*Watching* GREEDY *and* POSEYO) If you mean I ought to feel bad because Jasper died last night, the answer is I don't think I ought to feel bad at all. What did you expect him to do? Live? What did everybody expect Roosevelt to do? Live? And Mussolini and Hitler and all the little guys who die every day? Did everybody expect them to live? Well, they *did* for awhile. Joe Palooka will live longer than any of them, and Joe Palooka ain't even real.

BRICK. Poseyo, your music's making a fool out of that poor man. What do you say we try another record?

POSEYO. That's all right.

BRICK. What do you say we take a chance on the first record I pick up? Maybe it'll give Georgie Porgie some new ideas about Roosevelt and Joe Palooka and all the little guys who die every day?

GEORGIE. Play any kind of music you like, I'll still know what I know. I'll still know *I* ain't going to make any difference. *Much.* Joe Stalin himself ain't going to make any *real* difference *much*, either. I'm satisfied to sit here and try to guess what lunch is going to be. Hash, most likely. I hate the stuff, but I know I'll eat it and like it, because that's the way it's got to be until I'm good and ready to cross the bridge. Sickness ain't going to make a monkey out of *me*.

BRICK. Why don't you wait till the new music starts before you make a monkey out of yourself?

GEORGIE. Go ahead, start the new music.

BRICK *puts needle to disc and the music turns out to be* Heartaches, *very loud, played by Ted Weems and his orchestra.*

GREEDY. There you are! More Mozart! Seem like everything around here Mozart—Mozart—Mozart! (*Shifting his cards around swiftly and slapping them down in front of him*) Mozart, Andy Boy!

ANDY BOY. Gin?

GREEDY. That's right. That's exactly right. Old Mozart talking to me now. Talking my language for a change, too. Viper talk. (*He claps his hands, gets up, prances around the table, and half-sings to the rhythm of the music*) Moz—art, Moz—art, I hear you talking, little sweetheart. (*He examines* ANDY BOY's *cards*) How much I catch you with?

ANDY BOY. Twenty-one, and twenty for gin, forty-one.

He writes on the score pad, as GREEDY *sits down and shuffles the cards.*

GREEDY. Poseyo, you know what old Mozart saying to me now? He saying, Yeah man! That's exactly what he saying over and over again. (*He sweeps up his cards and looks at them quickly*) And he just about the biggest liar that ever live!

POSEYO. Oh?

GREEDY. That's right, Poseyo. Mozart tell me yeah, cards tell me no. Music tell me maybe, numbers tell me never. Drum tell me sure, hospital tell me scat. (*He studies his cards with distaste*) Scat! (*He folds them together, places them on the table face down, and looks straight ahead at nothing. He looks around and notices that* GEORGIE *is asleep on his folded arms. He gets up and shuts off the machine.* BRICK *is sitting on the piano stool, looking down at the keys of the piano.* ANDY *holds his cards, waiting for* GREEDY *to come back to the game.* GREEDY *looks at* POSEYO, *as if he were trying to find out what it is he thinks* POSEYO *knows. He speaks slowly and quietly*) What you keeping back, Poseyo? I know you keeping something back.

POSEYO. I don't know.

GREEDY. Is this the way to live? Ignorant and mad this way all the time? Sick and ugly, and nothing right to do before we go? Why you keeping back what you keeping back, Poseyo?

POSEYO. I don't know. I forget.

GREEDY. (*As if he had suddenly learned a great secret*) Forget? (*Pause*) Is that the secret, Poseyo? Is that what you been keeping back? Is that the way to live? Just forget? Just let everything go? Forget my name? Forget my color? Forget I'm here? Forget I was ever born? Is that the way, Poseyo? How you learn to forget? (*He picks up the 12-inch record and looks at it*) Mozart teach you? This music here teach you? Man, I hear this music all morning. This music don't teach me to forget. (*He puts the record back*) Make me remember worse than ever. Make me remember stuff I been forgetting all my life. Make me remember the half dozen different men I been, the half dozen different lives I live. Make me remember all the years I try to find out how to live, what to do. Make me remember the time I believe I know what to do— preach the gospel!

BRICK. (*With amazement*) Oh, Jesus!

GEORGIE looks up at BRICK, unnoticed by anyone.

GREEDY. Make me remember something I been forgetting all my life. Enjoy life and preach the gospel of enjoyment. Too late to enjoy now. Too late to preach the gospel now, but I got to find me something right to do before I go, something to teach me to forget, too.

BRICK. Oh, Christ!

GREEDY. Now, if I could read, I believe I'd like to sit down with a great big book and read it. I'd like to bury myself in the biggest book there is and just read it and forget everything.

BRICK. You ain't going to be buried in any *book!* You're going to be buried in a box, just like Jasper and all the rest of us. You'll forget everything in the box all right.

GREEDY. (*Turning on him, as* GEORGIE *watches*) You been teasing me long enough! No need to tease me any more! I hear every teasing word you say, but I keep my mouth shut because I don't want to hurt a man already almost dead. From now on you better speak to me when I speak to you, and you better speak with respect. I invite you to play cards because I want to be polite. You don't have to play cards if you don't want to, but you got to be polite, too. You got to look at me like a man when you tell me you don't want to play, instead of looking somewhere else, because I got to know we talking about the same thing. I got to know you ain't talking about color. Right now I see your eyes saying nigger to me. Any man—any man in this whole world—say nigger to me *now* with his *mouth*, I shut him up forever, I choke him to death! You hear? (*Pause*) I been talking to Poseyo, not you. Why you start new trouble for me first thing in the morning?

BRICK. What the hell's the matter with you? I was only kidding.

GREEDY. I been kidded long enough. I been kidded all my life, all over this country. Everything in this whole country been kidding me about my color, my smell, the shape of my head, my ignorance, the way I walk and talk and everything else. I been kidded long enough. No need to be kidded *here*, too.

BRICK. I was only talking. Everybody likes to talk once in awhile. You been talking ever since I come in here. (*Pause*) I ain't proud of my color.

GREEDY. What you proud of, then?

BRICK. I ain't proud.

GREEDY. What you mean?

BRICK. I just ain't proud *at all—of anything.* I don't think you ought to threaten anybody just because your color happens to be black—just because you happen to be sensitive about it.

GREEDY. What you talking about *now?*

BRICK. I almost never look at anybody when I talk to them. I remember what they look like, so I don't *have* to look at them. Looking at them makes me feel sorry for them. It embarrasses me. If you want to know the truth, I've never before noticed your *color*.

GREEDY. I *know* you ain't teasing no more. What you trying to say to me?

BRICK. I'm saying I ain't got time to notice little things about myself or anybody else any more. Color is one of the little things I've *never* bothered to notice.

GREEDY. You trying to say you wasn't laughing at me?

BRICK. I was laughing at *myself*. I was laughing at an old friend who's turned out to be a bore. If I get on your nerves, don't forget you get on mine, too. So does Poseyo and everybody else around here. So what? Doctor Stark gets on my nerves. The janitor mopping the floor gets on my nerves. I get on my own nerves. So what? I don't have to kill myself for that, do I? You don't have to threaten anybody for *that*, do you?

GREEDY. You sure you talking straight?

BRICK. I couldn't talk any straighter.

GREEDY. I'm sorry, then. I swear to God, I'm sorry I threaten you.

GEORGIE buries his head in his folded arms again.

BRICK. If you don't mind, then, I'll stop looking you in the eye. It makes me ashamed of both of us. (*Pause, softly*) Only the eyes of animals have the dignity and peace men want—especially the most savage animals, like the lion, the tiger, and the panther. The eyes of men stop at details. The eyes of animals never notice them. I wish you hadn't called my attention to your color. (*He stands*) A lot of people think the Bible's a nice book. Maybe that's the book you're looking for.

GREEDY. I'm much obliged to you, but maybe there's a bigger book than the Bible.

BRICK. Well, the dictionary's a pretty big book, too.

GREEDY. Bigger than the Bible?

BRICK. Two or three times.

GREEDY. Then that's the book I want.

BRICK. It's only words.

GREEDY. That's all right. That's exactly what I want. Words. All the words in the world. (*He goes to the book shelf*) Which one of these books is the dictionary?

BRICK. That great big one there. I'm going to walk around the ward. I'm sick and tired of myself. (*Softly*) I'm sick and tired of you, too.

GREEDY. Ah, don't go away mad, Brick.

BRICK. I ain't mad.

BRICK goes out. GREEDY takes the dictionary off the shelf, opens it and looks into it.

GREEDY. Poseyo, you hear that man? You hear what he say? Sick and tired of himself and sick and tired of me, too. He not a bad man, Poseyo. Just seem like I too ignorant to understand anybody. I been thinking all the time he look down at me, but he *don't* look down at me. Leastaways no more than he look down at himself, look down at everybody. He tell me he don't even notice my color, and I know he tell me the truth. I been thinking all the time he hate me, call me nigger in his heart, and I been hating *him*. Man, I got to stop being ignorant. I got to learn. I got to learn something besides hate. I got to understand. I been thinking that man my worst enemy, but he no enemy at all. If he ain't no friend, he ain't no enemy, either. He too sick and tired to be *either* a friend or a enemy. Man, I got to understand about *that*. Now, here's this big book right here in my hands—the holy dictionary, full of all the words in the world. I got to understand the words. (*He sets the book down on the card table and turns to the front of the book*) Andy Boy, you been to high school right here in San Francisco. I know you can read. Read the dictionary to me.

ANDY BOY. The whole dictionary?

GREEDY. Sure, Andy Boy. Every word in the holy dictionary, one by one. I been greedy for food, for money, for clothes, for women and fun and everything else, now I greedy for words. I greedy for understanding. Man, look at all the words right here on the first page, look at all the beautiful words. Do us *good* to read the words, Andy Boy.

ANDY BOY. Take a month to read the whole dictionary.

GREEDY. Take more than a month, Andy Boy. Take *three* months, maybe four! Three or four beautiful months with the dictionary, Andy Boy. Come on, read me the first word. Words better than cards any day, Andy Boy. Words tell us who we are, what we doing, where we going. (ANDY *gathers up the cards as* GREEDY *moves around the table, so that* ANDY *can start reading*) Now here, Andy Boy. Here's the first word, right here. What is it?

ANDY. (*Reading*) A.

GREEDY. (*Delighted*) A! Now, we're on our way, Andy Boy. Read about A to me. What do A mean?

ANDY. (*Reading*) A. The first letter of the alphabet in most of the known languages of the earth. In the Ethiopic, however, it is the thirteenth.

GREEDY. Wait a minute! In the *what?*

ANDY. The Ethiopic. That's a language of some kind, I guess.

GREEDY. What language that?

ANDY. The Ethiopian, I guess.

GREEDY. You talking about that man in Africa?

ANDY. What man in Africa?

GREEDY. That skinny man with the whiskers? Poseyo, who that man in Africa with the whiskers?

POSEYO. I don't know.

GREEDY. Andy Boy, you remember before the War a country someplace in Africa that Mussolini take away from that man with the whiskers.

ANDY. I don't remember.

GREEDY. (*Shaking* GEORGIE) Georgie Porgie, you awake?

GEORGIE. (*Sitting up with a start*) What's the matter?

GREEDY. Andy Boy reading me the dictionary. We working on the first word right now.

GEORGIE. Ah, for the love of Mike! I was fast asleep. I dreamed I was drinking Coca-Cola. What do you want?

GREEDY. Who that man in Africa with the whiskers that Mussolini attack with his army and take away his house and tigers and country?

GEORGIE. What the hell are you talking about? House and tigers and country? You mean Haile Selassie?

GREEDY. Yeah, that's the man. That Ethiopic, is that *his* language?

GEORGIE. I guess so. What difference does *that* make?

GREEDY. He was the King of some kind of black people in Africa. That Ethiopic, is that the language of them black people?

GEORGIE. I guess it's the language of *some* kind of black people. Why? What are you so excited about?

GREEDY. Andy Boy, read about that A again for Georgie Porgie, so he know why I excited this way.

ANDY. (*Reading*) A. The first letter of the alphabet in most of the known languages of the earth. In the Ethiopic, however, it is the thirteenth.

GREEDY. Hear that, Georgie Porgie? Now, what does thirteen mean?

GEORGIE. If you're superstitious thirteen means bad luck.

GREEDY. Everybody superstitious.

GEORGIE. If you're not superstitious every number means bad luck.

GREEDY. What you mean, every number mean bad luck? I hear *thirteen* the unlucky number.

GEORGIE. Ah, let me go back to sleep, will you? I was sitting on a porch in the summertime, listening to carpenters building a house, hammering nails into wood far away, and I was drinking a bottle of Coca-Cola. You come and shake me out of the best dream I ever had.

GREEDY. I'm sorry I wake you out of that nice dream, Georgie Porgie. You sure thirteen ain't the unlucky number?

GEORGIE. O.K., have it your way. Thirteen *is* the unlucky number. Now, leave me alone, will you?

GREEDY. Ah, man, don't get mad.

GEORGIE. (*Lazily*) Go ahead, read the dictionary. I'm wide-awake *now*.

GREEDY. I'm sorry I spoil your nice dream, Georgie Porgie.

GEORGIE. Forget it. Maybe if you didn't wake me up, I wouldn't remember the dream, and then where would I be?

GREEDY. You all right now?

GEORGIE. Sure.

GREEDY. You want to tell me about thirteen?

GEORGIE. Sure.

GREEDY. What do that number mean? I got to know before I go on reading the dictionary. What do it mean?

GEORGIE. Nothing. It's the number between twelve and fourteen.

GREEDY. You sure?

GEORGIE. That's all it is.

GREEDY. You sure you ain't being superstitious?

GEORGIE. Hell no. Thirteen's just another number, no different from any other number.

GREEDY. No different from one or three, twenty-one or thirty-three?

GEORGIE. Or two or four, twenty-two or forty-four.

GREEDY. Then if the letter A is number thirteen in the Ethiopic language instead of number one, that don't mean black people unlucky?

GEORGIE. Of course not.

GREEDY. I take your word for it, Georgie Porgie. Go ahead, Andy Boy, read the next word.

ANDY. There's some more about A.

GREEDY. Yeah?

ANDY. And after A, there's a lot of words I never heard of before.

GREEDY. What kind of words?

ANDY. (*Reading slowly*) Abaca. Abaciscus. Abacot. You don't want me to read *every* word in the dictionary, do you?

GREEDY. Well, *almost* every word. You can skip abaciscus and words like that, I guess. No harm in skipping abaciscus, I guess. What else the dictionary say about A?

ANDY. (*Reading slowly*) A is the first letter because it represents the first vocal sound naturally formed by the human organs, being the sound uttered with a mere opening of the mouth without constraint, and without any effort to alter the natural position or configuration of the lips. (*Weary pause.*)

GEORGIE. (*To* GREEDY) You know what that means?

GREEDY. Sure. A. Just like the book say, the first talking a man do. Go ahead, Andy Boy, read some more. (*Gently*) What's the matter, Andy Boy?

ANDY. I don't know. I don't feel so good. (*Reading slowly*) Hence the letter A is found in many words first uttered by infants, which words are the names of the objects with which infants are first concerned, as the breast and the mother and the father. Hence in Hebrew Am is mother, Ab is father. In Chaldee, Syriac and Arabic, father is Abba; in Ethiopic, Abi; in Malayan and Bengalese, Bappa; in Welsh, Tad, whence we retain Dad; in Old Greek and in Gothic, Atta; in Irish, Aithair; in Cantabrian, Aita; in Lapponic, Atki; in Abyssinian and Amharic, Aba; in the Shilhic and Melindane African dialects, Baba; and Papa is found in many languages.

GREEDY. I *know* this the right book for *us*, Andy Boy. You just hang on now, and read and read. Any more about A?

ANDY. Yeah. (*Reading*) Hence the Latin word for the breast, Mamma, in popular usage is the name of mother.

GREEDY. Well, what do you know?

ANDY. (*Reading*) This list might be greatly extended, but these examples prove A to be the first natural vocal sound, and entitled to the first place in alphabets.

GREEDY. You just hang on now, Andy Boy! What else do the book say?

ANDY. (*Wearily*) Well, it says, A, as a symbol, in Hebrew, Syriac, Chaldee, Samaritan and Arabic, denotes *one* or unity.

GREEDY. Hot dog! Now, let me just stand here a minute, Andy Boy, and remember all that stuff. (*Pause*) I got it! I got the first word in the book now. Pappa, Mamma! Read the next word, Andy Boy.

ANDY. All right to leave out some of the words I told you about?

GREEDY. I hate to think we going to lose something, Andy Boy. On the other hand, if we leave out some of the words now, when we finish the whole book, we going to have something to go back to. We *always* going to have something to fall back on.

GEORGIE. (*Watching* ANDY) We've always got something to fall back on *anyway*.

GREEDY. What that? God?

GEORGIE. Well, I was thinking we've always got sleep to fall back on, but let's put it your way. Let's say it's God we've always got to fall back on.

GREEDY. You *believing* man, Georgie Porgie?

GEORGIE. Oh, I believe all right.

GREEDY. You believe about God?

GEORGIE. Why not?

GREEDY. What you believe about God?

GEORGIE. Everything I hear.

GREEDY. What you hear?

GEORGIE. I hear God loves every one of us.

GREEDY. You believe *that*?

GEORGIE. Yes, I do.

GREEDY. What else you hear?

GEORGIE. I hear God's got good reasons for everything that happens to every one of us.

GREEDY. (*Pause, thinking*) You believe about Heaven at all?

GEORGIE. Quite a bit.

GREEDY. What you believe about Heaven, Georgie Porgie?

GEORGIE. I believe Heaven's a nice idea.

GREEDY. You believe you going there?

GEORGIE. Yes, I do. (*Pause, softly*) Let's hear the next word.

GREEDY. Yeah! You like hearing the words, too, Georgie Porgie?

GEORGIE. Sure.

GREEDY. What's the next word, Andy Boy?

ANDY. Abandon.

GREEDY. What do abandon mean?

ANDY. (*Reading*) Abandon. To forsake entirely. To leave and not come back. To give up. To evacuate.

GREEDY. Yeah. About time I learn some words. About time I get me a little education. About time I get me a big vocabulary. Man, we got something *right* to do now, Andy Boy. We got a job *worth* doing. When me and you evacuate for lunch, Andy Boy, you keep the place in the book, so that when we— What's a good word for come back?

ANDY. Return?

GREEDY. Yeah. So that when we— Ain't there a bigger word than return? Something with a nice sound like evacuate?

ANDY. No, I 'think return is the only word there is for come back. You know any other word for come back, Georgie Porgie?

GEORGIE. Reincarnation has something to do with coming back, I believe, but not from lunch.

GREEDY. From what, then, Georgie Porgie?

GEORGIE. From another life. Some people believe every one of us is a reincarnation from another life.

GREEDY. No fooling, Georgie Porgie?

GEORGIE. A lot of people believe we come and go all the time.

GREEDY. Where I come from?

GEORGIE. A long time ago in Africa, I guess.

GREEDY. Where I going?

GEORGIE. Well, that's hard to say because by the time any of us are ready to come back there may not be anything to come back to.

GREEDY. What you mean?

GEORGIE. If there's no human life left on this earth, what are we going to come back to?

GREEDY. Who says there ain't going to be no human life left on this earth?

GEORGIE. A lot of people do. We ain't the only people who're dying, you know. The whole human race is.

GREEDY. What the whole human race dying from?

GEORGIE. Starvation, homelessness, exhaustion, fear, anger, anxiety, despair, nervousness, overwork, worry.

GREEDY. You mean all them things killing everybody?

GEORGIE. That's what I read in the newspapers. That's what I hear over the radio.

GREEDY. Everybody dying right now?

GEORGIE. So I hear.

GREEDY. Ah, you just saying that to make me feel good. The whole world seem just about the same as ever to me.

GEORGIE. It ain't, though.

GREEDY. You talking about that lousy Adam bomb? Go on, man, no little old Adam bomb going to finish human beings.

GEORGIE. Maybe not, but it's going to help. They've made a weapon out of diseases, too, you know.

GREEDY. No Adam bomb and no disease going to finish human beings. If we going to come back some time, we going to have something to come back to all right. Question is, are we going to come back?

GEORGIE. A lot of people have always thought so. (*Pause*) I guess *return* is just about the best word there is for coming back from lunch, though.

GREEDY. Well, that ain't no new word for me, but it's all right, I guess. You keep the place in the dictionary when we evacuate for lunch, Andy Boy, so that when we return we can pick up right where we left off.

ANDY. O.K.

GREEDY. Let me hear the next word. Seem like I can't wait to hear the next word.

ANDY. (*Reading*) Abbreviate.

GREEDY. What do abbreviate mean?

ANDY. (*Reading*) To shorten. To abridge by the omission of a part.

GREEDY. Read that again, Andy Boy. I like the way that go.

ANDY. (*Slower*) To shorten. To abridge by the omission of a part.

GREEDY. And that will be exactly what me and you ain't going to do, Andy Boy. No, sir. We been abbreviating all over the place up to now, but from now on we going to go slow and easy. From now on we going to get on no bridge and take no short cut. We going to read the whole dictionary. What's the next word, Andy Boy?

ANDY. Abdicate.

GREEDY. I hear that word long time ago when that King of England step down from his throne, but I sure glad to hear it again, Andy Boy. Abdicate. That means to quit your job when you're King, but what do the book say?

ANDY. In a general sense, to relinquish, renounce, or abandon.

GREEDY. Yeah. That's right. What else do the book say?

ANDY. To abandon an office or trust without a formal resignation to those who conferred it, or without their consent. Also, to abandon a throne without a formal surrender of the crown. Blackstone.

GREEDY. Who that?

GEORGIE. That's the man who said that.

GREEDY. He must know a lot to say that. What else do the book say?

ANDY. To relinquish an office before the expiration of the term of service.

GREEDY. Yeah. Relinquish. There's a real nice word to say, but so far the best I hear is that Mamma and Pappa. Any more about abdicate in the book there?

ANDY. In civil law, to disclaim and expel from the family, as a father his child. (*Pause*) That's all for abdicate.

GREEDY. You hear that, Poseyo? You see the good job I find for me and Andy Boy? I ain't holding back no secrets from nobody. Read the next word, Andy Boy.

ANDY. Abdomen.

GREEDY. You sending me straight to Heaven with the words, Andy Boy, and we got the whole big book full of them. (*Suddenly*) What you looking for over there, Poseyo? Your record right there on top. Put your record on the machine if you tired of listening to words.

POSEYO. I not tired. I like words. I find new music.

GREEDY. Yeah, Poseyo. Let's hear some new music to go with the words. We up to abdomen now. (*He pats his belly*) That's right in here some place. Read what the book say, Andy Boy.

POSEYO searches through the records.

ANDY. (*Reading*) Abdomen. The belly or that part of the body which lies between the thorax and the bottom of the pelvis. It contains the stomach, liver, spleen, pancreas, kidneys, bladder, and intestines.

GREEDY. Yeah, man! I know the way to live now, Poseyo. Andy Boy and me, we got ourselves the best of everything now! We got words. On purpose words, not accidental words. Straight words. Words that mean what they say.

DOCTOR STARK, a tired-looking, hulking old man with a red face and a gentle manner, accompanied by the DAY NURSE, an elderly woman, steps into the room. GREEDY falls silent. The DOCTOR nods absently, as if to everyone in the room, studies one of the many charts he is holding, then goes to POSEYO.

DR. STARK. How do you feel this morning, Poseyo?

POSEYO. Fine, thank you.

DR. STARK. Sleep all right?

POSEYO. Little bit.

DR. STARK. Any severe pain?

POSEYO. Not much.

DR. STARK. (*To the* NURSE) Same treatment. (*He goes to* GEORGIE) How do you feel, Georgie Porgie?

GEORGIE. (*As to an equal*) Ignorant but still hungry.

DR. STARK. (*Trying to smile*) I can go along with you halfway. I'm scarcely ever hungry any more. (*To the* NURSE) Same. (*He goes to* GREEDY) How are you this morning?

GREEDY. I feel all right.

DR. STARK. Sleep all right?

GREEDY. Oh, I sleep *last* night, not like them first two nights.

DR. STARK. Wake up at all?

GREEDY. Two three times, but just for a little while.

DR. STARK. Feel any pain when you woke up?

GREEDY. Just the pain I'm used to now.

DR. STARK. Scared?

GREEDY. (*Embarrassed*) Little scared, I guess.

DR. STARK. That's good.

GREEDY. Good to feel scared, Doctor?

DR. STARK. Helps me a little to know what to do for you. (*He writes something on a piece of paper, hands it to the* NURSE, *then turns toward* ANDY.)

GREEDY. Doctor—

DR. STARK. (*Looking at chart*) Yes?

GREEDY. (*Almost stuttering*) How—how long—

DR. STARK. From what I know so far, I'd say you're doing all right.

GREEDY. (*Relieved*) Yes, sir. Thank you, sir.

DR. STARK. (*Looking at* GREEDY) Just try to pass the time pleasantly. Try not to get excited. Panic kills swifter than any
disease.

GREEDY. (*His voice low and soft*) Yes, sir.

DR. STARK. (*To* ANDY) How are you, Andy Boy?

ANDY. All right, I guess.

DR. STARK. Any trouble getting out of bed this morning?

ANDY. Yes, sir.

DR. STARK. More than yesterday morning?

ANDY. Yes, sir.

DR. STARK. Sleep all right last night?

ANDY. No, sir.

DR. STARK. (*Studying the chart*) Sleep at all?

ANDY. A little, I guess.

DR. STARK. Why didn't you call the Nurse?

ANDY. (*Slowly; softly*) I don't know. I guess I was afraid to.
I guess I was afraid if I took some medicine to put me to
sleep, I wouldn't wake up again. I been having a lot of bad
dreams. Animals—all kinds of animals coming after me.
(*Pause.*)

DR. STARK. Nurse, will you please see if Doctor Bohan's still in
the ward? (*The* DAY NURSE *steps out of the room. The* DOC-
TOR *notices the dictionary*) Reading the dictionary?

ANDY. Yes, sir.

GREEDY. We reading the dictionary from the first word to the
last.

DR. STARK. How many words have you read so far?

GREEDY. Andy Boy's read me six or seven so far, I guess. We
been taking them slow and easy, talking about them as we
go along.

DR. STARK. How do you like the words?

GREEDY. Oh, they're fine. They're mighty handsome when you
find out what they mean.

DR. STARK. (*To* ANDY) How do you like them?

ANDY. They're all right, I guess. Greedy Reed asked me to read
the dictionary to him.

DR. STARK. Greedy Reed? (*To* GREEDY) Who gave you that name?

GREEDY. I give it to myself, Doctor.

DR. STARK. Just lately or long ago?

GREEDY. Long, long ago, Doctor. I been greedy all my life.

DR. STARK. It's a good name for any man. (*To* ANDY) Doctor Bohan and I may want to try to make you a little more comfortable, if it's all right with you.

ANDY. I'm afraid of the animals, Doctor.

DR. STARK. Yes, I know. If you like we can let things go as they are.

ANDY. (*Slowly*) Could we let things go as they are for a month?

DR. STARK. You wouldn't be very comfortable, I'm afraid.

ANDY. How long would it take to make me comfortable?

DR. STARK. Well, if we're lucky, a couple of hours. Three, at the most.

ANDY. If we're *not* lucky, how long will it take?

DR. STARK. If we're *not* lucky—I think you ought to know we may not be lucky. Perhaps you shouldn't take a chance.

ANDY. Yes, sir.

The DAY NURSE and DR. BOHAN, a sharp, swift young man, come in. DR. STARK hands DR. BOHAN the chart, which DR. BOHAN studies for some time.

DR. STARK. What do you think?

DR. BOHAN. I'd say take a chance. (*To* ANDY) What do you say, son? You're the boss, you know. It would help us a lot if you made your decision *now*, though. (*He looks at his wrist watch.*)

ANDY. (*Softly, to* GREEDY) I don't know what to say. I guess I'd like to read the dictionary all right. I could read *some* of it anyway, I guess. (*Pause*) I don't know what to say.

GREEDY. (*Softly*) Maybe you better get comfortable, Andy Boy. (*He looks from one doctor to the other*) Maybe you better let the Doctors make you a little more comfortable. If we going to read the whole dictionary, Andy Boy, maybe you better take a chance.

ANDY. (*To the* DOCTOR, *after a long pause*) I'll take a chance, I guess. (*He tries to get to his feet.*)

DAY NURSE goes out, leaving door open.

DR. STARK. Better sit still. It's much too far to walk. (*To* POSEYO, *as the* DAY NURSE *pushes a stretcher on wheels into the room*) All right, Poseyo, put the record on the machine and let's have a little music.

GREEDY. (*Helping* ANDY *get on the stretcher*) That's right, Poseyo. Let's have the music to the words Andy Boy going to read just as soon as the Doctors make him more comfortable.

ANDY is helped onto the stretcher as POSEYO puts needle to disc. The record is Asch Records No. 4101 A Side 1, Masquerade Suite by Khatchaturian, Valse, Santa Monica Symphony, conducted by Jacques Rachmilovich. BRICK comes in and he and GEORGIE stand behind GREEDY, looking down at ANDY.

GREEDY. I'd like to go along with my friend and keep him company, Doctor.

DR. STARK. No, I think you better stay here and take things easy.

GREEDY. (*Almost shouting over the music*) Listen to me, Andy Boy, you hear? You go along with the Doctors now and get comfortable and come right back. I be here waiting for you with the dictionary. Man, we going to read the whole book. You remember how all the different people say Mamma and Pappa! You go along now and come right back and see me sitting over there at the table with the dictionary right in front of me, waiting. You come back and we start reading the words again. (*The* DAY NURSE *and the* DOCTORS *move with the stretcher out of the room. At the door* ANDY *sits up and turns around*) You come back, you hear? You come back, Andy Boy. You come right back. (*He looks around at* GEORGIE, BRICK *and* POSEYO.)

Scene II

It is sundown now. The room is almost dark in spite of
the faint streak of red in the light from the sinking sun.
The red is not for long, though, and there is no warmth
in it. The MEN seem smaller and more insignificant than
ever, perhaps because their shadows are so much larger
now than themselves. They seem strangely unaccountable,
too, as if they were being noticed by the eye for the first
time; and the place seems overtaken by a coldness which
can only increase. One almost feels the iciness of approach-
ing death, so that the room, in spite of its gaudy trappings,
seems a painfully fantastic place in which to spend one's
last hours.

POSEYO is sitting in front of the phonograph, listening
to his favorite music. GEORGIE is sitting at his table, looking
at a comic book. BRICK moves silently back and forth in
front of the window, stopping now and then to look out,
or to look with amazement at someone in the room.

GREEDY is sitting at his table, looking into the open dictionary at the words he cannot read, fretting about the man
he hopes is going to come back and read them to him.
He mumbles inaudibly, apparently saying to himself,
"Mamma," "Pappa," then waves his right arm slowly over
the book, an action which has the effect of restoring some
of his irrepressible humor.

GREEDY. Look here, Georgie Porgie! Look at this. (*He waves his
arm again*) Who do like this?
GEORGIE. Do it again.
GREEDY. Now watch! (*He waves again*) Who you see do that
before?
GEORGIE. I don't believe I've ever seen anybody do that before.
GREEDY. That's the Pope, Georgie Porgie. I see him do that in
the last newsreel I see.
GEORGIE. Is that so?

GREEDY. Yeah. Just like this. (*He performs solemnly*) Why he do that? Every time I see the Pope he do that. What do the Pope mean when he do that?

GEORGIE. It's a kind of blessing, I believe.

GREEDY. Is that what it is? Must be, to make a man feel so good. How come *everybody* don't do that?

GEORGIE. Everybody's not the Pope.

GREEDY. Make *me* feel good to do that, too. (*He does it again, and laughs*) What else the Pope do like that?

GEORGIE. Well, the Pope prays, too. I heard him pray over the radio once. That was away back in 1939, before the War. He prayed for peace on earth, of course. I heard him say some things in Latin, too.

GREEDY. I believe Andy Boy read something about Latin this morning. What is that Latin?

GEORGIE. That's a dead language.

GREEDY. No fooling? You know how to talk that dead language, Georgie Porgie?

GEORGIE. Oh, no. Nobody knows how to *talk* it; there's nobody to talk it *to*; but a few people know how to read and write it.

GREEDY. If nobody talk it, how come the Pope talk it? Who he talk it to, God?

GEORGIE. I suppose so. It's supposed to be a wonderful language, anyway.

GREEDY. (*Thinking, dreaming*) Yeah. Must be. Must be wonderful all right if the Pope talk it. I never even hear of it before. I see the Pope do like this, though. (*He does the imitation*) Seem like I can't wait to find out all about these things just as soon as Andy Boy come back. (*Pause*) Big man like the Pope believe in praying, Georgie Porgie. How about you?

GEORGIE. Oh, it's better than nothing, I suppose, but I don't suppose it's *much* better.

GREEDY. Better than nothing but not much better? (*He does the imitation*) You hit the nail on the head that time, Georgie Porgie, but seem like that nail got such a big head no matter which way you swing you *got* to hit it. Praying better than nothing but not much better. Pope better than me but not much better. That right?

GEORGIE. Yes, it is, I suppose.

GREEDY. And you always supposing, too. I suppose this and I suppose that. I suppose we're all here because I suppose, I suppose. (*He does the imitation and bursts into laughter*) Man, I ain't heard nothing like *that* before. (*Suddenly*) Make me *hungry*.

GEORGIE. Hungry? Why?

GREEDY. Why? Because all that I-suppose-I-suppose stuff make me feel dead and gone before I *am* dead and gone. Make me feel all of a sudden maybe I ain't *never* been alive. Make me feel it wasn't *me* who do all that poor living in the first place. I suppose, I suppose. Which was me back there and which was not me? Which is me now and which ain't? (*Slight pause*) Answer me that, Georgie Porgie.

GEORGIE. Ah, nuts. This morning you woke me up out of the best dream I ever had. Now you keep asking me all these foolish questions.

GREEDY. You mean that dream about Coca-Cola?

GEORGIE. Yes, Coca-Cola. Once upon a time I must have had a drink of Coca-Cola that made me feel I could never die and never be ignorant, and now that I'm about to die—now that I'm as ignorant as it's possible for any man to be—well, I had to go to work and remember my one good moment.

GREEDY. You ain't as ignorant as me.

GEORGIE. Oh, yes, I am. Who else has ever come to the end of his life, haunted by the memory of Coca-Cola?

GREEDY. What's Coca-Cola? I'll go get you a bottle from the machine in the hall right now.

GEORGIE. No, thanks. I had a bottle this afternoon. It's not the same. Oh, the Coca-Cola's the same all right, but *I'm* not. (*Pause*) I was the same in the *dream*, though. I could hear the carpenters hammering the nails in the wood, making a house half a mile away. And I was just sitting there on the porch, breathing. I wasn't thinking. I was just there.

GREEDY. How old was you?

GEORGIE. (*Very clearly*) One day, that's how old I was. I was forever. I was the original. And I'm not the original any more.

GREEDY. Who is the original?

GEORGIE. Oh, a couple of hundred million kids some place or other, out in the right weather, and I wish to God every one of them could have the weather forever.

GREEDY. (Amazed) Yeah.

GEORGIE. (Suddenly) Listen! You want Andy Boy to come back, don't you?

GREEDY. (Softly) You know damn well I want him to come back, Georgie Porgie. You know the worse I feel the more I carry on, the way I been carrying on, doing like the Pope do, and all that—and that's another thing I can't figure out. Here I am sitting over the dictionary this way, looking at the words I can't read, asking every minute what's happened to Andy Boy, at the same time waving my arm around like I see the Pope do in the last newsreel I see, talking this way and that, and every now and then laughing, too. What license I got to laugh? Why I laugh at a time like this, Georgie Porgie?

GEORGIE. Because you feel good.

GREEDY. No! Mostly I feel bad, Georgie Porgie. Only when I do like the Pope—like this—I feel good. I guess that's because he such a big important man and I such a little no-account one, doing the same thing. Average Pope live a long time, live longer than me, but sooner or later every Pope got to go along, too, just as if he ain't no bigger than the smallest man in the world, and that make me feel good. That's what make me laugh and carry on the way I been doing, but I know that ain't right!

GEORGIE. Well, it ain't wrong, either. Anyhow, if you want Andy Boy to come back, I think you'd better say a prayer for him.

GREEDY. (Slowly) Yeah. I got to pray. I got to pray for Andy Boy. Let me see now.

GEORGIE. (Helping) Our Father—

GREEDY. No, no, that ain't no prayer for Andy Boy. I got to remember about that Mamma and Pappa stuff he read to me this morning. (Trying to remember) Pappa! (He looks upward as if in prayer) Get in the sleep of Andy Boy, lying alone in the ether room, help him win the fight—a little more air and a little more light. (*He imitates the Pope, then turns to* GEORGIE) You hear that, Georgie Porgie?

GEORGIE. Yeah, but go ahead, pray some more.

GREEDY. Mamma! Give back to Andy Boy his abdomen—stomach, liver, kidneys, all of it—let him be comfortable. Christ, I still got mine—right here. (*He pats his belly, then imitates the Pope.*)

GEORGIE. Ah, go ahead, will you?

GREEDY. I just thinking, Georgie Porgie. I just thinking how a man don't stop to notice he got his whole abdomen until he about to lose *everything* he got.

GEORGIE. All right, so you've got your whole abdomen. Finish your prayer for Andy Boy, will you?

GREEDY. (*Earnestly*) Yeah. I got to forget my abdomen long enough to pray for every *bit* of Andy Boy. (*He looks up again, as if in prayer*) Mamma and Pappa—both of you— bring back my partner for the little time we got left to read the book and learn the way to go.

He falls silent, slowly hangs his head, as if in shame, while BRICK moves toward him, and even POSEYO watches. The music is heard clearly now.

BRICK. What's the matter?

GREEDY. (*He turns and speaks softly*) I been having fun, Brick, and now I ashamed. Right now Andy Boy fighting for a few more minutes of life and here I am carrying on, acting like a healthy man. Acting like all the people who ain't sick. Seem like I just ain't got no control at all. I never feel so bad as I feel right now, but here I am having fun. (*Suddenly*) Is this the way to live? Poseyo, what's the matter with me, anyway?

POSEYO. What?

GREEDY. I been thinking all my life black the trouble with me, but black ain't the trouble with me at all. Lots of good men black. Lots of good men white, red, or some other color. Color ain't the trouble with me or anybody else. Something else the trouble with me. Who fool around with me this way all the time, make me carry on? Who make me ornery? Who make me proud of my abdomen right here in this sad place, at this sad time, Poseyo?

POSEYO. Who?

GREEDY. Man, I wish I know. I wish I know who do that to me. I wish I know why. Time come to pray for my friend, and I pray like a man laughing at everything good we got—friendship and kindness. Here I am still proud of the little things I got that somebody else ain't got. Somebody make me ornery long enough. From now I going to be the boss of this here black man, and I tell him right now get on his knees like this, and pray for Andy Boy like a man. (*He kneels at the table.*)

BRICK. Andy Boy's going to be all right.

GREEDY. (*Earnestly*) Ah, that's nice of you to say that, Brick. Sure he's going to be all right. And when I *know* he's going to be all right I going to know *I* going to be all right, too. And I going to know something else, too. I going to know friendship way down deep inside that ornery secret we all trying to figure out, and I going to thank God for letting me know at the last minute, in the nick of time. I going to know friendship deeper and stronger in that ornery old secret than anything else, deeper and stronger than everything else *put together* maybe, and I going to hate no more, trouble my heart no more to get even. Get even on *who? People?* Why, people need somebody to *pray* for them. Every one of them need somebody to pray for him, even the Pope, doing like this. (*He does the imitation without pleasure*) Pope ain't no better off than any of us, either—all that church work to do. From now on *I* boss me, nobody else. What the boss say, I got to do, and now the boss say pray for Andy Boy. (DAY NURSE *comes in, holding a drinking-glass containing half a dozen thermometers in alcohol*) Nurse, I fixing to pray for Andy Boy right now, but tell me first, how is he?

NURSE. He's as well as might be expected under the circumstances.

GEORGIE. You mean he's dying?

NURSE. (*Placing a thermometer in* GEORGIE'S *mouth*) Now,

there's no need for anybody here to excite himself about Andy Boy. He's in good hands and if his life can be saved, Doctor Bohan will save it. (*She places a thermometer in* POSEYO's *mouth, then in* BRICK's, *then in* GREEDY's.)

GEORGIE. He had a good month to live *without* any help from Doctor Bohan.

NURSE. Never mind trying to talk with the thermometer in your mouth, Georgie Porgie. You can all just be quiet for a minute or two while I take your temperatures.

POSEYO's music is heard while the DAY NURSE holds each man's wrist and looks at her wristwatch, taking their pulses, after which she removes the thermometers from their mouths, examines them, writes on each of their charts, beginning with GEORGIE.

GEORGIE. You don't think Andy Boy's got a chance, do you?

NURSE. Now, you be quiet, Georgie Porgie. I didn't say he hasn't got a chance.

GEORGIE. (*To* GREEDY) Well, if you're going to pray, you'd better get going, and you'd better make it good this time.

GREEDY tries to say something.

NURSE. (*Removing the thermometer from* POSEYO's *mouth, turning to* GREEDY) Never mind trying to talk just yet, please. (*She examines* POSEYO's *thermometer. Then removes the thermometer from* BRICK's *mouth. She examines the thermometer, looks at* BRICK *curiously, at the thermometer again, then touches his forehead*) I think you'd better get to bed.

BRICK. No, I always get a little fever about this hour of the day.

NURSE. It's not a *little* fever, I'm afraid.

BRICK. This happens every evening. I'm all right.

NURSE. Well, you know where your bed is. You'll be wanting it soon enough, I can tell you that, and I'll be around later on with some pills. As long as you are up, though, see that you keep quiet. I wouldn't have any louder music than the music you're listening to now, Poseyo.

GEORGIE. We've gotten so used to Poseyo's music we don't hear it any more.

NURSE. I hear it, and I must say it's quite nice. (*She removes* GREEDY's *thermometer*) What is it?

GREEDY. (*Glum and troubled*) That's Mozart.

NURSE. It is? Now, all of you be nice and quiet, will you? Poseyo, you didn't eat your supper again. Who did?

GREEDY. (*Raising his hand like a schoolboy*) Me. Greedy Reed.

NURSE. Poseyo ought to eat a little more. You ought to try to get him to eat a little more instead of gobbling up everything on his tray.

GREEDY. Yes, ma'am.

NURSE. See that you eat your breakfast in the morning, Poseyo. I'm not sure you shouldn't get to bed, Brick.

BRICK. No, I'm all right.

NURSE. Georgie Porgie, look after Brick, will you? If Doctor Bohan weren't already so overworked I'd ask him to come in and have a look at Brick after he's through with Andy Boy. Anybody want anything? (*Pause*) All right, then, no excitement, please. (*She goes out, sliding the door shut behind her.*)

GEORGIE. What's the matter with you, Brick?

BRICK. I never told you I used to ride in the amateur bike races, did I?

GEORGIE. No, you never did.

BRICK. Well, I used to.

GEORGIE. That's good. Why don't you sit down?

BRICK. (*Looking straight ahead at nothing, as if in a trance*) I never cared much for the sprints, but I used to like the distance races. Fifty miles, a hundred miles, a hundred and fifty, two hundred. I never cared much about winning, either. I just liked to ride. There was a race one summer when I was sixteen or seventeen from Fresno to San Francisco, up Highway 99, two hundred miles. I got off to a good start, with the nearest riders about half a mile down the highway when I got to Madera. It was a hot morning in August and it was all I could do to keep from hollering at the top of my lungs, I felt so good. Seemed like I just couldn't get tired. By the time I got to Merced I couldn't see any of the other racers at all. I felt glad to be out in front that way and all alone, but pretty soon I got lonesome—lonesome for the rest of the guys in the race, I *thought*—so I slowed down and let three of them pacing along together catch up with me. I got in with them and we paced along together, talking and telling jokes, but pretty soon I felt lonesomer than ever, so I picked up a swifter pace and moved out in front again. By the time I got to Modesto I couldn't see them, and I wasn't even beginning to get tired, so it looked as if I ought to win the race easy. It was one of those Sundays you see in the San Joaquin Valley, everything hot and half-asleep and very still. You could hear little noises from far away as if they were from real close, like a screen door banging, or some kid hollering out to another. There's a small park in Modesto where they have a band concert Sunday afternoons in the summer, and I had been hearing the band four or five minutes when I reached the park. The band was playing something I seemed to know that I hadn't heard in years, and the park was full of girls. There must have been three or four dozen of them at least: all kinds of American girls, and all kinds of Mexican and Portuguese and Japanese and Negro girls, and I went riding around the park looking at them instead of racing. I kept trying to remember the words of the song the band was playing, and then finally I remembered them. (*He tries to sing*) "You know you belong to somebody else, so why don't you leave me alone?" (*He whistles a little more of the song*) Pretty soon the boys racing behind me reached the park, and there I was sitting under a tree instead of racing, because I loved every girl in the park. (*Pause*) Well, that's the way I feel now.

He looks around, whistling the song softly, then goes out slowly, shutting the door behind him. EVERYBODY remains silent a moment, as POSEYO turns the volume dial up and the music is heard softly but clearly.

GEORGIE. (*Suddenly to* GREEDY, *who's been kneeling at the table all this time. He speaks powerfully*) All right, you heard what the nurse said. If you're going to pray, get going, before it's too late.

GREEDY. (*His voice hushed*) I been praying all the time, Georgie Porgie. I praying *now*.

GEORGIE. I don't *hear* you praying.

GREEDY. I ain't using words this time, Georgie Porgie. The boss tell me to pray with everything I got—abdomen and all—and it don't come out in words. I hear every word Brick say about that bike race and the park in Modesto and the girls there. Seem like the words Brick say was a prayer. Maybe when Andy Boy come back and read me the dictionary I learn some words good enough for a real prayer for everybody, white and black and red and man and woman and rich and poor and strong and weak and everything else, but right now I don't know any words for a prayer like that.

GEORGIE. (*Standing*) O.K., O.K., I'll read the dictionary to you until Andy Boy comes back. I'm half blind, but I can still see good enough to read, I guess.

GREEDY. That's awful nice of you, Georgie Porgie. You know I dying to hear the words in the dictionary, but I couldn't doublecross my partner that way. What kind of partner I be if I go ahead and let somebody else read the dictionary while he fighting for his life? Andy Boy's got to read the words. Nobody else.

GEORGIE. He may not come back.

GREEDY. Ah, Georgie Porgie, why you say that? Why you go to work and jinx Andy Boy that way? The boss got me kneeling here this way praying for him with all my might. Why you even let yourself think *maybe* he ain't coming back? That ain't right, Georgie Porgie. He *got* to come back.

GEORGIE. It wasn't his idea to read the dictionary in the first place. It was your idea.

GREEDY. What that got to do with it?

GEORGIE. Plenty. Wasn't I telling you this morning about one of the theories of personal continuity?

GREEDY. No, Georgie Porgie. You tell me something about everybody in this world being here from long ago, and everybody leaving this world maybe coming back again.

GEORGIE. That's one of the theories of personal continuity. Well, there's another theory about another matter, too.

GREEDY. What theory about what matter that?

GEORGIE. The theory about the matter of dying. This theory says nobody dies until he's *willing* to die. Now, how do you know Andy Boy ain't willing to die right now, in spite of your praying? I don't mean the Andy Boy we see on the outside, I mean the one we don't see—the man in you that you call the boss. I mean the man in Andy Boy who's come back to this world so many times he's sick and tired of it. A man's got to have something going to keep him from being willing to die, and according to this theory as long as a man *has* got something going, he just naturally can't die, no matter how sick he is. In other words, the theory says you die when you yourself are willing to die, and not before—not even by accident. It's a theory, of course, but everything we believe is a theory. All right, suppose Andy Boy just ain't got anything going to keep him from being willing to die? Suppose he doesn't care about reading the dictionary enough to stay alive? What's the use kidding ourselves? Maybe he doesn't want to bother about anything any more.

GREEDY. Georgie Porgie, how you expect me, a religious man, kneeling here in prayer right now, know what you talking about? Religious man like me ain't got no brains. Friendship all I got, and right now my best friend dying and I praying for him because I give him my word. The boss tell me not to break my word, Georgie Porgie. He tell me to pray for Andy Boy until he come back, and that's what I doing. Andy Boy going to read the dictionary, nobody else.

GEORGIE. (*Sitting down*) O.K., have it your way, but I think you're keeping another friend from a good chance to round out *his* poor life by doing something generous and unselfish.

GREEDY. Who that?

GEORGIE. Me, that's who. Don't you think it would make my last hours easier if I felt I was making you happy by reading the dictionary?

GREEDY. Praying man like me don't understand so much peculiar friendship all of a sudden, Georgie Porgie. The dictionary stand up there on that shelf all the time. Nobody open it. When I look for something right to do before I go, and find the dictionary, nobody volunteer to read it to me.

GEORGIE. Did Andy Boy volunteer?

GREEDY. No, but sick as he was he accept my invitation right away. This morning when I invite Brick and you to sit down and play a little casino, you turn me down, make me feel cheap and black. Man, I don't understand this brand-new friendship you talking about.

GEORGIE. People ain't necessarily the same in the evening as they were in the morning. I'll just read some of the dictionary, not all of it. Just as soon as Brick gets over his fever and feels a little better, maybe he'll read some of it, too, and I can rest and listen. And then when Andy Boy comes back, he can read as much of it as he likes, or he can rest, too, and listen while Brick reads. We're all friends.

GREEDY. You talk good, Georgie Porgie, but what you say ain't right. I know it ain't right because the boss tell me so. He tell me not to break the word I give Andy Boy. Nobody else going to read the dictionary. Lots of books over there on that shelf. Anybody want to read, let him read one of them books, not the dictionary. I kneeling here in prayer for Andy Boy with the open dictionary in front of me waiting for him to win his fight and come back and read the words, just like I promise him.

GEORGIE. I can see you haven't learned very much from the words he read you this morning.

GREEDY. What you mean, Georgie Porgie?

GEORGIE. You're still the same man you always were. You just ain't willing to let something good happen to anybody but yourself. You're getting a lot of pleasure out of kneeling and praying for Andy Boy and not letting me read the dictionary. You're still getting even. Keeping the dictionary for Andy Boy is just another way for you to get even, that's all. It's not an act of friendship or understanding, it's an act of revenge. Like all religious fanatics you feel sorry for yourself alone. You don't care what happens to anybody else just so you can find out how to become willing to die. Well, I'm trying to find out, too, and I ain't got much time. It's true you discovered the dictionary, but that don't mean you got to keep me from reading it. (*Suddenly*) Unless of course you don't want to have the dictionary read to you at all. Unless you're just building up all that stuff so you can enjoy feeling sorry for Andy Boy and yourself and anybody else whose skin happens to be something like the color of yours. Maybe you don't want to have the dictionary read to you at all.

GREEDY. Ah, what you talking about, Georgie Porgie? What you trying to make me feel low and crooked for? (*Painfully, earnestly*) I give Andy Boy my word. What you twisting everything around for? I been feeling almost decent kneeling here, trying to pray these few minutes, but you spoiling it all, making a monkey out of me, and the boss tell me that ain't right. You playing games on a ignorant man, Georgie Porgie.

GEORGIE. *I'm* not playing games, you are! You keep putting yourself over to one side, away from Brick and me. You're hogging the dictionary because your skin and Andy Boy's skin is darker than ours, and because you're proud—yes, proud—that you—a black man who can't even read—discovered in this miserable place the only occupation for the anxious heart and the troubled mind that can soothe them both, and let a man turn away from this world of his own free will instead of having his life *forced* out of him as if he were an insect, or had never lived at all. Now, isn't that so?

GREEDY. No, it ain't so, and you know it ain't so, Georgie Porgie. You talk and talk and make me feel low and crooked, kneeling here, but what you say ain't so, Georgie Porgie. Reading the dictionary Andy Boy's job, and nobody going to take his job away from him. You saw him sit up and turn around when they wheel him out of here this morning. He look at me, to tell me to keep my word, and he look at the dictionary, to see the way it lie here on this table, the way it going to lie here when he come back to go on reading. Everything got to be the same when he come back. Now I ain't going to talk no more. I ain't going to listen no more, Georgie Porgie. I going to pray, and pretty soon you going to see

the nurse come and say Andy Boy going to be all right,
Andy Boy going to come back. (*He shuts his eyes, folds his
hands, bows his head.*)

GEORGIE. (*Softly*) For your sake, then, I hope he *does* come back.

GREEDY. (*His eyes shut, softly*) Oh, he coming back all right.
(POSEYO *shuts off the phonograph.* GREEDY *speaks softly without opening his eyes*) Why you stop the music, Poseyo?

POSEYO. I go lie down now. (*He goes.*)

GREEDY. (*Softly*) Seem like I can't pray no more. I still trying
to pray, Andy Boy, but seem like I need some help from
Mozart, or Brick telling about the bike race that time he
fell in love with all the girls, or even Georgie Porgie badger-
ing me to let him take your place at the dictionary. Seem
like a man need a lot of help, one kind another, to say a
decent prayer even, Andy Boy. I just can't pray worth a
damn all alone this way, so I going to get up off my knees
now and go look for help. Amen. (*He opens his eyes, unfolds
his hands, stands up, straightens the dictionary on the desk,
and notices* GEORGIE *lost in the comic book*) If I say anything
wrong while I praying, Georgie Porgie, I sorry.

GEORGIE. (*Abstractedly*) What?

GREEDY. I say I sorry.

GEORGIE. (*Still looking in the book*) What for?

GREEDY. If I say anything wrong while I praying. (*Pause*) Seem
awful cold around here now without Mozart and Poseyo and
Brick and Andy Boy. Almost make me shiver, so cold around
here now. Cold and dark. You want me to switch on the
lights, so you can see what you looking at there?

GEORGIE. No, I kind of like the dark, and I know these pictures
by heart anyway.

GREEDY. I going out to ask the nurse about Andy Boy now.
You want me to fetch you something? A Coca-Cola, maybe?

GEORGIE. No, thanks.

GREEDY. I done my best.

GEORGIE. What?

GREEDY. Praying for Andy Boy, I mean. (*Softly*) Seem awful
cold around here. (*Pause*) You mad at me, Georgie Porgie?

GEORGIE. Why should I be mad at you?

GREEDY. I feel awful cold, Georgie Porgie. Seem like somebody mad at me.

GEORGIE. I'm not. Let me know what the nurse tells you about Andy Boy.

GREEDY. Yeah. I let you know, Georgie Porgie. (*Pause*) When you hear the workmen hammering them nails in the wood, how come that make you feel so good?

GEORGIE. I told you how come. I was somebody who was forever. I was the original. The whole place was for me. Everything was made for me. Everything belonged to me.

GREEDY. Yeah. (*Pause*) I feel awful cold, Georgie Porgie. Seem like lots of freezing and dying going on around here. (*He goes out.*)

ACT TWO

Scene I

GEORGIE waits until the door is shut by GREEDY REED, then gets up quickly and goes to the dictionary. He looks down at the words, trying to see if he can make them out, then hurries to the light switch and switches on the lights, which are very dim. He goes back to the dictionary and again tries to make out the words, moving his head closer and closer to the page. He lifts his head suddenly, shakes it, rubs his good eye, tries again, but is obviously unable to make out the words. He thinks about this a moment, then goes back to his table, sits down, and takes up the comic book, whistling BRICK's song softly. BRICK comes into the room, slides the door shut behind him, goes to the window and looks out, as GEORGIE watches with interest.

GEORGIE. I thought you went to bed.

BRICK. Well, I didn't.

GEORGIE. I was afraid you weren't going to be able to get out here any more.

BRICK. Is that so?

GEORGIE. Yeah. The nurse scared me, and so did that story of yours about the bike race. It was all I could do to keep things alive for myself playing games on poor Greedy Reed. He just went out to get the latest news on Andy Boy. Now that you're back, though, I don't feel so bad. (*Slight pause*) Got any more stories?

BRICK. No, just the one.

GEORGIE. You'd think we'd all have dozens of stories. Take the twenty years or so I gambled for a living. There wasn't one day that wasn't full of accidents of luck that only I knew

55

about, that I thought I'd want to tell somebody about some day, but I'll be damned if any of it seems worth telling now. (*He waits a moment for* BRICK *to say something, then goes on easily*) There was a place on O'Farrell Street where I was always good for a couple of hundred dollars' credit. Many times I sat down to a game of stud with nothing to my name but my guts, and five or six hours later got up rich enough to spend a whole year loafing and traveling first-class, the way I'd always wanted to do but never did. And then three days later all I'd have to my name again would be my guts. (*Slight pause*) But there it is—it just doesn't seem to be worth telling now. I always wanted to loaf and travel, though. (*He watches* BRICK *at the window, then goes on softly*) I say, I always wanted to loaf and travel, though.

BRICK. I heard you. (*Pause.*)

GEORGIE. Well, if you don't feel like talking, I'm glad you're going to be up and about for a while longer yet, anyway.

BRICK. Thanks. (*Pause.*)

GEORGIE. Poseyo turned off the phonograph and went to bed, but I don't think it's anything serious. He'll be out here in the morning before anybody else, the same as ever, most likely. (*He pauses ever so slightly for some show of interest, then goes on, determined to draw* BRICK *out*) As far as I'm concerned, I never expected to live almost fifty years, anyway. After I was twenty, I always believed I didn't have more than another year to go at the most. That's when I started gambling. There's a lot of fast living in one night of gambling, let alone a whole year of it, and it's the kind of living that takes you pretty close to—whatever's next. After I was forty, though, I began to believe I could go on living as long as I felt like it, because one day was exactly like another, and I had forgotten all about noticing time going by, the way you do before you're twenty. And then all of a sudden I felt I'd lost something somewhere along the line. Not time or money—something else. That's when I *quit* gambling. Of course I didn't know I'd quit when I had. I just found myself spending a lot of time *not* gambling. I began to sleep a lot more than I had been sleeping. I'd stayed in some games as long as thirty-six hours, fighting to get even, or to win a little, so of course I'd missed a lot of sleep. After I'd caught up on my sleep, I began to read. Newspapers at first, then magazines, and finally books—from the public library. I guess I was looking for what I'd lost. I once read a whole book about bacteriology, for instance. I remember reading about a man named Noguchi who lost his life trying to find out something or other. Seemed kind of strange and—handsome—that a man could be that interested in something. Finally, I found out why I'd quit gambling. It was because I hated enslavement of any kind, especially the enslavement that comes from having to work for a living—for money, I mean, so you can keep your body warm and alive, so you can stay enslaved a little longer. I didn't like that at all, but that was exactly what had happened to me, gambling, so I quit. After awhile I found out what I'd lost during the years of gambling, too. I'd lost the memory of ever having been out in the weather. (*Almost laughing*) That doesn't seem like much to lose, but it's really a hell of a lot—everything maybe. I got it back this morning in that Coca-Cola dream I had. You'd think a man about to die would have something better to remember. (*Slight pause*) Are you listening to me at all?

BRICK. Sure I'm listening.

GEORGIE. I'll shut up if you want me to.

BRICK. No, I don't mind listening.

GEORGIE. Well, anyway, I'll never forget the corny remarks professional gamblers used to make to some sucker who'd gone broke. They never got tired of saying, "Easy come, easy go," for instance. The fellow might be a stevedore or a bricklayer with a week's wages pissed away, and an anxious wife and maybe a couple of hungry kids to go home to without any money. He'd get up from the table and try to laugh at the corny remark, but anybody could see how hurt he was. I always felt sorry for workingmen trying to get hold of easy money.

BRICK. So what?

GEORGIE. Nothing. I just hate enslavement of any kind, that's all. (*Slight pause*) Maybe you ought to go to bed after all, like the nurse said. Maybe you're worse off than you think.

BRICK. No, I'm all right.

GEORGIE. (*Eager to keep the talk going at any cost, swiftly*) The nurse didn't think so. What makes you think so?

BRICK. Oh, I know I'm all right—now.

GEORGIE. *Now*? What do you know now that you didn't know when the nurse took your temperature?

BRICK. I know how I'm going to spend the rest of my life.

GEORGIE. Is that so? How? (*Pause.*)

BRICK. I'm going to stand here until I see the lights go on at Alcatraz.

GEORGIE. That ought to be soon enough. Then what are you going to do?

BRICK. Then I'm going to sit down at the piano.

GEORGIE. After that, what are you going to do?

BRICK. After that, I'm going to go back and look at Alcatraz some more.

GEORGIE. What are you always looking at Alcatraz for? (*The conversation collapses. There is a long pause*) What's the matter? I said, what are you always looking at Alcatraz for?

BRICK. And I said, I heard you.

GEORGIE. Something's the matter with you besides fever. What the hell is it?

BRICK. Play your little games on Greedy Reed. He'll be back in a minute.

GEORGIE. You're worse off than I thought. I'm not playing any games. Why shouldn't I be on the level with you?

BRICK. I don't know, unless it's because you can't be on the level with *anybody*, even yourself.

GEORGIE. Oh, I'm on the level with myself all right, don't worry about that.

BRICK. If you're on the level with yourself, you'd get in bed and stay there instead of hanging around out here, stalling for time. You're as far gone as anybody in bed. You just want more time. (*Pause*) More time for *what*, though?

GEORGIE. I'd like to know how Andy Boy makes out, for one thing.

BRICK. Andy Boy's dead. You know it and I know it, so who do we think we're kidding?

GEORGIE. He may be, and then again he may not be. I'd like to know for sure.

BRICK. You just haven't got guts enough to give up, that's all.

GEORGIE. Why don't you sit down at the piano, like you said you were going to do after you saw the lights go on at Alcatraz?

BRICK. I didn't see the lights go on. I missed seeing them go on because I was talking to you. Now they're on, but I didn't see them go on. Why don't you get up and put on the clothes you were wearing when you came here a month ago and walk out of here, like you said this morning you could do any time you felt like it? Why don't you do *that*, as long as you're asking me why I don't do this and that?

GEORGIE. I don't feel like it. I feel like sitting here and looking at these pictures of Joe Palooka.

BRICK. I don't believe you've *ever* looked at those pictures. (*Suddenly, desperately*) Christ, can't we get out of here? Can't we go to a bar on Pacific Avenue and drink ourselves to death?

GEORGIE. Ah, sit down at the piano.

BRICK. I'm sick and tired of hanging on. I'm sick and tired of having you provoke me into hanging on. What are you doing it for all the time? Three weeks ago when I got here I expected to get in bed and stay there and let it go at that, but every morning you get me out of bed and bring me out here to this God-forsaken room and provoke me into forgetting I'm dead.

GEORGIE. I've got to have somebody intelligent to talk to, don't I? I've got to have somebody with a little sense in his head to listen to me, don't I?

BRICK. Pick on somebody else from now on. You won't get me out of bed tomorrow.

GEORGIE. I'll try. I got you out of bed this morning. You heard me make up all kinds of lies about Poseyo, so Greedy Reed would get out of bed, too. I want anybody who comes to this ward to get out of bed as long as possible.

BRICK. (*Whispering desperately*) I wish to Christ I was in a bar on Pacific Avenue!

GEORGIE. You'll be all right. (BRICK *sits at the piano, begins to play his song softly*) I didn't know you could play the piano. (*He listens a moment. Suddenly* BRICK *stands, clutching his belly, and* GEORGIE *gets to his feet*) Now don't get excited! Take it easy! You'll be all right again in a minute. Hang onto the piano. (BRICK *sprawls over the piano, hanging on and trying not to moan*) That's right. Hang on. That pain ain't going to last forever.

BRICK. (*In terrible pain*) I wish to Christ I was in a whorehouse on Pacific Avenue.

GEORGIE. Take it easy! You'll be all right in a minute.

BRICK. Oh, Christ! It's too late now! (*Suddenly*) Help me! Help me to my bed, will you?

GEORGIE. You'll be all right in a minute, I tell you!

BRICK. No! This is it! Oh, Jesus, this is too much pain for one man.

GEORGIE. You don't know what pain is! You've got to have it in the head to know what it is.

BRICK. Oh, Christ, cut it out, will you? You know you're in no pain at all! (*Suddenly, helplessly, writhing with pain*) Oh, Mamma, Mamma, Mamma! (*He stops writhing; whispers*) Help me to bed, Georgie Porgie, for the love of God! Get the nurse. Get me something for this pain! I promise to get out of bed in the morning.

GEORGIE. Oh, no, I'm not going to fall for that! If you're going to kick the bucket, kick it out here like a man, not in bed like a baby looking for Mamma to rock him to sleep. You ain't finished yet, but you will be if you take any pills the nurse gives you. Most of your pain's gone now, anyway, isn't it?

BRICK. (*Moaning*) No! Jesus! No!

GEORGIE. I began having attacks like that two weeks ago. The first one scares you a lot, but that's about all. You've got plenty of time. Let yourself go, though, and you're gone, that's all. Don't tell the nurse or anybody else about this. Keep it to yourself. You'll be all right again before you know it, wait and see, and then you'll really know what living is. This is only the first attack. You won't have another until to-morrow night maybe, or the next, but you've still got at least half a dozen more coming if you don't let yourself go, so don't let yourself go. I could keep Andy Boy going longer than the Doctors ever could if I knew how to talk to him. Anybody knows we're past help in the body. The Doctors just don't know how to give us any other kind of help. I'm finding out how, though. I can still help myself, at any rate, and if you'll hang on a little longer and listen to me, I can help you, too. I swear to God I can. What can you lose? Turn yourself over to the hospital—tell them about this—and you know you're finished. So don't tell them. Don't go to bed and die. Stay here. I'll help you find out how to help your-self.

BRICK. Don't stop talking, Georgie Porgie. For God's sake, keep talking. Just keep talking. Recite the alphabet. Say anything. I'm listening. I can't think straight any more, but I know I need more time—just a little more time—so keep talking, will you? (Moaning painfully) Oh, Jesus, Jesus, Jesus.

GEORGIE. Sure you need a little more time. A man never needs time the way you and I need it now. Time never means very much until it's this kind of time—time that we make our-selves, out of nerve and guts, for ourselves. There's a lot of anesthesia in every one of us when we're hurt and mad this way, and it's the only anesthesia that works when we're past getting help for our bodies.

BRICK. Keep talking, Georgie Porgie. Oh, Jesus, my guts, my guts. Keep talking. Keep talking.

GEORGIE. Don't worry, I'll keep talking. I've got pain of my own to get rid of, you know. Your pain's in a bad place but not as bad as where mine is—in the head, behind the eye that's eaten away, and now—Christ, now it's behind the other eye, too. We belong to the same race for sure now. Pain's our life, and the anesthesia for both of us is the same now, too—arrogance, contempt and hate. Hate for anything and everything, anybody and everybody. That's all. (He watches BRICK straighten up slowly. BRICK's face is white *and wet.* GEORGIE *speaks softly*) You'll be O.K. for at least twenty-four hours now, maybe thirty-six or forty-eight. That's a lot of time, Brick. And I gave it to you. (*Painfully*) I gave it to you because you're the only son of a bitch around here I can talk to, and the only one who's going to be able to give me a little help when I'm not going to be able to help myself any more, when I'm going to want it and need it most. (*Slight pause*) You all right now?

BRICK. I'm a lot better, thanks. My guts still hurt, but not the way they did a little while ago. Something seemed to be tearing them to pieces. I'm scared. Christ, I'm scared! (*He goes to the window.*)

GEORGIE. You'll get over *that* in a few minutes, too. (*Long pause*) How do you feel now?

BRICK. I can't believe I'm still *alive*. That pain scared me, Georgie Porgie. I guess I'm O.K. again for a little while, but what the hell for? I keep thinking I need a little more time. I keep expecting something to happen, something better than anything that's happened in my whole life, and that's what's scaring the hell out of me because I know the only thing that can happen now is another attack, only worse than the one I just got over. Yeah, I'm O.K. again for a little while, I guess. So what? For God's sake, Georgie Porgie, so what? (*He goes back to the piano and sits down*) Yeah, I'm O.K.

GEORGIE. I can see you are. Well, I'm not O.K., see? I got you over your first attack, but *this* is my ninth or tenth. Yes, and one *is* worse than the other. I'm in more pain than you'll ever know, but that's all right.

BRICK. I'm sorry, Georgie Porgie.

GEORGIE. Never mind. I still know how to keep myself alive, and I've still got guts enough not to need any help from you or anybody else. Tomorrow or the next day when you get your next attack I'll try to keep you going again. But *I'll* go when I get good and ready to go. I'll go because I've had enough and *feel like* going, not because I'm getting the bum's rush.

BRICK. I'll help you, Georgie Porgie. I swear to God, I'll try my best to help you, if you'll let me. I've never known how bad it was with you until now. I'll help you, Georgie Porgie.

GEORGIE. Never mind. I'll go hating, like I said, because I know what I am—what every man is—a dirty crook who kids himself into thinking a little measly health entitles him to some kind of life everlasting, and then when his health is gone whimpers and wails and rocks himself back to sleep in Mamma's big warm lap. I'll go knowing I've *had* my life everlasting—one little memory of breathing easily, drinking Coca-Cola. I'll go the way I want to go, after I've done everything I want to do, and I still want to do a few more things.

BRICK. (*Softly, with real sympathy*) Sure, Georgie Porgie.

GEORGIE. Never mind. You just stand there at the window and look down at Alcatraz and feel sorry for yourself

BRICK. (*Looks at him curiously. Softly*) I'm not standing at the window, Georgie Porgie.

GEORGIE. You're a dirty liar!

BRICK. No, Georgie Porgie. I'm sitting at the piano.

GEORGIE. (*Standing in anger, pointing at the window*) You're standing right there at the window. I can see you.

BRICK. No, I'm not, Georgie Porgie. I'm sitting here at the piano. (*Long pause.*)

GEORGIE. (*Very softly*) Touch the keys of the piano if that's where you are.

BRICK. Sure, Georgie Porgie.

He plays several chords of his song very softly, then stops, as GEORGIE turns to the piano, stares a moment, then slowly sits down.

GEORGIE. (*Whispering*) Oh, Christ! (*There is a long pause. GEORGIE speaks with power and anger*) All right, I can't see. I'm blind now, too, but everything I said still goes. (BRICK *stands*) You just stood up, didn't you?

BRICK. Yeah, Georgie Porgie.

GEORGIE. Well, I can still see *that* much, anyway. Sit down and finish playing what you started to play.

BRICK. I'll help you get around, Georgie Porgie.

GEORGIE. Sit down. Sit down.

BRICK. I'll stick by you, Georgie Porgie. (*He sits.*)

GEORGIE. I saw you sit down. I can still see a little. Go ahead, play the piano.

BRICK. Sure, Georgie Porgie.

BRICK plays half a minute or so. He stops when the DAY NURSE comes in with a shy little MAN (BUSTER) of fifty or so who appears to be stunned and lonely and on the verge of tears, as lost children are.

DAY NURSE. (*To the* MAN) This is the Sun Room. It's not much now, but during the day it's very nice, and the view from the window is a sight for sore eyes. (GEORGIE *barely winces.*)

BUSTER. Yes, ma'am.

DAY NURSE. Not many of the boys get out here any more, so you and these two and one or two others will have the whole place to yourselves—piano, phonograph, radio, magazines, books, games, view and all. Do you play the piano?

BUSTER. No, ma'am.

DAY NURSE. Well, it's there anyway. (*Brightly*) Now don't be bashful. You'll find everybody here the same as everybody anywhere else. (*She turns to* GEORGIE *and* BRICK) Boys, I want you to meet— (*She examines the chart she is holding for the man's name.*)

BUSTER. (*Shyly, softly*) My son calls me Buster.

BRICK. This is Georgie Porgie, Buster. I'm Brick.

DAY NURSE. Now, it's not going to be half bad, is it? You'll find everybody just as nice and friendly as they can be.

BUSTER. (*Softly*) Yes, ma'am.

DAY NURSE. We've got three vacant beds in the ward, boys. Please help Buster pick one out for himself, and then if you don't mind, please show him where to put away the clothes he's wearing and put on the hospital pajamas and robe. Now, you'll make him feel at home, won't you?

BRICK. Sure we will.

BUSTER. (*Almost speechless with sudden panic, almost stammering*) I'd like to stay in these clothes until bedtime, if I may. (*He brushes a sleeve nervously.*)

DAY NURSE. Well, it's not exactly according to hospital regulations, but I don't think anyone will mind very much. Bedtime's at nine, so about half-past eight you'd better let the
boys show you around.

BUSTER. Yes, ma'am.

DAY NURSE. (*Suddenly, with forced cheerfulness*) My, you're
quiet tonight, Georgie Porgie! I see you're still on your feet,
Brick. Are you sure you're all right?

BRICK. I'm all right.

DAY NURSE. Well, all right, if you say so. Night Nurse is up
front if you want her. Now, take good care of each other.
I'll see you all bright and early in the morning.

GEORGIE. Where's Greedy Reed?

DAY NURSE. Why, he's in bed, isn't he? Of course he is. I just
saw him lying in bed.

GEORGIE. How long has he been there?

DAY NURSE. I don't know, Georgie Porgie. Why?

GEORGIE. We had two vacant beds this morning, didn't we?

DAY NURSE. (*Softly*) Yes, that's right, Georgie Porgie. (*Pause.*)

GEORGIE. Well, when did it happen?

DAY NURSE. Oh, about an hour ago. (*Slight pause*) Let the Night
Nurse know which bed Buster takes, will you please, boys?

GEORGIE. Sure. He'll probably take Andy Boy's. It's by a window.

DAY NURSE. Good night, then.

The DAY NURSE goes out, sliding the door behind her. BUSTER
stands at the window looking out. BRICK goes to the table
on which the dictionary lies. He looks down at the book,
toward the glass door, at GEORGIE, at BUSTER, and then down
at the book again.

BRICK. (*Reading softly*) Abide. To rest. To tarry or stay awhile.
To continue. To be firm and immovable. To endure. To suffer
the consequences. (*He closes the book*) You want to listen to
the radio or anything, Buster? (BUSTER *does not hear him.
After a moment he turns to* GEORGIE) Do you, Georgie Porgie?

GEORGIE. No, thanks. I just want to sit here and look at these
pictures of Joe Palooka.

BRICK. Sure, Georgie Porgie.

GEORGIE. What are you going to do?

BRICK. Abide, I guess. Tarry. Suffer the consequences.

GEORGIE. Why don't you sit down and read *Time* or something?

BRICK. Sure, Georgie Porgie. (*He gets a copy of Time off a shelf, sits down across the table from* GEORGIE) *Time*.

GEORGIE. What's it say?

BRICK. (*Turning several pages*) Well, it starts out with letters.

GEORGIE. What do the *letters* say?

BRICK. (*Reading, with great effort*) Sir. *Time's* definition of the Man of the Year is the man who had the biggest rise in fame during the year and more than anyone else changed the news for better or worse. That man is Secretary of State George C. Marshall. The year 1947 spotlighted his rise to fame from military genius to the even nobler role of defender of human democracy, and the inspiring plan which bears his name is 1947's most effective challenge to the Russian threat of world domination. Marshall is the Man of the Year, the Marshall Plan is the hope of the world. (*He stops, as if being inwardly attacked by pain again.*)

GEORGIE. All right, read some more. What's the matter?

BRICK. (*Softly*) I didn't do a damn thing this year, Georgie Porgie.

GEORGIE. Well, I guess it's Marshall's year all right, then.

BRICK. Oh, I don't know. (*He stands suddenly, moved more by pain than by will. He half clutches at his belly*) Listen, Georgie Porgie! Let's get out of here quick and die in the world. (*He opens his robe, revealing a tan suit with the trouser cuffs rolled up to his knees*) I've got my clothes on, and I can get yours, too. You can put them on in the can, the way I did. I've got twenty dollars, and I know you've got a little. So what the hell are we waiting for? Let's die in the world, Georgie Porgie. We're still free men. Let's die as if we didn't have this disease. I know a half dozen places in the North Beach. I can't stay here any more. I can't stand this silly smell of death any more. I've got to get out in the streets again. I've got to smell life again. (*He bends, holding his belly in silent pain, his eyes shut in agony.*)

GEORGIE. All right. Tell me more. I'm listening. (*Pause*) What's the matter *now?*

BRICK. (*Whispering painfully, staring at* GEORGIE) Can't you see at all, Georgie Porgie? For God's sake, Georgie Porgie, can't you see enough to give me a *little* help? I'm going to need somebody to hold me up every once in awhile.

GEORGIE. Take it easy, will you? You've got to learn to take it easy!

BRICK. (*Almost weeping*) Ah, can't you see at all, Georgie Porgie? I've got to get out of here. I'm still a free man. Can't you see enough to—

GEORGIE. (*Severely, whispering*) Listen to me a minute, will you, Brick? (*Slight pause*) You're not up to being free, and neither am I. If we were we wouldn't be here in the first place. We're not bodies any more. Bodies are a lot of crap all right, but bodies are where we've got to spend our time whether we like it or not. We're not the prison any more, we're the prisoners. Like the boys on Alcatraz, we spend our time looking at San Francisco and the Golden Gate Bridge. But we can't escape from Alcatraz until we're ready to cross the Bridge, and you know damn well the Bridge doesn't go to San Francisco. You know damn well even if you could get to San Francisco, you couldn't have any fun because you'd still be enslaved by your own Alcatraz. The Bridge is next for us, Brick, and I'm not ready to cross it yet. Now, in the dark, I need you more than ever, so gather yourself together and hang around.

BRICK. (*Sober now*) Sure, Georgie Porgie.

GEORGIE. Go back to the can, take off your street clothes, put them back where they belong. We're not up to any more side trips. (*Slight pause*) Go get Greedy Reed out of bed. Get Poseyo. Bring them out here. We've still got as much time as anybody else in the world. (*Softly*) Go get the boys, Brick.

BRICK. Sure, Georgie Porgie.

GEORGIE. (*Slight pause*) Listen, Brick. I know you had another attack a minute ago.

BRICK. It wasn't much.

GEORGIE. You could take some pills and go to bed, you know.

BRICK. No, I don't think I want to do that.

GEORGIE. If you feel like going to bed, Brick, go ahead. Don't stay up on my account. What the hell, it's no disgrace, it's just painless, that's all. I can't know how bad it is with you. A lot of new pain has made me irritable, but for God's sake don't be a fool. Go to bed if that's what you want to do, and no hard feelings.

BRICK. No, I don't want to go to bed, Georgie Porgie.

GEORGIE. Well, thanks, then. Thanks a lot. It wouldn't be the same around here without you. I can't see worth a damn any more, and I'd like to hear you play the piano again. We've had some laughs, and I swear to God I've always been on the level with you. That's the truth, Brick.

BRICK. Sure it is, Georgie Porgie.

GEORGIE. You're not mad at me for going blind this way, are you?

BRICK. No.

GEORGIE. I'll be waiting for you. (BRICK *looks around the room, smiling pathetically. He begins to walk to the door, falls silently to one knee, clutches his belly, and tries not to cry out with pain.* GEORGIE *turns*) Brick?

BRICK. Yeah.

GEORGIE. You all right?

BRICK. Yeah, sure.

GEORGIE. You want me to go with you?

BRICK. No, I'm all right.

BRICK draws himself to his feet, clutching the handle of the door. He slides the door open, steps out, slides the door shut, stands outside staring into the room a long time, his face in agony, and then disappears. There is a long pause.

GEORGIE. (*Softly*) Buster? (*Pause. Louder*) Buster?

BUSTER. (*Turning*) Yes?

GEORGIE. You've been crying, haven't you?

BUSTER. Yes, I'm afraid I have.

GEORGIE. Everybody does when they first get here. When they first realize how foolishly a life can end.

BUSTER. I miss my son.

GEORGIE. You're lucky to have a son.

BUSTER. (*Moving to table*) If I could just see him once more, that's all I'd want, and I could die in peace.

GEORGIE. When did you see him last?

BUSTER. (*Slowly*) Two years ago, when he was almost five. His mother left me then. I can't say I blame her, either. I married late in life, and I've always been a litttle ridiculous. I used to be at the Bank of America, Sunset Branch. I guess I liked my wife all right, but the only person in the world I've ever *loved* is my son. My wife used to go out with people her own age. I didn't mind, though. I didn't mind when she stayed out all night, even, because I was with my son. My son and I had almost five years together. When my wife left, she was going to have another baby. (*Pause*) I mean I knew it wasn't mine. I asked her to stay anyway, but I guess she was pretty sick and tired of the sight of me. She must have been to scream at me the way she did. (*Softly*) She said my son *wasn't* my son. Oh, I know she said it because she hated me so, but I wish she *hadn't* said it. Last year she married a fellow who works in a bar on Ortega Street, but I left my job soon after she went off with my son to live with him. I was fired, I mean. (*Pause, as he brings odds and ends from his pockets and examines them oddly*) I was just no good any more. I'd known for years something was the matter with me but I hadn't done anything about finding out what. I guess I was afraid to find out. When my son was born I didn't care *what* it was. I had *him* and that's all I wanted, so I let it go some more. I let it go until my wife left me, and then I found out. That's when they fired me. I was glad they did. I wrote to my wife and asked her to please let me see my son, but she never answered my letters, so one night I went to the bar on Ortega Street to talk to her. She made fun of me in front of everybody. And the man she's married to now put me out. She wasn't married to him then, though. (*Pause*) He lifted me by the seat of my pants and put me out. (*Pause*) I've been moving ever since. First, I walked all the way to town because I was too ashamed to get on a streetcar. Then I took a bus to Reno because there was a bus going there when I got to the bus station, but when I got to Reno I decided to keep going. I'd always wanted to get to New York. When I ran out of money in New York, I got a job in a department store, but I was too old and tired to work, so I didn't last very long. I held my first job twenty-seven years, so you can see how tired I was. I started traveling by bus again, and finally, last week, I got back to San Francisco. I tried to see my son, but I guess I didn't try hard enough.

GEORGIE. Why not?

BUSTER. I don't know. I guess I was afraid. I guess I was afraid of my wife. I guess I was afraid of the man she's married to now. (*Pause; very softly*) I guess I was afraid my son wouldn't remember me, too.

GEORGIE. Yeah.

BUSTER. I spent a whole afternoon near the house, hoping to see her come out of the house with my son, but she didn't, so then I went to a drugstore and telephoned the house and my son answered. (*Pause*) At first I couldn't talk, I was so excited, but after a moment I said, "This is your father." (*Pause*) "Who?" my son said, and then a man got on, so I hung up.

GEORGIE. Why have you come here?

BUSTER. I was *brought* here. I'm broke and, as you know, very sick.

GEORGIE. Do you have a lot of pain?

BUSTER. Quite a lot. I've had quite a lot for a long time now, but not as much as I've had since I got back to town.

GEORGIE. If you had some money, what would you do? (*Pause*) I mean, tonight. Right now.

BUSTER. I'd go back and see my son.

GEORGIE. Yeah. Sure. So would I. Why does he call you Buster?

BUSTER. That's what I used to call *him*. We used to pretend we were the same person, so he used to call *me* Buster, too. I've always felt we were the same person.

GEORGIE. Yeah.

BUSTER. But when I said, "This is your father," all he said was,

"'Who?" (*Pause*) W*ho?* I can't believe he's forgotten me.

GEORGIE. Why don't you forget *him?* He's all right. He's alive.

BUSTER. I *can't* forget him. How can a father forget his son? If I could hold him in my arms once more, I'd feel I wasn't going on alone. I'm too alone. This is no way to go. If I knew he loved me, I wouldn't feel I was dying *at all.* I'd be *glad* to go. But this is no way at all. I hate being here. I *hate* being here. I believe I hate everybody in this world but my son.

GEORGIE. Feeling the way you do, you might scare him.

BUSTER. Yes, I know, but I can't help wanting to hold him in my arms once more, so I can die in peace.

GEORGIE. You better forget him. No use scaring the only person in the world you love.

BUSTER. He's got to love *me,* too, the way he used to love me, so I can stop being so alone, and so afraid to go. He's my son. He's got to love me.

GEORGIE. Maybe he can't do that any more. Maybe he loves the man your wife's married to now.

BUSTER. (*Quietly*) Then, I'll kill that man.

GEORGIE. You know you wouldn't do that.

BUSTER. (*Softly*) I know I *would.*

GEORGIE. How?

BUSTER. (*Bringing a small pistol out of his pocket*) With this. (*Pause*) I bought it from a man on a bus. He was broke, but all I could spare was three dollars. I told him to keep the gun, but he said he was *afraid* to keep it.

GEORGIE. Gun? Are you sure it works?

BUSTER. I fired one shell. It works all right. I wanted to be sure it works because on the way back to San Francisco I decided to— Well, I thought I'd take a room and see my son every day until I knew I was finished anyway, and then go out to the ocean and use this. (*Long pause.*)

GEORGIE. You've still got your clothes on. You've still got time.

BUSTER. (*Looking at a button in his hand*) I haven't got any more money.

GEORGIE. (*Bringing out some currency from the inside pocket*

of his robe) Here's a little. It's enough for food and a room
at a hotel somewhere for six or seven days anyway.

BUSTER. *(Taking the money)* My name's Harry West in case
we don't see each other again. I didn't expect anybody to be
so kind. I wish there was something I could do for you. *(He
searches through his pockets)* I've got two snapshots of my
son. I'd like to leave one of them with you. *(He looks at
one of the pictures, then puts it in front of* GEORGIE) Well,
I'll be going now. Thanks very much.

GEORGIE. I hope your son remembers you.

BUSTER goes out. GEORGIE picks up the snapshot and tries
to make out what's on it, but obviously fails to do so. He
goes to the door and stands there, looking into the ward
and listening. Then he wanders to the piano and touches
several keys, one at a time. Then he goes back to his chair,
obviously almost blind now. He is looking at the picture
when POSEYO comes in.

GEORGIE. Is that you, Brick?

POSEYO. Brick very sick, Georgie Porgie. *(He holds a candy bar
out to* GEORGIE) You want candy?

GEORGIE. Thanks. *(He reaches out, finds the chocolate bar, tears
off the paper, and puts almost half the bar into his mouth)*
I can't see any more, Poseyo.

POSEYO. That's all right. I help you.

GEORGIE. *(Softly)* What's the matter with Brick?

POSEYO. He cut his hand with razor in toilet. Nurse take him
away on wagon.

GEORGIE. Ah, for God's sake! *(Pause)* What's the matter with
Greedy Reed?

POSEYO. He crying.

GEORGIE. *Crying?*

POSEYO. He crying because Andy Boy die. *(Softly)* You want
more candy?

He hands GEORGIE PORGIE another candy bar which GEORGIE
unwraps and begins to stuff into his mouth.

GEORGIE. I tried my best to keep Brick going, Poseyo. He promised to hang on. He promised to help me.

POSEYO. I help you, Georgie Porgie.

GEORGIE. Thanks. Thanks a lot. (*Pause*) Listen, Poseyo. (*He holds out the snapshot* BUSTER *left with him*) What's on this picture?

POSEYO. (*Looking at picture*) Boy.

GEORGIE. What kind of boy?

POSEYO. Small boy.

GEORGIE. What do you think of him?

POSEYO. Nice boy.

GEORGIE. If he was your son, Poseyo, and you loved him, what would you do if *he* didn't love *you?*

POSEYO. (*After thoughtful pause*) Nothing. What I can do?

GEORGIE. If he was the only person in the whole world you *ever* loved and he loved you almost five years, and then his mother told you he *wasn't* your son, what would you do?

POSEYO. (*After pause*) Nothing.

GEORGIE. If she took him away from you, what would you do?

POSEYO. (*Swifter*) Nothing.

GEORGIE. If you wanted to hold him in your arms once more, and the man your wife went off with wouldn't let you, would you *kill* that man?

POSEYO. No.

GEORGIE. Why not?

POSEYO. I don't know.

GEORGIE. (*Suddenly*) Slide open that door, will you?

POSEYO. (*Sliding door open*) What's matter?

GEORGIE. Put a record on the phonograph and make it loud.

POSEYO. Everybody sleeping.

GEORGIE. Greedy Reed ain't sleeping. He's crying, and I don't want him to cry. A little loud music will bring him out here, and I'll straighten him out. (POSEYO *puts a record on the machine: it's the Mazurka of Khatchaturian's Masquerade Suite*) Yeah. That's good.

They listen to the music. After a moment GREEDY comes in, sliding the door behind him. He moves to the phonograph helplessly, sits on a folding chair and listens in despair until the record ends. He shuts off the machine, goes to the table on which the dictionary rests.

GREEDY. (*Softly, almost to himself*) Who close the dictionary?

GEORGIE. Brick, when he heard about Andy Boy.

GREEDY. Who tell him close the dictionary? Cut hisself?

GEORGIE. Nobody told him.

GREEDY. What right he got close the dictionary?

GEORGIE. He didn't know what he was doing.

GREEDY. He lose the place. We was up to abdomen. (*Suddenly*) God damn my black luck! (*The* NIGHT NURSE, *a heavy woman of fifty or so, obviously upset but trying to control herself, comes in*) Nurse, where's Andy Boy?

NIGHT NURSE. What in the world are you talking about?

GREEDY. He was here this morning. Where is he now?

GEORGIE. What's happened to Brick? Is he all right?

NIGHT NURSE. Just a moment please, *both* of you! (*Looking at chart*) Harry West, the new patient. Day Nurse said I'd find him in the Sun Room.

GEORGIE. He's gone to change his clothes.

NIGHT NURSE. Please let me know the minute he comes back.

GEORGIE. Sure. (*Slight pause*) Is Brick all right? Is he going to be all right? (*Pause.*)

NIGHT NURSE. I'm afraid not. (*Slight pause*) He must have been in terrible pain to do what he did.

GEORGIE. He said something was tearing his guts to pieces.

NIGHT NURSE. He should have come to me about it. He shouldn't have waited until the pain was unbearable.

GEORGIE. What could you do for him?

NIGHT NURSE. *Doctor Bohan* might have been able to help him.

GEORGIE. Brick was here three weeks. Doctor Bohan had plenty of time to help him. Why didn't he?

NIGHT NURSE. Oh, stop it! You needn't be sarcastic about Doctor Bohan. He can't do the impossible, he can't work miracles, but he *can* give any man at least a little temporary relief from pain.

GEORGIE. Temporary? He gave Andy Boy *permanent* relief.

NIGHT NURSE. Just a minute! I suppose it's perfectly natural for all of you to be ungrateful, but if you don't mind I'd rather you kept your feelings to yourselves. If you don't know how lucky you are to have Doctor Bohan looking after you, I do, and I'd rather not hear you speak of him as if he were some sort of witch doctor.

GEORGIE. Oh, we're lucky to have him looking after us all right, but not as lucky as he is to have us to *fool around* with. Jasper yesterday. Andy Boy today. Greedy Reed tomorrow.

GREEDY. *Greedy Reed* tomorrow? Nobody going to fool around with *Greedy Reed* tomorrow.

GEORGIE. Or Poseyo, or myself, or somebody else in the ward.

GREEDY. Nobody going to fool around with Greedy Reed the day after tomorrow, *either*.

NIGHT NURSE. Oh, stop it, please!

GREEDY. Just because Greedy Reed black, don't mean Doctor Bohan going to fool around with *him*. Nobody going to fool around with Greedy Reed.

NIGHT NURSE. Oh, stop it, I say! (*Slight pause*) I wish you'd try to be a little helpful, Georgie Porgie.

GEORGIE. I *do* try. I kept Brick alive three weeks. I tried to get him over his pain tonight, too, but— (*He falls silent.*)

NIGHT NURSE. (*Softly*) You should have come to me about his pain. (*Slight pause*) When the new patient comes back, please let me know. (*She goes.*)

There is a long lonely pause.

GREEDY. (*Softly*) You still willing to read the dictionary, Georgie Porgie? You still willing, like you was a little while ago?

GEORGIE. I'm still *willing*.

GREEDY. (*Lifting the dictionary and setting it down in front of* GEORGIE) Ah, thanks, Georgie Porgie. We was up to abdomen. Now, what is the next word, and what do it mean?

GEORGIE. (*Opening dictionary, trying hard to read*) Well, the next word is— (*He rubs his good eye and tries again*) The next word—is—

GREEDY. What's the matter, Georgie Porgie?

GEORGIE. I'm *willing* enough, but I guess I just can't see any more.

GREEDY. Ah, no, Georgie Porgie. Try again, now. Look real hard. What is the word after abdomen?

GEORGIE. Abide.

GREEDY. No fooling? What do abide mean?

GEORGIE. To tarry awhile.

GREEDY. Yeah, that's right. What else do it mean?

GEORGIE. To hang around and hang around, and then hang around some more.

GREEDY. Is that what the book say?

GEORGIE. That's what *I* say. I can't read the book. I can't see to read it. I can't even see faces any more. Everybody is a shadow to me now.

GREEDY. (*Desperately*) God damn my black luck! Somebody got to read the dictionary, Georgie Porgie. Poseyo, read the word after abdomen!

POSEYO. I no can read.

GREEDY. Sure you can, Poseyo.

POSEYO. Only Greek.

GREEDY. Where's the new patient, Georgie Porgie? He can read. Where is he?

GEORGIE. I don't know.

GREEDY. I go find him, bring him here. New patient read the dictionary. (*He goes. There is a pause.* GEORGIE *laughs softly.*)

POSEYO. (*Softly*) I help you, Georgie Porgie.

GEORGIE. Thanks, Poseyo. (*Slight pause.*)

POSEYO. I feel bad when Jasper die.

GEORGIE. Yeah. He was a lot of fun with his sarcasm and wise cracks.

POSEYO. I feel bad when Andy Boy die.

GEORGIE. Yeah. It was good seeing a quiet man like that every morning. A man out of China.

POSEYO. I feel bad when Brick—

GEORGIE. Yeah. Brick was good company. (*Pause.*)

POSEYO. Greedy Reed tell me this morning you say I hate everybody.

GEORGIE. Everybody hates everybody, Poseyo. I only said that

to make Greedy Reed get out of bed and stay alive. If I said
you loved everybody that would be true, too, but it wouldn't
make Greedy Reed get out of bed. Everybody *does* love
everybody. Why not? But staying alive's a fight and the fight
always seems to stop when hate stops. I said you hate everybody because I knew you'd understand. You're an older man
and you've been here longer than the rest of us. Greedy Reed
needs medicine no hospital's got. Everybody here does. You
understand, don't you?

POSEYO. (*Softly*) I understand. (*Slight pause*) Man is funny man.
More he hate more he help, more he love more he hurt
Then who can help who? Father help his boy? Husband his
wife? Mother her girl? Brother brother? Friend friend? No.
Nobody help nobody. Because man is man. Man is great
foolishness. Man is important joke. Oh yes, I feel bad when
Jasper die, but I no tell lie, Georgie Porgie, I feel *good*, too.
I feel glad. (*Slight pause*) You understand, Georgie Porgie?

GEORGIE. I understand, Poseyo.

POSEYO. So hard to understand, Georgie Porgie. I try, I try very
hard but pretty soon I don't know. Pretty soon I don't
understand no more, and I listen to music. Now, I sick of
music, too. I go sleep now, Georgie Porgie. Maybe I see you
in morning.

GEORGIE. Good night, Poseyo. (POSEYO *goes*) Good night, Brick.
Good night, Andy Boy. Good night, Buster.

GREEDY. (*Comes in, excited and breathless*) He come here, that
new patient? I look all over the ward for him, inside and out,
but I don't find him. He come here?

GEORGIE. No, he didn't.

GREEDY. Where he go, Georgie Porgie? I hear the nurse ask
about the new patient. Where *is* the new patient?

GEORGIE. I don't know.

GREEDY. (*Almost sobbing*) Somebody got to read the dictionary,
Georgie Porgie. We was up to abdomen when the Doctors
come and take Andy Boy away. We was going strong when
they take him away and kill him.

GEORGIE. (*Softly*) The Doctors didn't kill him.

GREEDY. What they do, then?

GEORGIE. They tried to make him more comfortable.

GREEDY. The Doctors know Andy Boy ain't got no chance. Why they fool him that way?

GEORGIE. (*Softly*) Poseyo didn't tell Andy Boy to take a chance. Poseyo kept his mouth shut, the way any real friend would do.

GREEDY. What you mean?

GEORGIE. I didn't tell Andy Boy to take a chance. I kept my mouth shut, too.

GREEDY. What you talking about?

GEORGIE. You could have kept your mouth shut, too.

GREEDY. My fault Andy Boy dead?

GEORGIE. You could have kept your mouth shut.

GREEDY. (*Taking* GEORGIE *by the throat*) Don't you say I kill my friend! Don't you say that, Georgie Porgie!

GEORGIE. (*Calmly*) I ain't saying you killed your friend. I ain't saying anybody killed him.

GREEDY. (*Releasing him*) Don't *nobody* say I kill my friend! Doctors kill him.

GEORGIE. He didn't *have* to take a chance. He had time enough to read the whole dictionary the way he was.

GREEDY. No! Don't say that, Georgie Porgie! You know you lying.

GEORGIE. I'm not lying. How do we know he might not be here *three months* from now the way he was?

GREEDY. (*Almost sobbing again*) Doctors fool me, Georgie Porgie. Doctors act like Andy Boy got a good chance.

GEORGIE. No use being sore at the Doctors. They did everything they could. All you had to do was keep your big mouth shut. Andy Boy didn't want to take a chance.

GREEDY. Man, I ain't no Doctor. They act like they know what they doing. I want to *help* Andy Boy.

GEORGIE. I know you *meant* well, but you could have kept your mouth shut just the same, just in case they didn't know what they were doing. Doctors don't know very much more than anybody else, you know.

GREEDY. I didn't know, Georgie Porgie. I believe Doctors know everything. I would have kept my mouth shut, but the way they act, I believe they know what they doing, so when Andy Boy ask me what to do, I tell him to take a chance.

GEORGIE. Well, maybe you're right at that.

GREEDY. What you mean?

GEORGIE. Maybe they *did* know what they were doing. The *young* Doctor, at any rate.

GREEDY. What you mean *now*?

GEORGIE. *He* knew Andy Boy *didn't* have a chance.

GREEDY. Then why he act like Andy Boy got a *good* chance?

GEORGIE. How should I know? Maybe he wants to find out everything he can about disease.

GREEDY. He kill Andy Boy to find out?

GEORGIE. How should I know? He's the one who does all the operating around here.

GREEDY. Old Doctor, he don't do no operating?

GEORGIE. Not any more. He doesn't take any chances, and he doesn't ask anybody else to take any. You should have kept your mouth shut just the same.

GREEDY. (*With despair*) I don't know why my luck so bad. I don't know why I don't keep my mouth shut, Georgie Porgie, but the Doctors fool me, make me tell Andy Boy to take a chance because I don't want him to be in so much pain when he read the dictionary. I believe with all my heart they going to make Andy Boy comfortable, bring him back here to read the dictionary in peace, and that make me so glad I remember the Pope doing like this, and *I* do it, too. For the first time in my life I feel so good I don't want to get even on nobody about nothing no more. I feel so good I get down on my knees and pray and I feel sure God going to answer my prayer, but He *don't* answer it, Georgie Porgie. He let Andy Boy go. Why? Because Greedy Reed black? Because Andy Boy Chinese? I don't ask for much. I only ask for one comfortable month for my friend, so we can read the dictionary. Why God refuse me just when I getting a little education? Just when I beginning to *like* this life? Just when I beginning to laugh at my poor color because I know skin color don't mean nothing? Just when I beginning to know the way to live? Why God do that to me, Georgie Porgie?

GEORGIE. I don't know.

GREEDY. Awful cold around this place now, Georgie Porgie. I feel the cold in my bones now, and the murder in my blood.

GEORGIE. (*Soberly*) I'm blind and finished, anyhow. Anybody wants to murder me is welcome to do it.

GREEDY. Oh, I ain't going to choke the life out of any dying man, Georgie Porgie. I'm sorry I grab you by the neck that way. The murder in my blood and hands ain't for you, Georgie Porgie.

GEORGIE. (*Standing*) Then, help me to my bed, will you?

GREEDY. (*Helping him*) Oh, I help you, Georgie Porgie. I help you as long as I live. Ain't you blind and ain't I black? (*Almost with contempt*) The hell with praying! God no friend of mine. He too high-tone to listen to my prayer! He too busy listening to the Pope. The hell with being polite! Now, the little kindness I still got in my hands is for everybody like me—ugly and sick and ignorant—but all the murder in my hands—all the hate—is for the strong and proud and wise —because they don't know—they don't know, Georgie Porgie. And they is always safe—safe!—all of them, except one, and I going to get him before I die. I going to get him, Georgie Porgie! (*They go.*)

Scene II

POSEYO is alone in the Sun Room listening to his favorite record. The day is wet and foggy again, and the foghorns seem nearer than ever. MOPPER comes in with bucket and mop.

MOPPER. Nurse wants you to go back to your bed, Poseyo. (*POSEYO doesn't hear him. MOPPER begins to mop around the piano, stops, leans on the handle of the mop and listens to the music*) Nurse, Poseyo. (*He sits at the table on which the dictionary rests, turns a page, then turns to POSEYO again*) She wants you to go eat your breakfast. (*Slight pause*) What you doing?

POSEYO. (*Softly*) What you say?

MOPPER. (*Earnestly, helplessly*) What you doing?

POSEYO. (*With kindness*) Why you say what you doing?

MOPPER. Huh?

POSEYO. What you want?

MOPPER. (*Getting up and mopping a little*) Nurse told me to tell you to go back and eat your breakfast. (*Slight pause*) What's the matter, Poseyo?

POSEYO. (*Almost mocking*) What's matter! What's matter?

MOPPER. She told me to tell you, and I told her I would, that's all I know. If somebody tells me to tell somebody something, I tell them, that's all, and nurse told me to tell you. It's not my fault. I don't know what's the matter. I do what I'm told. I don't want any dirty looks from anybody. Everybody's sore out there. Everybody's giving everybody dirty looks. You ain't the same, either, Poseyo. I see you out here every morning alone, but not like *this*. Not mad at *me*, the way you are this morning. I didn't do anything. Every morning except today I see you out here taking life easy. Why ain't you taking life easy any more? What are you mad at me for?

POSEYO. I not mad. (*Slight pause*) You know death?

MOPPER. No, Poseyo.

POSEYO. Death and Poseyo fight very hard last night. You know new patient?

MOPPER. What new patient?

POSEYO. In Andy Boy's bed.

MOPPER. Yeah? What about him?

POSEYO. Come here last night, go away, come back three o'clock in morning, very sick. Nurse shake him, shake him, make him cry, give him medicine so he sleep. You know this music?

MOPPER. Yeah, sure, Poseyo.

POSEYO. I find this music when I come here three months ago. I listen every morning.

MOPPER. Yeah. Why do you do that, Poseyo?

POSEYO. Every morning this music cry. I listen, but I don't know why this music cry. This morning I *know* why.

MOPPER. Yeah? Why?

POSEYO. Because no man is what he want to be.

MOPPER. Oh.

POSEYO. Nobody *know* what he want to be.

MOPPER. *I* know.

POSEYO. You know what everybody want to be?

MOPPER. (*Pause, slowly*) Yes, I do.

POSEYO. What they want to be?

MOPPER. (*Pause, thinking*) Warm. Warm and soft and covered up. They don't want eyes. They don't want hands and feet. They want to be warm and small and round. That's why everybody's always mad at everybody. Always giving everybody dirty looks. (*He mops to the door, slides it open, pushes the mop beyond the door, turns to* POSEYO) It's not my fault.

He goes out, sliding the door behind him. The music is heard clearly now. After a moment, the DAY NURSE slides the door open and looks in.

DAY NURSE. Poseyo! You haven't touched your breakfast!

POSEYO. I drink orange.

DAY NURSE. (*Comes in, leaving door open*) It's not enough to drink your orange juice. Now, you come right back to your bed and eat everything on your tray. (POSEYO *just looks at her*) Oh, Poseyo!

POSEYO. What's matter?

DAY NURSE. (*Trying to straighten herself out*) You must try to eat, Poseyo. You musn't sacrifice your breakfast every morning for a few minutes of privacy out here. You've lost too much weight. Doctor Bohan spoke to me about it yesterday.

POSEYO. Oh?

DAY NURSE. Yes, Poseyo.

POSEYO. Doctor Bohan want me to be fat?

DAY NURSE. No, of course he doesn't want you to be fat, but he doesn't want you to lose any more weight, either.

POSEYO. Why?

DAY NURSE. Oh, Poseyo, you *must* eat, that's all.

POSEYO. I eat. (*Slight pause*) I eat little bit every day.

DAY NURSE. You don't eat half enough. (*Slight pause*) Why don't you *eat*, Poseyo?

POSEYO. I not hungry.

BUSTER, wearing hospital clothing, comes in. He is in a daze. DAY NURSE looks at him bitterly, then turns back to POSEYO.

DAY NURSE. Remember, Poseyo, in this life we must think of others, not ourselves alone. Sometimes in this life we must do things because they make *others* happy.

BUSTER. (*Softly, bewildered*) What?

DAY NURSE. I'm not talking to you. I'm talking to Poseyo! You just behave yourself from now on. (*She turns to POSEYO again while BUSTER watches*) Don't you see, Poseyo, when you don't eat, I'm not happy.

POSEYO. Oh?

DAY NURSE. Yes, Poseyo, and the reason I'm not happy is that when you don't eat Doctor Bohan's not happy. He's learned a great deal from you, Poseyo. In this life we must try to make others happy.

POSEYO. I don't like this life.

DAY NURSE. Oh, Poseyo, I wish you'd stop talking nonsense. You must try not to be so selfish.

POSEYO. You want me to eat breakfast?

DAY NURSE. Indeed I do—because I want you to keep yourself alive as long as possible. The longer you stay alive the happier you make Doctor Bohan, and the happier he is the happier I am. Doctor Bohan would be brokenhearted if you were to leave us, too.

POSEYO. Why?

DAY NURSE. Poseyo, don't you see Doctor Bohan finds out new things from every patient in this ward. I wish you only knew how much you've helped him already. The more he learns, the more he's able to help others. Now, how can you stay alive if you don't eat?

POSEYO. Maybe if I eat, I lose no weight but die very quick. Doctor Bohan, he think about that?

DAY NURSE. (*Startled*) Poseyo, do you mean you don't eat, so you'll stay alive longer?

POSEYO. I don't know.

DAY NURSE. You've been here longer than anyone else, Poseyo. Do you think it's because you eat so little?

POSEYO. I don't know. (*Slight pause*) You want me to eat breakfast?

DAY NURSE. Are you pulling my leg, Poseyo?

POSEYO. What means that?

DAY NURSE. Are you making fun of me?

POSEYO. I don't know. If you want me to eat breakfast, I eat breakfast.

DAY NURSE. Well, under the circumstances, perhaps you'd better not. Perhaps I'd better report to Doctor Bohan first and find out what he thinks. (*She turns to* BUSTER, *who is standing at the window. She speaks bitterly*) As for you, young man, you behave yourself from now on, do you hear? You had the whole hospital in an uproar last night. You can thank God we took you back. This is not a gentlemen's club, you know, that you can come to and leave whenever you like. We're here to take care of very sick men, and you're a very sick man. I'm not sure you ought to be out of bed, even, so behave yourself until Doctor Bohan makes his morning rounds and tells me what to do with you. (*She turns back to* POSEYO *and speaks softly*) He's very sick, Poseyo. Please look after him.

She steps out and slides the door behind her. POSEYO goes to BUSTER.

POSEYO. You come sit down in big chair.

BUSTER. (*Turns*) What?

He half collapses. POSEYO catches him and gets him into the big red leather chair.

POSEYO. What's matter?

BUSTER. (*Very softly*) I want to go home.

POSEYO. You rest in big chair. Listen to music.

BUSTER tries to speak, begins to weep softly, then covers his face with his hands. GREEDY comes in, sliding the door behind him. He looks at BUSTER a moment, then turns to POSEYO.

GREEDY. (*Softly, pointing*) Why he crying?

POSEYO. I don't know. (*POSEYO turns off the phonograph.*)

GREEDY. (*Standing over* BUSTER) Why you crying?

BUSTER. (*Taking his hands away from his face*) What? (*He stares at* GREEDY *a moment, then hides his face again.*)

GREEDY. No use crying, man. No use hiding your face. They kill Andy Boy, but you don't see me crying.

BUSTER. (*Taking his hands away from his face again*) What?

GREEDY. They kill Andy Boy.

BUSTER. Who?

GREEDY. Andy Boy, man. Andy Boy. He was reading that dictionary right there, and they take him away and kill him.

BUSTER. Who killed him?

GREEDY. I know who. Georgie Porgie tell me all about him last night.

BUSTER. Georgie Porgie?

GREEDY. He be out here pretty soon. He just about the sickest man in this whole ward, almost *blind* now, too, but he be out here pretty soon. He sicker than ever now that his friend Brick kill himself.

BUSTER. Brick? Kill himself?

GREEDY. Yeah, Georgie Porgie and Brick was out here last night, trying to keep each other company, waiting to hear about Andy Boy. Well, they hear about him all right. Andy Boy dead. And I know who kill him.

BUSTER. What?

GREEDY. Man, you sleeping? I'm talking about the man who kill Andy Boy.

BUSTER. (*Dazed, stunned*) I want to go home.

GREEDY. What's the matter with you, man? You can't go home no more. No use being scared about it, though. We all in the same boat here. We all at the end of the line. We all tagged. We all homeless and homesick, the same as you.

Today or tomorrow or the next day, we all got to go, ignorant and all alone, but nobody going to push me. If there's going to be any pushing around here, I going to do it! I ain't going to push somebody who ain't got far to go, either. I going to push somebody who *think* he got a long way to go.

BUSTER. Push? What for?

GREEDY. What *for?* Man, ain't I just told you what for? He kill Andy Boy. You know, Poseyo, I ain't scared of this dying business no more, because I got my man to get even on now. Nobody going to cheat me out of my revenge *now.* Today or tomorrow or the next day, I going to kill the man who kill.

BUSTER. No! You can't do that! It's not right.

GREEDY. What you know about right?

BUSTER. It's not right to kill!

GREEDY. Tell that to the man who kill Andy Boy. Tell that to the man who young and strong and healthy and kill the sick and dying. Tell that to the man who cheat my friend out of three months of life. Cheat me out of the first right thing I ever find to do. Tell that to the man who kill, and get up in the morning and sit down with his wife and children and eat a big breakfast. Tell that to the happy man.

BUSTER. No! It's not right to kill!

GREEDY. At last I got my man, Poseyo. I got him and I ain't going to let him go. I find him at the end of the line, but it's going to be the end of the line for *him,* too. (*To* BUSTER) Oh, I ain't saying it ain't better to be nice when you're going to die. I ain't saying it ain't better to forgive. I ain't saying it ain't better to love. I ain't saying it ain't better to lie down and die all alone and be glad it's only you. I ain't saying it ain't better to die nice that way. I just saying I ain't going to pick and choose at the end of the line. I never find out the way to live. I ain't going to pick and choose the way to die. I been waiting forty-four years, and I got my man at last. I got him the way disease got me, but he don't know the terrible disease *he* got. Greedy Reed *his* disease!

BUSTER. (*Standing, excited*) No! You don't know what you're saying! Tell me who the man is. Tell me, so I can warn him.

GREEDY. Oh no! Nobody going to cheat me out of my revenge.

BUSTER. Revenge for what?

GREEDY. Never mind! I know for what! I know!

BUSTER. No! Let me help you. Tell me who the man is. I must warn him, for your sake!

GREEDY. Never mind, never mind! You just sit down again. You got something to hide your face about and cry. You just sit down and hide your face and cry.

BUSTER. (*To* POSEYO) Who is the man? You must tell me. (*To* GREEDY) For *his* sake, you must tell me. Who is the man?

GEORGIE comes in, unnoticed. He seems hushed and feeble until he speaks.

GREEDY. Poseyo don't know who the man is.

BUSTER. I don't believe you. (*To* POSEYO) I want to help this man. I have no right to sit by and let him kill another man. You have no right to do that. Tell me who it is he plans to kill. Tell me, for God's sake!

GEORGIE. Is that you, Buster?

BUSTER. (*Is stunned*) Buster? My name is Harry West.

GEORGIE. (*He sits at a table and picks up a comic book*) I know. You told me last night.

BUSTER. (*Almost stammering*) Last night? (*Quickly*) This man is planning to kill someone, and I want to help him. I have no right not to help him.

GEORGIE. Did you see your son, Buster?

BUSTER. (*Stunned*) What?

GEORGIE. Your son, Buster. (*He brings the picture of* BUSTER'S *son out of his pocket*) This boy. Did you see him? (BUSTER *walks slowly to* GEORGIE, *takes the picture out of his hand, and looks at it a long time. He then sits down in the big leather chair and hides his face in his hands*) Oh, don't be ashamed, Buster. I knew you wouldn't. Why should you? Why should you scare the only person in the world you've ever loved? An innocent child who could never be blamed for forgetting someone he hasn't seen in two years? Why should you hate the poor boy's mother? Somebody's got to be everybody's mother. Why should you hate the man she left you for? You never loved *her* anyway, and even if you had, she never loved you. Sure you wanted to hold your son in your arms again. Everybody wants to do a lot of things they can't do any more. It's no disgrace to know you can never get back anything you ever let go. It's the only thing that gives people the little dignity they have. I knew you'd be back, Buster. I gave you the money and told you to go because I wanted you to find out for yourself that the son you love is no more. I wanted you to let him be, whoever he is. I wanted you to find out for yourself that your love is the only thing you have by which to die in peace—the *only* thing, Buster—your love for a child who takes you for an ugly stranger. Now, I'm glad you're back, safe and sound. It's all right, Buster. It's all right to cry. You're among friends.

BUSTER. (*Excited, whispering to* GREEDY) Listen! Listen to me, before it's too late! Do not scheme to take the life of another. Lie down like a man and die in peace, hating no one. If you want to do the right thing, do *nothing!* Nothing! Love nothing! Hate nothing! Be nothing! Lie down, lie down and forget you ever lived. That is the right thing to do. Anything else is wrong.

GREEDY. (*Earnestly*) What he talking about, Georgie Porgie? (*Softly*) He break my heart. (BUSTER *hides his face in his hands*) There you go hiding your face again! If you want to help me, like you say, why you hide your face and cry? You break my heart, man.

BUSTER. (*Stands*) I want to go home. (*He looks around desperately*) I want to lie down in my own bed in my own house and forget I ever lived. (*He goes.*)

GREEDY. (*Deeply touched*) That man break my heart, Georgie Porgie. I never see a man like *that*. Why he hide his face and cry?

GEORGIE. How would you feel if the only person in the world you love doesn't love you? How would you feel if your own son doesn't even *remember* you? How would you feel if your wife told you your son *ain't* your son?

GREEDY. Oh man, is that why he hide his face and cry?

GEORGIE. How would you feel if the man your wife went off

with made a fool out of you in public because you wanted *him* to let you see your son? How would you feel if you were sick and small and old, the way Buster is, and the man was healthy and strong and young, and picked you up by the seat of your pants in front of your wife and a lot of other people and bounced you out of a cheap saloon? How would you feel if you didn't have the courage to stand up to people who were stealing your son's love away from you? You'd want to hide your face and cry, too, wouldn't you? You'd want to crawl into your bed and forget you ever lived, too, wouldn't you?

GREEDY. Oh man! I don't know *what* I do. If all that stuff happen to *me*, I go crazy, I guess. Buster do the right thing all right to crawl in his bed and die, but man, I know *I* wouldn't do the right thing. I guess I go crazy and kill that man. I kill that dirty man!

GEORGIE. No, you wouldn't. You'd just feel bad, stay alive a little longer, and then die, the way everybody else does, the way Buster's doing now. I know.

GREEDY. How you know, Georgie Porgie?

GEORGIE. Buster didn't want to be here last night. He wanted to go home. He wanted to see his son. He had a pistol he'd bought from somebody on a bus, and he said he'd kill anybody who tried to keep him away from his son, only he didn't have any more money, so I gave him all the money I had. I wanted him to get out of here. I wanted him to see his son. But most of all I wanted him to kill the man who took his son and his wife away from him, and put him here to die like a dog instead of in his own house, in his own bed, with his son in the house to listen to and see and smell and hold in his arms. He's a little man, but I thought maybe he'd do it. I thought maybe he'd have guts enough to fight back against the strong, but he didn't. He came back. He didn't do it because human beings can't hate. I always *thought* they could, but they can't. They can't love, either. (*He stops.*)

GREEDY. What can they do, Georgie Porgie?

GEORGIE. (*Softly*) Breathe.

GREEDY. Is that all?

GEORGIE. That's all. But even *that's* done for them, the same as it's done for *all* animals. Human beings might as well be sheep. And now, I'm tired of being one of them. I can't even *pretend* to hate any more. When Doctor Bohan makes his rounds this morning I'm going to ask him to do something about my head.

GREEDY. No, Georgie Porgie! He kill you!

GEORGIE. Oh, I know he can't help me, but I'm finished and I know it, so there's no use kidding any more.

GREEDY. No, Georgie Porgie, you got a *lot* of time. We ain't finished yet.

GEORGIE. You may not be finished yet because you can still pretend, but I can't. I can't pretend anything any more.

GREEDY. What you mean, Georgie Porgie?

GEORGIE. You can still pretend you want to hear somebody read the dictionary. You can still pretend hearing the words *means* something to you. You can still pretend there's a good way to spend the rest of your life. You can still pretend there's something you can do that will give your life some kind of meaning. You can still pretend you hate. You can still pretend you're *yourself*, a whole man, and not a small part of the incurable disease all men are. Our disease is just one of the many names for it, and I can't pretend any more that I'm not a small part of it and nothing else. Now, all I want to do is give my head back, and everything else. God help us in our naked and blind loneliness.

GREEDY. I don't know what you saying, Georgie Porgie, but don't go put yourself in the hands of Doctor Bohan and leave me all alone. If it's pretending you need to stay a little longer, *pretend* something, Georgie Porgie. Pretend something!

GEORGIE. My head's on fire. My eyes are blind. I can't pretend any more.

GREEDY. Ah, sure you can, Georgie Porgie. Don't go leave me now when I need you so bad. Pretend, and stay a little longer. Stay and keep me company. Pretend we ain't dying at all, Georgie Porgie. Pretend we're getting ready to get born.

GEORGIE. I can't, I can't. I wish to God I could, but I can't.

GREEDY. Pretend we ain't scared to go, Georgie Porgie. Pretend we're on our way to something nice, like that time you dreamed about yesterday. Pretend we're on our way to sunshine and nothing to do but enjoy ourselves. Pretend things like *that*, Georgie Porgie, and keep me just a *little* more company.

GEORGIE. I'm sorry. I can't pretend *anything* any more.

GREEDY. Then, tell me what to do, Georgie Porgie. I can't fight my ignorance alone. (*He lifts up the dictionary*) The words, Georgie Porgie! They're the only thing can save me. (*His voice cracks with sobbing as he goes on*) Education! That's my only hope. I don't want to be ignorant no more. I don't want to hate no more. I don't want to kill no more. Pretend something, Georgie Porgie, keep me just a little more company, teach me the way to fight my ignorance.

MOPPER. (*Comes in with some newspapers and magazines*) Here's the new American Comics, Georgie Porgie. Anybody want the morning paper?

GEORGIE. What's the headline, Mopper?

MOPPER. (*Opening paper, reading headline*) Man Shot in Street.

GEORGIE. What street? Market?

MOPPER. (*Examining paper*) No. Ortega.

GEORGIE. Ortega? Are you sure, Mopper?

MOPPER. Sure I'm sure. Ortega Street is what it says right here.

GEORGIE. Who killed who?

MOPPER. Somebody killed a bartender named James Valenti.

GEORGIE. Who did it?

MOPPER. Nobody knows. Nobody saw it happen. Bartender was walking home after work at two o'clock in the morning. Somebody shot him, that's all. Wasn't robbery, though. Bartender's wallet was in his coat pocket.

GEORGIE. (*Swiftly*) Any pictures?

MOPPER. Pictures on page twelve, it says. (*He turns to the last page of the first section of the paper*) Here they are. Here's James Valenti. Here's Mrs. James Valenti. And here's a picture of the four of them together on a picnic in Golden Gate Park. Husband, wife, son and baby daughter.

GEORGIE. Any other pictures?

MOPPER. No, just those three.

GEORGIE. Let me have that paper, will you, Mopper?

MOPPER. Sure, Georgie Porgie. Who wants *Time* and *Life*?

GEORGIE. I'll take them all.

MOPPER. (*Putting the bundle in front of* GEORGIE) Whoever it was killed the bartender must have had a good reason. Nobody goes to all that trouble for nothing. (*He goes to the door.*)

GEORGIE. How are things in the ward, Mopper?

MOPPER. Everything seems to be under control again, I guess. The man in bed nine died last night. Nurse asked me to help her get him on the wagon, and she took him away.

GEORGIE. Who was in bed nine, Poseyo?

POSEYO. Man who come here six seven days ago. Sleep all the time.

GEORGIE. Oh yes. Larson, the seaman. Thanks for bringing the paper and magazines, Mopper.

MOPPER. I hope the police don't find him because he must have had a good reason. (*He goes.*)

GEORGIE. Poseyo, look at this picture, will you? (POSEYO *looks at the picture*) How about it?

POSEYO. I don't know. I *think* so.

GEORGIE. Look carefully now.

POSEYO. Same boy, I think.

GEORGIE. What's the bartender look like?

POSEYO. Young, strong.

GEORGIE. And the woman?

POSEYO. Strong.

GEORGIE. Do you think she loved the bartender?

POSEYO. Maybe.

GEORGIE. Do you think she loved him enough to help the police?

POSEYO. What for? Strong woman. Good-looking. What for? He's dead.

GEORGIE. Maybe she's *glad* he's dead.

POSEYO. Maybe.

GEORGIE. (*His voice powerful again*) She won't help the police. (*Pause*) And neither will we. Will we, Poseyo?

POSEYO. What for?

GEORGIE. Greedy Reed? We won't help them, will we?

GREEDY. What you talking about, Georgie Porgie?

GEORGIE. Buster can *read*, you know. He can read the dictionary.

GREEDY. Buster? That little man kill the bartender?

GEORGIE. No, of course not. Buster's the man who come here to read the dictionary. We don't *know* who killed the bartender. The police don't know. The bartender's wife doesn't know. Buster doesn't know. All we know is that Buster's *here!*

GREEDY. (*Alive and hopeful again, going to* GEORGIE's *table*) Let me see that bartender! (*He looks*) Hot dog! Well, what do you know? A man about thirty-three years old. Handsome, too. Strong and proud. Well, *I* live longer than the bartender, anyway. (*He gestures with his arm over the picture as he cackles with joy*) Man, man, that Buster he sure come here to read the dictionary all right. He sure come here in the nick of time all right.

GEORGIE. He's an intelligent man, too, you know. Worked in a bank twenty-seven years.

GREEDY. Hot dog! A *banker* to read the dictionary. A man who been around a lot of money. I go get him right now. Tell him I ain't scheming to kill nobody no more. (*He gestures*) I go bring him out here to start reading.

GEORGIE. Not yet. Give him time to get used to everything. You know how friendless you felt when you first came here. Well, it's the same with him. There's no hurry any more. He's going to be with us a long time, don't worry about that. It's going to take him a little while to understand that he came all the way from New York to read the dictionary. He thought he came to see his son, but he's an intelligent man and he'll find out why he really came. He's feeling pretty bad now, but he'll be all right as soon as he finds out he's among friends.

GREEDY. Oh, he among friends, all right, Georgie Porgie. Everything warm and friendly around here now, Georgie Porgie. (*He puts his arms around* GEORGIE *and* POSEYO, *and hugs them as he laughs*) Little while ago that Buster break my heart, but now he make me proud and give me hope. *Real* hope, Georgie Porgie. Hope for everybody, for every lonesome incurable in the world. He just the man to read the dictionary, Georgie Porgie.

GEORGIE. (*Almost gaily*) That is correct!

GREEDY. He make me *proud* to be incurable. Proud to be *lonesome*. Proud to be *black*, even. (*He stands alone.*)

GEORGIE. That is *also* correct!

GREEDY. He make me feel so good you know what I going to do, Poseyo?

POSEYO. What?

GREEDY. I going to smoke a cigar! (*He lights a cigar.*)

GEORGIE. (*Swiftly*) Now, listen! Listen carefully. You listen, too, Poseyo.

GREEDY. Yeah, Poseyo, you listen to Georgie Porgie, too.

POSEYO. I listen.

GEORGIE. We need Buster. We need him bad.

GREEDY. That's right, Poseyo. Buster going to read the dictionary.

GEORGIE. He's here and we don't want him to get away.

GREEDY. No, sir!

GEORGIE. We don't want the police to take him, or Doctor Bohan, or anybody else.

GREEDY. No, sir! We want him to read the dictionary. We don't want him to go to bed and stay there, or anything *else* like that. No, sir!

GEORGIE. Listen! A *long* time ago I felt finished—the way I been feeling all morning. And then Brick came along, and I'm still here. Well, if I could do it once, who says I can't do it again?

GREEDY. Yeah! Who says that?

GEORGIE. Who says any of us can't? As long as we're alive at all, we've got as much time as anybody else alive, and we're *still* alive.

GREEDY. That's right! That bartender he was alive last night, but he ain't alive this morning. Oh, that Buster he make me proud.

GEORGIE. Listen! When he comes out here let me do all the talking, do you hear?

GREEDY. You hear, Poseyo? Let Georgie Porgie do all the talking. He knows what to say.

POSEYO. I no talk.

GEORGIE. And don't play any more phonograph records.

GREEDY. That's right, Poseyo.

GEORGIE. Let's listen to the radio for a change. Let's move out of this bird-cage into the world again.

GREEDY. Yeah, Poseyo, that's right.

GEORGIE. And from now on let's act as if we're going to be around as long as anybody else because maybe we are. Switch on the radio, Poseyo.

GREEDY. Yeah, Poseyo, let's see what the radio got to say.

POSEYO. O.K.

He switches on the radio. They wait for the radio to warm up. After a moment, the voice of a radio singer is heard singing the ballad, Your Eyes Have Told Me So.

GEORGIE. That's fine. Just make it a little softer. (*Pause*) That's good. (*The singer is barely heard*) Now, listen. Look out into the ward and let me know what's going on.

GREEDY. (*Almost leaping to the sliding door*) I look out.

GEORGIE. Where's Buster?

GREEDY. He's in his bed, Georgie Porgie.

GEORGIE. Who's in the ward?

GREEDY. Just the men in bed. Nobody else.

GEORGIE. All right. Just stand there and let me know what you see.

GREEDY. I let you know, Georgie Porgie. (*Pause.*)

GEORGIE. You all right, Poseyo?

POSEYO. Sure.

GEORGIE. You want to look at Life?

POSEYO. Sure. (*He goes to GEORGIE's table and takes the copy of Life.*)

GEORGIE. Sit down by the radio, Poseyo, and be ready to make it louder or shut it off when I say so.

POSEYO. (*Sitting down*) Sure.

GEORGIE. I hope you don't mind not listening to Mozart any more.

POSEYO. That's all right.

GEORGIE. Anything new in the ward?

GREEDY. Everything the same, Georgie Porgie, except Buster tossing and turning now.

GEORGIE. That's good. Any good pictures in *Life*, Poseyo?

POSEYO. (*Turning pages*) Man standing on head.

GEORGIE. Yeah?

POSEYO. Old lady with thumb on nose.

GEORGIE. Yeah?

POSEYO. (*Turning page*) Girls.

GEORGIE. Yeah? Go on.

POSEYO. Boy crying.

GREEDY. (*Excited*) Buster tossing and turning some more.

GEORGIE. That's good.

GREEDY. (*Excited*) Now, he getting out of bed.

GEORGIE. (*Casually*) O.K., get the dictionary ready.

GREEDY. (*Leaping from the door to the dictionary*) Here it is, Georgie Porgie—open and ready to go. (*He leaps back to the door*) Here he come, Georgie Porgie. Here he come to read the dictionary, Poseyo. We going to read the whole book from beginning to end. We going to find out what every word in the book mean. We going to live and live *right* until we die. Oh, that Buster he make me proud. Here he come now. (*He bounds across the room to the piano. Softly*) I just lean here on this little piano and smoke my cigar. (*Whispering*) Here he is at the door.

BUSTER slides the door open, steps in, stops. GEORGIE turns, and BUSTER looks from one face to the other. EVERYBODY is just barely smiling at him. The radio singer's voice is heard softly. BUSTER steps toward GEORGIE timidly. He speaks very softly.

BUSTER. You were very kind to me last night. When I left here with the money you gave me I didn't expect to see you again, but now that I'm back I think you ought to know what happened.

GEORGIE. I *know* what happened, Buster. You don't have to tell me.

BUSTER. I thought perhaps if I tried to explain what happened, and how it happened, I might—I might still be able to—

GEORGIE. There's plenty of time to explain, Buster.

GREEDY. (*Unable to restrain himself*) You sit right down here, Buster, and rest yourself. (*He helps* BUSTER *into the chair*) Now, right here in front of you is this great big book. No one here but you can read the book, Buster. Georgie Porgie he can't see to read no more. Poseyo he read only Greek. And myself I never learn to read, so you got to read the book.

BUSTER. This book's the dictionary.

GREEDY. That's right. And we going to read the book from the beginning to the end, the four of us right here in this room. So far we reach abdomen. Now you look in the book there, Buster, and read the word after abdomen.

BUSTER. But why? Why do you want me to read the dictionary?

GREEDY. Do you good to read the book, Buster. Do me good. Do Georgie Porgie good to hear you read. Do Poseyo good. Now, what is the word after abdomen?

BUSTER. (*Searching the page*) Well, the word after abdomen is— Yes, here it is. (*Reading*) Abide.

GREEDY. (*Almost overjoyed*) Ah man, that's right! That's exactly the next word. Now, what do abide mean?

BUSTER. (*Reading*) To rest. To tarry or stay awhile. To continue. To be firm and immovable. To endure. To suffer the consequences.

GREEDY. Hot dog! You hear that, Georgie Porgie? You hear what Buster read out of the book, Poseyo? Now, you just make yourself comfortable, Buster, and you read and read because we got a lot of time to rest and continue and tarry and be firm and immovable and all that other stuff. You just settle yourself down like a small boy at school who all finished doing mischief and read us the whole dictionary. Oh, we going to eat lunch pretty soon, and tonight we going to lie down in our beds and remember the words, and tomorrow morning we going to get up and eat breakfast and come out here and go right on reading the words. Now, what is the next word, Buster?

BUSTER. (*Reading*) Ability.

GREEDY. Yeah! Ability. That's probably something very nice, but read what the book say. What do ability mean?

BUSTER. (*Reading*) Power, whether physical or mental, inherent or acquired.

GREEDY. Yeah, man!

BUSTER. (*Reading*) Skill in arts or science.

GREEDY. (*Beside himself with joy*) Go on now, Buster, that's right. Just go right on.

BUSTER. (*Reading*) The state or quality of being able.

GREEDY. I got it, Buster. Go right on.

BUSTER. Capacity, skill, talent, aptitude.

GEORGIE. (*Standing, leaning his head toward the radio*) Wait a minute. What's that I hear on the radio? Turn it up, will you, Poseyo?

POSEYO turns the radio up. The music is now the theme music of the Coca-Cola Company.

RADIO VOICE. Whoever you are, whatever you do, wherever you may be, when you think of refreshment, think of Coca-Cola, for Coca-Cola makes any pause the pause that refreshes, and ice cold Coca-Cola is everywhere.

GREEDY. You hear that, Georgie Porgie? You hear what the man say? Go on, Buster, read the next word. I can't wait to hear the next word.

SAM EGO'S HOUSE

A Play in Three Acts
and Seven Scenes

PREFACE

Sam Ego's House, like *Don't Go Away Mad* and *A Decent Birth, A Happy Funeral*, is an allegory, and in a moment I shall make some of its meaning clear. First, though, I must point out that everything I write, everything I have ever written, is allegorical. This came to pass inevitably. One does not choose to write allegorically any more than one chooses to grow black hair on his head. The stories of Armenia, Kurdistan, Georgia, Persia, Syria, Arabia, Turkey and Israel are all allegorical, and apart from the fact that I heard these stories as a child, told to me by both of my grandmothers, by great aunts and great uncles, and by friends of the family, I myself am a product of Asia Minor, hence the allegorical and the real are closely related in my mind.

In fact all reality to me is allegorical, and I cannot so much as hear a commonplace American joke and not know and enjoy its deeper humor and meaning.

The allegory, as I understand it, entertains as it instructs, and the writer whose work is allegorical is both an entertainer and a teacher. One may take his teaching or leave it, as one prefers, for the teaching is always incidental, frequently subtle, sometimes even obscure; but it is always there.

In Asia Minor stories were spoken, not written, even after the printing of books had become more or less universal and the profession of writing was well established. The favorite storytellers of a nation, a people, a city or even a family were those who looked as if they ought to know a great deal, who spoke clearly and effectively, and were themselves dramatic. The best of them were generally old men or old women, and each of them was famous for his particular way of telling a well-known story, for the important thing was not the story itself but the story-teller's way of telling it, which came out of his own mouth and life.

There was a good range of stories, but sooner or later one had heard them all and began to hear them over again. Many people preferred to hear the same story-teller tell the same story in order to enjoy the subtle changes in his manner of telling it. The older the story-teller the better the telling of the story, and no one ever presumed to tell a story to anyone older than himself, although a mother of twenty might tell a story to her son of four. Three years later he might hear the same story told to him by his older brother, aged ten or eleven; and a year or two later he might be telling his version of it to his younger brother.

In short, story-telling was an educational system. A story-teller who could make his listeners weep was highly esteemed, but it frequently happened that the same story might next be told in such a manner as to impel astonishing gladness and laughter. As this awareness of style became known to listeners a broader appreciation of the potentialities for variety in a given thing also became known, and in this manner the process of education continued.

My father's mother, Hripsime, when she was perhaps no more than fifty and I was seven or eight, told me a story that broke my heart, and then about twenty years later told it again with such sophistication and brilliance that it was hilarious. But it was still the same story, the story of the timid world-frightened man who was driven out of his house by his fierce and powerful wife and told not to come back until he had done heroic deeds and had a fortune consisting of twenty sacks of gold and a caravan of a hundred camels. By accident the timid man over a period of more than twenty years performed heroic deeds and came into possession of not twenty but forty sacks of gold and a caravan of not one hundred camels but two hundred; whereupon he went back to his wife. His adventures were what broke my heart: his loneliness, his fear, and his eagerness to make good and get safely home again. But the second time my grandmother told the story she ridiculed the man, his wife, and the story itself, for one was as foolish as the other, since

the man was too timid, the wife too fierce, and the story too
elementary and false to be worth anything better than ridicule.

This illustrates somewhat what happens in written story-
telling, too: the story is essentially always the same one—the
story of human experience—but literature exists insofar as the
telling of this story satisfies the development of both the story-
teller and the listener. The story of the timid man was always
an allegory, but it was a discredited allegory when my grandmother told it the second time.

Any allegory, any story, any work of literary art, may be
discredited immediately it is created or after a time, but the
discrediting of it, in order to be satisfying, must come out of
a greater and better understanding of it, of the story itself,
and not out of a refusal to take the time to acquire a greater or
better understanding of it, and of all experience.

Sam Ego's House is a rather difficult allegory to discredit, I
believe, for it is, itself, a discrediting of a great deal that is
allegorical in American experience. Sam Ego is the American
Dream: the dream of the national ego, the dream of individual achievement, of material wealth, of social importance,
of personal security.

Sam does very nicely for awhile. He achieves great fame.
He accumulates great wealth. He builds a great house. And
it seems as if not only is he himself to be forever secure,
so is his wife, his son and his daughter. *Sam Ego's House* is
of course the American nation itself. Something happens, however, that very nearly spoils everything. A War in Europe comes
to pass. Sam's son goes to the War, returns home safely, and is
killed in an automobile accident as he celebrates his home-
coming. Sam Ego's wife, distraught and desperate because of
this ironic destruction of her son at home, on his own door-
step, runs and hides and disappears in an overdose of sleeping pills. Sam's daughter comes home to have a secret child
and she and the child perish together. Sam himself tries for
a time to carry on, but one day in court, while he is arguing
on behalf of some trivial right, begins to laugh and is unable
to stop, whereupon he is placed in a home for the unbalanced,
and his great house locked. It soon becomes haunted, accord-

ing to gossip, the refuge of lonely lovers, and the fearful resting-place for the desperately homeless.

The play begins with a fifth or sixth annual attempt on the part of the Administrator of the Estate to auction off the house. This time it is sold for almost nothing to a man called Utmost Urge who represents common people: the majority of them, in short. Part of the bargain is that the house must be immediately removed from its present location, for the dream alone has been sold, and while it is a pretty badly damaged dream, Utmost Urge believes he can fix it up so that it will look like something again. On the property a moving picture theatre will be built. The house will be moved to Mr. Urge's Junkyard in the slums free of charge by two brothers who are professional house-movers. These brothers are working-men in general, and their equipment is obsolete and very nearly useless, but not their intelligence, which is elementary and courageous.

The house sets out on its journey across town, from the restricted residential district reserved for rich white people to the slums where everybody is not only welcome but forced by necessity to go. At this moment Sam Ego escapes from the asylum and hides inside his old house. Utmost Urge's son Easy witnesses Sam's arrival, befriends him, takes him food and drink. The entire town searches for the escaped lunatic, as he is described by the press, and falls upon the house while it rests on its journey beside the First Presbyterian Church. Between the Police and Fire Departments and the Boy Scouts the house is very nearly demolished, but Sam Ego's hiding-place inside the house is not discovered. He himself, however, after listening to a rattled preacher's madcap sermon in the yard of the church, after the searchers disrupted his services, emerges from the house, apparently determined to give himself up, in order not to make things too difficult for the new owner of the house and his family. Utmost Urge, however, refuses to listen to the old man and pleads with him to help in the reconstruction of the house. He insists that the house is still Sam Ego's and that Sam must live in it with the Urge family after the house has been restored. Officials from the asylum make a scene with the angry and outraged old Sexton of the church when the Sexton asks them a few intelligent questions about themselves. The officials imply that this old man is as crazy as Sam Ego, and they are about to put him to a test when he cracks one of them in the nose. The house-movers join the fight and the officials are subdued. The meaning of this episode in the play ought to be obvious, but I will explain nevertheless that this is not meant to be an attack upon the science of psychiatry, which is a science I happen to cherish deeply and which I believe is capable far more effectively and swiftly than the organized church, for instance, to restore, maintain and improve public health as well as liberate the world's mind and make it capable of growth. The episode is a scoffing at the little minds which muck up psychiatry by being little and by being in control of important jobs of administration. God help any man with an intelligent and impatient nature if he falls into the hands of such nitwits. And the episode warns against a leaping to conclusions about any man's mental balance, for it is possible from almost a dozen different planes of thinking to regard any normal man who is not also a piece of machinery as mentally unbalanced.

The journey of Sam Ego's house across town is a long and difficult one, full of ordeals of all kinds for the house-movers, one of the difficulties being the wild women who in celebration of the ending of the War crawl under the house and startle them almost to death with the violence of their sexual hunger, expressed in so many different ways on so many different occasions. The boys who have just recently talked about things in general, including the profoundly important matter of finding wives, and describing the kind they would like to find, are soon discovered married to women who were among the lot which celebrated under the house, and of course these women are scarcely what they had had in heart or mind.

The house is finally settled on Utmost Urge's property in the slums, it is restored, and the play ends with the return of Utmost Urge's sons from the War, a soldier, a sailor, and a marine. The sons return as friendly and appreciative strangers. They go into the house to sit down to a Sunday dinner of roast beef, pumpkin pie and coffee.

That's the long and short of it, except perhaps for the fun
and poetry along the way.

Is this play subtle propaganda for Communism, as some
people who read it in manuscript felt it might be? It is not.
It is propaganda, and not very subtle propaganda at that, on
behalf of the principle that art should teach while it entertains.
If I were a Russian Communist or an American Communist, I
am sure I should have to be proud of it; but the truth of the
matter is that I have not been able to respect any political
party or theory enough to be willing to subscribe to its plans,
purposes or techniques. I am as opposed to everything that
seems to me to be false, foolish or fierce in Russian Communism as I am to the same things in American Capitalism,
even though I am by birth both an American and a Capitalist.
Any money I happen to come into, after taxes, I spend as I
please, and I do not know how anybody who abides in a
Capitalist society can possibly help being a Capitalist by actual
practice. But I am not a political animal in the first place. I am
an esthetic one. And I will venture to guess that I will never
know an actual political system (as against a theoretic and
non-actual one, which can always seem perfect to some people)
that I will be able to wholeheartedly accept. Mr. George Bernard
Shaw has a right (because he is 93 years old) to believe he knows
what he is talking about when it comes to politics, but I do not
believe I have any such right, as I am 41 years old (was 20, will
be 60). I would be willing to say straight off, however, that everybody in politics seems to be trying to do his best under the circumstances, and I don't know how you can swiftly improve the
quality of anybody's best. It takes a lot of time and a lot of
art to do that. And that's the reason this play is propaganda on
behalf of more allegorical, more entertaining and instructive
playwrighting.

THE CHARACTERS

AMPLE URGE, *first angel*
INNER URGE, *second angel*
OUTER URGE, *third angel*
UTMOST URGE, *their father*
EASY URGE, *their younger brother*
DANCEY URGE, *their younger sister*
YESTER URGE, *their mother*
SAM EGO
AUCTIONEER
ADMINISTRATOR
HOUSE-MOVER
HIS BROTHER
PASTOR
SEXTON
FIRST BOY
SECOND BOY
THIRD BOY
FOURTH BOY
FIRST FIREMAN
SECOND FIREMAN
THIRD FIREMAN
HOUSE-MOVER'S WIFE
OTHER WIFE
WESTERN UNION MESSENGER
EXTRA BOYS, GIRLS, MEN *and* WOMEN

THE TIME
Summer and Fall, 1945.

THE PLACE
The town of Angels Aghast, California.

THE SCENE
Sam Ego's house in seven different places before, during and after the process of being moved across town.

Scene I

An old two-story white frame house is up for auction on a hot evening in the summer of 1945 in the city of Angels Aghast, California.

The front of the house has been covered with circus and side-show posters, patent medicine advertisements, pictures of candidates for public office, lovers' initials, and hand-painted mottoes of religious or amorous import. "The wages of sin is death, sayeth the Lord." "Is not, Sayeth Harry. Sinned here, feel fine."

THREE YOUNG MEN stand nearby, watching: a SOLDIER, a SAILOR and a MARINE, in uniform. They might be angels, and they are certainly frequently aghast, as they witness all of the scenes of the play, standing to one side or moving in close to the action. They respond to what happens, approving or disapproving. They are now stiff and straight, and they carry miscellaneous weapons.

Loud radio jazz of the summer of 1945 is heard, followed by applause so sudden, dynamic and unaccountable as to seem insane.

The effect of this national radio madness is evident on the BOY of thirteen who wears a red-white-and-blue striped jersey, white tennis trousers and white shoes, as he rehearses boogie dancing with his GIRL in the street. She wears the same model of jersey, white shorts, and red sandals which are laced high above the ankle. The fat AUCTIONEER, sitting on the steps, watches them with disgust, while the tall ADMINISTRATOR of the estate walks about on the porch, hawking and spitting as he goes.

AUCTIONEER. Get away from here! Scat! Scat! (*The* DANCERS *hug and kiss as they dance*) Scat, I say! You're in public! Boogie boogie boogie. The street is no place for the handsome likes of you. Get away! Get away from here! I've got a rotten house to sell at auction.

THE BOY. Ah, shaddap, fat man!

AUCTIONEER. Scat, I say! Off with you! Boogie boogie boogie! Off to the movies now! Kiss and slap about in the movies!

THE BOY. Shaddap, shaddap!

ADMINISTRATOR. (*Hawk-spit*) If you've come to see the auction, please behave like ladies and gentlemen.

THE BOY. Shaddap! The only way to get rid of that house is to burn it down. (*He strikes a match; holds out the flame*) I'll start the fire for you.

ADMINISTRATOR. (*Hawk-swallow*) Put out that match!

THE BOY. Shaddap!

ADMINISTRATOR. As the administrator of the estate, I'll put you in the hands of the police.

THE BOY. Shaddap, shaddap!

He lights cigarette, inhales deeply, places the cigarette in the lips of the GIRL, blows out the flame, flicks the matchstick at the ADMINISTRATOR, and goes off with the girl. The TWO MEN fall silent as the nearby radio fills the evening with more madness. The AUCTIONEER stands and stretches.

AUCTIONEER. I'm hungry.

ADMINISTRATOR. (*Hawk-spit*) They say the American people eat too much.

AUCTIONEER. I don't care what they say. I'm disgusted and I'm hungry, and when I'm hungry I like to sit down and eat. I don't eat with the rest of the family, you know. Can't stand the noise. I make them turn off the radio, too. The damn boogie boogie boogie makes me sick to my stomach.

ADMINISTRATOR. Is that so?

AUCTIONEER. Yes, and how much longer do you want me to hang around this time?

ADMINISTRATOR. Oh, we'll have the house sold in no time at all.

AUCTIONEER. You've said that every year since 1939. Nobody ever comes to the auctions, and you know it.

ADMINISTRATOR. Don't worry, we'll have a nice crowd this year. (*Hawk-spit*) Houses aren't easy to find these days, you know.

AUCTIONEER. *This* one is.

ADMINISTRATOR. Yes, it *is* a landmark in Angels Aghast, famous from one end of town to the other.

AUCTIONEER. Famous as a *haunted* house.

ADMINISTRATOR. Only children believe the house is haunted. The house is famous as the mansion of Sam Ego.

AUCTIONEER. Proud lawyer and prosperous lunatic. (*Slight pause*) How long *has* poor Sam been in the lunatic asylum?

ADMINISTRATOR. Twenty-five years. I've been the administrator of the estate twenty-five years.

AUCTIONEER. That long? It must be a nice place.

ADMINISTRATOR. Last year they planted one of the biggest institutional Victory Gardens in the country. You may have eaten some of the potatoes they sold in the open market.

AUCTIONEER. You mean the *lunatics* planted the Garden?

ADMINISTRATOR. Oh, yes. Not only that, the excitement of War restored the mind of a Brigadier General, whereupon he was put in charge of three divisions in Southern Italy.

AUCTIONEER. What about Sam Ego?

ADMINISTRATOR. He's still the same. Still shaking with uncontrollable laughter.

AUCTIONEER. The War didn't cure him?

ADMINISTRATOR. No, just the Brigadier General.

AUCTIONEER. I don't want to hear any more about it.

They fall silent again while the nearby radio goes on with its monkey business. The AUCTIONEER suddenly leaps to his feet in a frenzy.

AUCTIONEER. I see a man coming! For God's sake, stand in the street, and I'll open the auction. (*The* ADMINISTRATOR *hawks and spits as he stumbles down the rickety steps of the porch to the street*) Ladies and gentlemen! I am going to sell this handsome house at public auction to the highest bidder.

Built at the turn of the century by Sam Ego, the house was
designed for noble and gracious living. Although unoccupied
for some time, the mansion requires only a few minor repairs
to be as good as new.

A lean, hard, hungry-looking man appears.

ADMINISTRATOR. This is the house-mover, I'm afraid.

AUCTIONEER. Oh. (*He sits down wearily.*)

HOUSE-MOVER. I came to study the problem. (*He looks under
the house*) The rollers have sunk into the earth, I see, but
if they haven't rotted my brother and I can get them out
all right. He'll be along in a few minutes. We haven't moved
a house in six years, and we've never moved a house this big.
We'll need horses to hire, so you can see two hundred and
fifty dollars isn't going to be enough. Have you sold the
house?

ADMINISTRATOR. The auctioneer will sell the house in just a
moment. In the meantime, as the administrator of the estate,
let me repeat that two hundred and fifty dollars is all the
money I can permit to be spent on moving it. There is an
out-of-town house-moving concern which is eager to accept
the job, but of course I would rather keep the business here
at home.

HOUSE-MOVER. Well, if we didn't have to move the house too
far my brother and I *might* be able to do it for two hundred
and fifty dollars.

ADMINISTRATOR. You would be legally responsible for getting
the house to its new location in a reasonable amount of time,
you know.

HOUSE-MOVER. Oh, we'd get it there in a reasonable amount of
time all right. It's been sitting *here* forty-five years, six years
on our brand-new rollers which cost good hard money when
you offered us the job in 1939. The time we'd take would be
reasonable enough.

ADMINISTRATOR. A day and a half, perhaps?

HOUSE-MOVER. No, a good deal longer than *that*. It's to be *rolled*,
you know, but it will not go as an automobile does. Very

slowly—very slowly indeed, with my brother or myself under the house taking chances on getting squashed. I remember the foundations as having been well along in rot. Now, if they were to smash, moving the house would be more like *dragging*, which of course takes more time than rolling, and of course it's a good deal more dangerous, too. We've made a study of these things and understand the principles of physics involved. We know *any* amount of time we may take will be relatively reasonable. Mind you, I said *relatively*. Pay us enough to hire the horses, and then you may go home to bed, and the day after tomorrow see the house on its way down the street. That's the long and short of it, but we've got to have the money for the horses.

ADMINISTRATOR. At the most, how much time do you feel you and your brother would require to get the house settled on its new plot?

HOUSE-MOVER. Where *is* the plot?

ADMINISTRATOR. We don't know yet, but assuming the new plot is at the farthest point within the city limits, how much time would you and your brother require?

HOUSE-MOVER. The farthest point would be close to six miles, and six miles according to our experience might take a little time.

ADMINISTRATOR. How much time?

HOUSE-MOVER. A month perhaps. Two hundred and fifty dollars for a month of horses would not be enough.

ADMINISTRATOR. Surely you and your brother could do it in a week, and two hundred and fifty dollars for a week of horses would be quite adequate.

HOUSE-MOVER. We had imagined a profit of some sort might have entered into the matter.

ADMINISTRATOR. A profit of some sort *does* enter into the matter. It enters into the matter in your keeping your business alive, in not losing an opportunity—a most *valuable* opportunity, I might say—to demonstrate to the people of our city your skill at moving houses. Move this house and I'll wager you'll have more houses to move than there are horses in Angels

Aghast to help you do it, and that means enlarging your business!

HOUSE-MOVER. My brother and I have taken into account the advertising value of this particular job, but as I say the proposition isn't much better than a challenge. A man requires a great deal of plain food if he is to roll a house like this six miles, and plain food—the very *plainest* food—costs money. When there isn't a house to roll, my brother and I are satisfied to have only a reasonable amount of plain food, but when the job is upon us, and we're rolling, we're called upon to eat *enormous* amounts of plain food, and by plain food I mean bread, beans, greens, and the cheaper cuts of beef which we know how to prepare.

ADMINISTRATOR. Two hundred and fifty dollars. Take it or leave it.

HOUSE-MOVER. My brother and I will take it if you'll let us have it in full when we shake hands, but of course you understand we'll be doing it for advertising purposes alone.

ADMINISTRATOR. Agreed, House-mover! When the house is sold, we shall shake hands, you and your brother shall have your money in full, I shall go home to bed, and the day after tomorrow see the house on its way down the street, is that right?

HOUSE-MOVER. That is right.

UTMOST URGE pauses in the street.

AUCTIONEER. (*Leaping to his feet*) Here, now! Here comes somebody else. Ladies and gentlemen, the auction is open. Make a bid for this house as it stands, moved to where you want it within a reasonable amount of time free of charge, and let us all get along with our private lives. (*Shouting desperately*) Make a bid, friend, make a bid!

UTMOST. (*Looking around*) Who?

AUCTIONEER. You, friend! You!

UTMOST. Me? Oh, I'm not here to *buy* the house. I've only come to *see* it. It *is* a handsome house, but such a house is not for me.

AUCTIONEER. How many of you are there?

UTMOST. Oh, seven of us.

AUCTIONEER. Ah! Now, let me ask, you have work, an income, and you are a family together?

The HOUSE-MOVER'S BROTHER arrives.

UTMOST. Oh, yes. I have a place in Sundown Slums, but I could never buy a house like this and move it *there*.

HOUSE-MOVER. (*To his* BROTHER) Sundown Slums? That's at the very edge of the city limits. That's *more* than six miles as the crow flies, and the crow would have to fly straight through the heart of the city. (*To the* ADMINISTRATOR) A route like that with people watching all the time would require an enormous amount of plain food.

AUCTIONEER. Now, I want you to know the man who just spoke is a professional house-mover. He and his brother there under the house have been hired by the estate to move this house safely to the place within the city limits of Angels Aghast designated and owned by the purchaser. These men, these house-movers, *both* of them under the house now, as you see, studying the problem, will move the house to its new location within a reasonable amount of time. Now, let me ask further, you have in Sundown Slums—*what?*

UTMOST. A small house—not a house like this at all—and a place of business.

AUCTIONEER. What sort of business, let me ask?

UTMOST. Junkyard.

AUCTIONEER. Ah! Now let me ask, friend, this junkyard is sufficiently spacious to accommodate the house that I am auctioning off to the public, is it not?

UTMOST. Oh, the yard is big enough all right, but of course a good deal of the junk in the yard would have to be moved.

AUCTIONEER. (*Warming up*) I understand perfectly. Some of the junk must be moved—*piled*, no doubt—to make room for this splendid dwelling. Now, I want to make a point: you and your family would want the house as a *home* of course. That is to say, you would make certain minor repairs

—using an item here and an item there from the yard itself—
and then move into the house lock, stock and barrel. I mean,
you must understand that the estate is permitted to sell the
house only on condition that the house serves as a private
dwelling for *people*. I might add, you would be permitted
to entertain guests, although not for profit. You understand,
I trust.

UTMOST. Oh, I *understand* all right. I would like the house for
my family very much, but my business is not large or profit-
able. I finished paying for the yard last year, after twenty
years. The little house I built myself is paid for, I have a
fair assortment of junk in the yard, but very little money.
I came only to *see* the house.

AUCTIONEER. Now, understand that the house-mover there and
his brother will put the house where you want it, facing any
direction you like—am I right, House-mover?—free of charge
and within a reasonable amount of time? Now, let me hear
a bid, please.

HOUSE-MOVER. I hope you understand that by a reasonable
amount of time, my brother and I mean a measurement of
time consistent with the laws and limits of physics, horse-
power, and quantity of food we eat on the job, with scarcely
any regard for quality.

AUCTIONEER. Oh, yes, I understand—a *reasonable* amount of
time.

HOUSE-MOVER. Through the heart of the city, and with many
problems. Narrow streets to be avoided, spectators to be gotten out of the way, possible dragging rather than rolling.
And of course my brother and I could not be responsible
for any damage to the house during the night while we are
at home eating and reading.

AUCTIONEER. (*Impatiently*) Yes, those are all definite— Now,
my friend, you've heard for yourself, so let me ask, how
much money have you put away for a rainy day?

UTMOST. Oh, I've got eighty or ninety dollars in the bank, a
few dollars in the cigar box at the junkyard, a few nickels
and dimes in the teapot in the cupboard—but I haven't come

to make a bid on the house. I'm sure somebody else will buy it.

AUCTIONEER. Let me put it this way? What is your name?

UTMOST. My name is Urge—Utmost Urge. Ridiculous, I know, but I was born and christened so. Urge is a common name among my people. Utmost was my father's idea.

AUCTIONEER. And your friends, they have a nickname for you, Mr. Urge? Utmo, or Ut, perhaps? I want us to understand one another.

UTMOST. I don't believe I have a nickname.

AUCTIONEER. The reason I brought up the matter of nicknames, Mr. Urge, was to carry us into a friendly relationship. I'd like you to know that my friends call me Fatso, a fitting nickname, no doubt—because of my size and shape—and if you'll think of me not as an auctioneer but as a friend—as Fatso—I'll think of you as—well, Mr. Urge. Now, then. Let Fatso ask you as a friend, Mr. Urge, how much money have you got in your pocket? Call me Fatso.

UTMOST. Oh, I've got a dollar and fifty cents. I'm to buy some wine for Sunday dinner, Fatso.

AUCTIONEER. Now, about *water* at Sunday dinner *instead* of wine, Mr. Urge. Why not bid a dollar and fifty cents and have the house instead of the wine? Understand, *delivered* to the junkyard within a reasonable amount of time free of charge.

UTMOST. A dollar and fifty cents for *this* house? You must be joking.

AUCTIONEER. I assure you I'm *not* joking! I have here the necessary authorization to make the sale, the necessary papers calling for signatures—and the necessary witnesses! Make your bid, please!

UTMOST. I bid a dollar and fifty cents for Sam Ego's house, Mr. Auctioneer.

AUCTIONEER. (*He strikes the porch railing with his hammer*) Sold! Sold to Mr. Utmost Urge!

The railing topples over into the weeds, half the porch creaks, groans, and slowly sinks several feet, forcing the

HOUSE-MOVER to scramble to safety from under the porch.
The AUCTIONEER leaps down the steps to shake hands with
UTMOST, while the ADMINISTRATOR shakes hands with the
HOUSE-MOVER. The BOY and GIRL come up the street danc-
ing boogie to the radio jazz.

Scene II

Now, about forty-eight hours later, the hind end of SAM
EGO's house sticks out around a corner and blinks in the
hot glaring light of sunset. The house has escaped from
Rich Angel Street where it has stood for forty-five years
and has plunged down Infant Angel Street. The names of
the streets are on signposts, and another sign pointing
down Infant Angel Street says, Sundown Slums, 6 miles.

The ANGELS are more relaxed now, and only the MARINE
carries a gun, but the bayonet has been removed from it.

Large and small billboards stop the eye from seeing more
than the hind end of the house or any of the neighbor-
hood. The largest billboard advertises AN INSPIRED PIC-
TURE: BACELY DANDER IN THE DIRTY DOG, WITH ANNA MOLE,
AND INTRODUCING MISS GAY MUCKAGE (ALMOST RHYMES WITH
LUGGAGE), now playing at the Infant Angel. Bacely Dander
has turned his back but not his head (his profile shows)
on Anna Mole who lies in negligee on a floor, weeping
and clutching a man's shoe, and on Miss Muckage who,
wearing the costume of a chorus girl, sits at a table in a
night club, counting a stack of currency. Part of the advertisement says, Buy Bonds and Help Win the War. A GIRL
of seven or eight with a piece of red crayon draws a
moustache on Miss Mole's upper lip, after which she
draws moustaches of various styles and sizes all over Miss
Mole and revises the Treasury Department's share in the
advertisement to read Buy Bonds and Help Win the
Money. She then writes, *I am a girl.*

Smaller billboards advertise lipstick, perfume, soap, dia-
monds, furs, cigarettes, smoking pipes, razor blades, canned

pork and beans, chewing gum, beer, whiskey, the Marine Corps, airplanes, and the new cola, Publicola (The Favorite of the People). In every advertisement there is one pretty girl, half-naked, so that the scene swarms with female flesh larger than life.

A basketball basket has been attached to the house and two small GIRLS are trying to toss empty cans into it.

THREE OTHER GIRLS, all of them no more than six or seven, are skipping up and down the steps of the back porch.

FOUR BOYS of eleven or twelve arrive with a basketball, which they dribble and pass to one another as they come. They drive the GIRLS away without a word, pushing or shoving them if they are big, or walking slowly after them if they are little, and then start a game of one-basket basketball. They are very good at the game, play smartly, and make the basket quite often.

A MAN in shirt-sleeves smoking a pipe comes along, glancing at the girls in the advertisements, lingering an extra moment near one of them. He compares Bacely Dander with himself, watches the basketball game, lights his pipe six or seven times, and then sits down on the steps of the back porch.

A GIRL of seventeen or eighteen, bathed and fresh in a summer dress, comes walking down the street, her buttocks rolling helplessly. The MAN on the steps watches her until a match burns his fingers and goes out, and the BOYS stop the game.

FIRST BOY. Who's that?

SECOND BOY. Ah, that's my sister.

THIRD BOY. Your sister?

FOURTH BOY. Since when does your sister walk like that?

SECOND BOY. Don't ask me. Come on, let's play.

FIRST BOY. Doesn't she even say hello to you when she sees you in the street?

SECOND BOY. Naah.

THIRD BOY. How come?

SECOND BOY. How should I know, how come? Come on, let's play.

FOURTH BOY. What's your hurry? Does she talk to you when you're at home?

SECOND BOY. Sure she talks to me when I'm at home. Why wouldn't she talk to me when I'm at home?

FIRST BOY. If she talks to you when you're at home, why doesn't she say hello to you when she sees you in the street?

SECOND BOY. For the love of Mike, if we're going to play, let's play. Maybe she doesn't say hello to me in the street because she doesn't want the whole world to know I'm her brother.

THIRD BOY. Why not? Is she too good to be your sister just because she walks that way?

SECOND BOY. Ah, lay off, will you? She can't help the way she walks. Things happen to girls as they get older.

FOURTH BOY. I'll say they do! Won't say hello to her brother when she sees him in the street. If I had a sister like that I'd beat her up.

SECOND BOY. Lay off, will you? What do I care if she doesn't say hello when she sees me in the street? I didn't say hello to her, did I?

THIRD BOY. That's different. You were in the game.

SECOND BOY. Come on, come on, give me the ball and let's get going.

He tries to take the ball out of the hands of the FOURTH BOY, who hangs onto the ball and pivots.

FOURTH BOY. Take it easy. What's the matter, ashamed to talk about your sister just because she walks like that?

SECOND BOY. Who wants to talk about the way my sister walks, for the love of Mike?

THIRD BOY. You must be blind. Haven't you ever watched her walk?

SECOND BOY. What do I care how my sister walks?

FIRST BOY. I never saw anybody roll the way she rolls.

THIRD BOY. You just know she knows everybody watches the way she rolls.

FOURTH BOY. A girl just don't get a roll like that from sitting.

FIRST BOY. A roll like that just don't happen by itself.

THIRD BOY. You just know she knows she's got a roll like that.

FIRST BOY. I once saw a colored girl with a roll that wasn't half as big as *that*.

THIRD BOY. If I had a sister with a roll like that who wouldn't say hello to me in the street, I'd catch her coming out of the bathroom some night and teach her some manners.

FOURTH BOY. What I'd do to a sister like that who wouldn't say hello to me!

FIRST BOY. Ever see your sister come out of the bathroom at night?

SECOND BOY. Sure I've seen her. We live in the same house. I've seen her all my life.

THIRD BOY. Does she roll that way coming out of the bathroom?

FIRST BOY. Do you see her *naked*?

FOURTH BOY. I'd teach her some manners if she came out of *my* bathroom naked.

SECOND BOY. She doesn't come out of the bathroom naked. She comes out in a bathrobe. I don't have to teach my sister any manners.

THIRD BOY. Well, if you don't, *somebody* does!

FIRST BOY. Some day somebody's going to teach a girl like that a *lot* of manners.

FOURTH BOY. Beat her up good!

SECOND BOY. You guys lay off my sister! She's got manners! Just lay off her, that's all!

THIRD BOY. What are you getting tough about? Who do you think your sister is anyway?

FIRST BOY. Since when do you come around telling us what we can talk about and what we can't talk about?

FOURTH BOY. Do you think your sister is somebody nobody can talk about?

SECOND BOY. I said lay off!

THIRD BOY. We don't want to lay off. We want to talk about your sister.

FIRST BOY. What are you going to do about it?

FOURTH BOY. Going to beat up the three of us for talking about your sister?

SECOND BOY. (*Beginning to sob*) Sure I'm going to beat the three of you up!

He swings at the FOURTH BOY, who ducks, pivots, catches him by the arm, while the THIRD BOY hits him from behind and knocks him down, and the FIRST BOY falls on him. The MAN on the porch stands and watches.

FOURTH BOY. (*As they fight*) Oh, yeah?

THIRD BOY. We'll teach you a little manners, too.

FIRST BOY. (*Leaping on the SECOND BOY and laughing*) Poor little crying tough boy. Sister's little lover.

SECOND BOY. (*Taking a beating*) I'll show you dirty sons of bitches!

FIRST BOY. (*Lifting him up*) Show us your sister coming out of the bathroom naked.

FOURTH BOY. (*Pushing the SECOND BOY's head swiftly many times*) Poor little crying boy, crying for his sister.

SECOND BOY. (*Kicking and crying*) I'll get you sons of bitches, you wait and see!

THIRD BOY. Wait till we get your sister. All three of us will teach her some manners, and you can watch us do it. (*He slaps the SECOND BOY front-and-back hand.*)

SECOND BOY. (*Sobbing bitterly and trying desperately to break free*) I thought you dirty bastards were my friends, you dirty bastards!

FOURTH BOY. We are your friends. We're just teaching you a little manners.

FIRST BOY. We're going to teach your sister a little manners, too.

SECOND BOY. I thought you sons of bitches were decent!

THIRD BOY. Look whose sister's decent!

FIRST BOY. Poor little crying boy!

SECOND BOY. I thought you bastards would want to be decent, the way any decent fellow would want to be!

FOURTH BOY. (*Grabbing the SECOND BOY as he almost wrenches himself free*) Not yet, crying boy! We'll let you go home when we get good and ready! (*He pushes the* SECOND BOY's *head swiftly again and again.*)

SECOND BOY. I thought you'd fight one at a time, like any decent fellow would, you dirty bastards!

THIRD BOY. We're not fighting, crying boy! We're just teaching you a little manners. (*He slaps the* SECOND BOY *very hard.*)

SECOND BOY. You're dirty cowards! (*He almost breaks free, but the* THREE OTHERS *fall on him, laughing as they do so*) If you weren't such dirty cowards, you'd fight one at a time, you dirty cowards! (*They struggle in silence.*)

FOURTH BOY. I'll rest awhile. You two guys wear him down. (*He disengages himself from the struggle, lights a cigarette, smokes it casually.*)

SECOND BOY. I'll get you sons of bitches, you wait and see! I'll get every one of you! (*He is almost exhausted, and his sobbing has almost stopped*) I thought you wanted to be decent. You're decent when you play basketball. (*He stops struggling, and the* OTHERS *relax their holds a little. The excitement begins to wear away. The* SECOND BOY *looks down helplessly as he tries to catch his breath. The* TWO BOYS *holding him watch his face*) I thought you guys were my friends. I thought I'd do anything for you guys, and I thought you'd do anything for me. I've known every one of you all my life, you dirty bastards! I thought we were all decent. You guys are dogs, you dirty stinking yellow dogs! If two of you guys jumped on one of us, I'd fight against you. I wouldn't be a dirty dog like you dirty dogs! (*The* BOYS *drop their arms. The* SECOND BOY *stands free. He looks up at the* THIRD BOY, *who is ashamed to look him in the face*) I thought you were my best friend!

THIRD BOY. I'm sorry. (*Barely able to speak*) I don't know what happened to me.

SECOND BOY. I thought you were decent, you dirty son of a bitch! (*He slaps the* THIRD BOY *very hard. The* THIRD BOY *turns his back in shame and moves away a little. The* SECOND BOY *turns to the* OTHERS) You guys call yourself men, don't you? You make me ashamed of myself! (*He straightens him-*

self out and walks off, turning once to look back with contempt. *The* MAN *on the porch sits down.*)

FOURTH BOY. (*Throws away his cigarette, picks up the basketball, bounces it several times. He tries to make a basket and
follows the ball. He tries again, then stops and turns to the*
FIRST BOY) All right, get in the game! What's the matter with
you?

FIRST BOY. I don't feel like playing. (*The* FIRST BOY *watches the*
THIRD BOY *walk off. The* FOURTH BOY *passes the* FIRST BOY
the ball very swiftly. He catches it and throws it away) I said
I don't feel like playing, didn't I? (*He walks off.*)

The FOURTH BOY goes after the ball, taking a lot of time and
turning to watch the FIRST BOY go. He picks up the ball,
as the HOUSE-MOVER and his BROTHER come along with tooth-
picks in their mouths. They now wear coveralls whose many
pockets are weighted down with all kinds of working tools.
The FOURTH BOY bounces the ball as he returns to the basket.
He is about to try for another basket when he changes his
mind. He walks off slowly.

The HOUSE-MOVER and his BROTHER stand before one of the
billboards and study the picture of the girl on it. They bring
out cigarettes, light them, inhale, exhale, and begin examining the rollers on which the house rests.

The MAN on the steps lights his pipe, puffs at it, gets up
slowly, yawns, and goes off.

The HOUSE-MOVER and his BROTHER get under the house.

The little GIRL with the red crayon comes back and contin-
ues her drawing of moustaches.

The HOUSE-MOVER and his BROTHER begin a duet of hammering under the house.

The little GIRL turns and listens a moment and then prints
the word Me on a billboard.

The hammering takes on a rhythm which gradually grows swift, and acquires form.

The other little GIRLS come back and try to toss cans into the basketball basket, and dance up and down the steps of the house.

It is almost night now.

The BOY and the GIRL in the red-white-and-blue jersey sweaters come along and dance to the rhythm of the HOUSE-MOVERS' hammering.

The SECOND BOY'S SISTER comes back on her way home, rolling her buttocks, followed by a YOUNG MAN who looks something like Bacely Dander. She carries two books which are obviously library books, and she looks straight ahead as she walks.

The HOUSE-MOVER'S BROTHER crawls to the edge of the house to watch her walk. The YOUNG MAN brings his thumb and forefinger together for the BROTHER as commentary on the perfectly wonderful way the girl walks. BROTHER scrambles out from under the house to stand in the street and look, with his mouth open.

The HOUSE-MOVER scrambles after his BROTHER and stands with him and watches.

The little GIRLS stop playing and dancing.

The LOVERS in jersey sweaters walk off.

The HOUSE-MOVERS sit on the steps of the porch and once again light cigarettes and inhale deeply.

The little GIRLS wander off.

The HOUSE-MOVERS stare at the pictures of the girls in the advertisements.

The street light comes on.

Three radio programs come into hearing range simultaneously. One is a concerto for piano and orchestra; one is a soprano singing; one is a man's voice in speech. The programs blend almost as if they were meant to do so. After awhile the man's voice and manner of speech is faintly recognizable. He is saying something about Nagasaki. The HOUSE-MOVERS listen attentively. The soprano sings and the piano and the orchestra play.

UTMOST, carrying a tool-kit, appears with EASY URGE, a boy of eleven or twelve. The father takes pride in the house, and EASY is amazed that it is now theirs.

UTMOST opens his tool-kit and takes out a hammer and a handful of nails, and with them tightens a loose board.

The HOUSE-MOVERS finish their cigarettes, take up their hammers, crawl back under the house, and begin hammering again.

The hammering of the three men joins the three radio programs and gradually drowns them out. The BOY unlocks the back door, pushes it in and stares into the gloom of the house. Unseen by anyone except EASY, an OLD MAN with a beard, shaking with laughter, enters the house and disappears. EASY runs down the steps, and stands beside UTMOST.

ACT TWO

Scene I

It is Sunday, several days later, a moment or two before daybreak, and SAM EGO's house has reached the First Presbyterian Church of Angels Aghast in its journey from Rich Angel Street in Sunup Heights to Poor Angel Street in Sundown Slums. Now a portion of one side of the house and just a little of the back porch is open to view, the remainder of the house being hidden by trees and the rear end of the church. Two windows of the lower floor of the house and two of the upper are in view, the panes of all of them broken almost to the frames. The window of the Minister's study looks across to the upper windows of the house.

All is dark and still, except for occasional Sunday morning chirps of waking birds in the church trees.

The ANGELS are now in battle dress. Their faces are dirty and they are desperate and weary.

The church SEXTON, a man of seventy or so with a gruff, casual manner as if he were always angry about something but not too angry, arrives at the back door of the church, unlocks it, enters the church, and a moment later lifts the lower half of the window of the Minister's study to let in fresh air. He stands at the window a moment, looking out at the broken windows of SAM EGO's house, then disappears.

When he is gone SAM EGO, the old man with the white beard who was seen by EASY entering the house, appears at one of the upper windows.

He is shaking with what appears to be silent laughter, but he is not by any means a frightening man to see. He thrusts his head out of the window, apparently looking for someone. When the SEXTON reappears in the Minister's study, SAM EGO leaps out of sight, and when the SEXTON leaves the study, closing the door behind him, SAM EGO reappears at the window again, thrusts his head out and looks around.

EASY, the junkman's boy, comes along carrying a full paper sack.

SAM EGO. (*Whispering*) There you are, my boy! But quiet now, there's someone in the church. Be ready if he should appear in that window or down below there, like the sharp fellow you are. (EASY *nods*) You've told no one? (EASY *shakes his head*) I knew you wouldn't. Not even your father, or your mother, or the dearest person you know in all the world, whoever that might be? (EASY *shakes his head*) You're not afraid? (EASY *shakes his head*) You know I'm only an old man who's done no more than come to his own house? (EASY *nods*) Then come up with the food you've brought, but quiet! (*He motions*) Around the back and up the stairs. It's almost morning now and I've been starved all night. Put the parcel in the place we know. I'll get it all and take it where I go to eat and sleep and not be found, my boy. They'll come looking for me soon, but only you and I know I'm here, and only I know the place. I'd tell you where it is, but plenty of time for that, my boy. Around the back, then, like the fearless fellow you are. I'm famished and weak. You've brought plenty of bread and a bottle of water? (EASY *nods*) Up softly, then, and again tomorrow. Good-bye, my boy. (SAM EGO *disappears into the house.*)

EASY looks around, then hurries to the back door, unlocks it, and goes in. The SEXTON comes out of the church with a broom and begins to sweep, as the light of the sun begins to make the day Sunday. The HOUSE-MOVER comes along in coveralls with a toothpick in his mouth.

SEXTON. (*Leaning on his broom*) Now, you're not going to make a racket with your moving on the Sabbath, are you?

You're not going to have the Sabbath a shambles of hammering and hollering at horses and creaking and groaning and not moving the house more than an inch the whole day, are you? The Pastor needs a lot of peace and quiet when it's time to give his sermon. You might have dragged the awful house another way, alongside the church of the Baptists, or the Episcopalians, or the Methodists, or the Catholics, or the Jews, instead of the First Presbyterian. The Pastor's sensitive to noise and stops his sermon if he hears so much as a sneeze in a handkerchief. And where are the horses now?

HOUSE-MOVER. They'll be out front before long, brought by my brother.

SEXTON. (Outraged) Out front? Out front to do what? To drag this wreckage on the Sabbath? Four sick and hungry horses?

HOUSE-MOVER. The horses we've hired are all in good health and well-fed. They brought the house this far, and my brother and I, we've added two more to the team.

SEXTON. Oh, you have? Well, the Pastor isn't going to like the noise of them. It's no noise for the peace of the Sabbath. And what do you think you'll be doing to the Sunday School classes?

HOUSE-MOVER. My brother and I hope to move the house a little before the Sunday School classes begin.

SEXTON. Oh, you do, do you? And how do you mean to do it?

HOUSE-MOVER. By the principles and laws of physics which we have studied.

SEXTON. Well, you've had the house sitting here since yesterday morning at nine by the principles and laws of physics, haven't you?

HOUSE-MOVER. We found a flaw in our system of ropes and pulleys, but we've corrected the flaw and we hope to move the house a considerable distance before Sunday School classes begin. What time do they begin?

SEXTON. They begin in four hours, at half-past nine. And what about the choir? Will they ever be heard? Where will your hammering and hollering be in five hours when the choir begins to sing? In Sundown Slums, I suppose, where you're dragging the miserable house!

HOUSE-MOVER. My brother and I estimate we can move the house to the next corner in four hours.

SEXTON. And is the Pastor so deaf he can't hear your hammering and hollering from there?

HOUSE-MOVER. Only faintly.

SEXTON. Oh. And you're right under the Pastor's study, where he makes his notes and gathers his thoughts together. What thoughts is he going to be able to gather together with you and your brother hammering and hollering and your six horses thrashing about and slipping and falling all over the place?

EASY comes up from the front of the house and stands beside the HOUSE-MOVER.

HOUSE-MOVER. The Pastor might gather together some thoughts about what will it profit a man if he gaineth the world and loseth his soul, as the man who built this house forty-five years ago might well have considered, from what I've heard about him.

SEXTON. And just what is it that you've heard about him? That he lost his soul? *I* heard he lost his *wits*. And he didn't gain the world in the first place—not by a long shot. He was a lawyer and a good one, and before he lost his wits I knew him well. I knew him as well as I know anybody in Angels Aghast, as well as I know the Pastor I've served these thirty years. Sam Ego and myself are men of the same age, allowing two or three years one way or the other, and so is the Pastor, God help him on this Sabbath day.

HOUSE-MOVER. He was a rich man to build a house like this, and being rich is what they mean by gaining the world. A *mind* lost is no different and no better than a *soul* lost.

SEXTON. Oh, isn't it? And who is it says the soul needs the cluttering of the mind? Who is it says *that*?

HOUSE-MOVER. My brother and I believe the mind is the best thing to hang onto that a man has. We believe a mind hung onto and cultivated can fix a man up with a *new* soul—a better one than the one he started out with. We're both men who live in the life of the mind.

SEXTON. You're both *imbeciles!* What mind do you think it is that you live in? What mind is there to a man who crawls under a house eaten with rot, hammering on the foundations and hollering to his brother?

HOUSE-MOVER. My brother and I move houses in order to earn the few dollars we require for plain food. It's honorable work and not beneath us because we've strong bodies and live in the life of the mind. If the lawyer whose proud house this once was hadn't pushed and crashed after the empty things of life and neglected his mind and the minds of his wife and children, perhaps my brother and I wouldn't be moving the house to Sundown Slums.

SEXTON. And who is it says Sam Ego pushed and crashed after the things you *say* he pushed and crashed after? *You?* The man was *overtaken*, as any man might be. He was overtaken, Lord help him. (*Suddenly*) And this boy here who's been listening all this time, who's *he*, to be up and about at this hour of the morning?

HOUSE-MOVER. This is the son of the man who's bought the house at public auction. His name's Easy. His father's name is Urge. He's a lively boy, with a good mind, and helps me under the house for the experience of it.

SEXTON. Is this the *junkman's* boy?

HOUSE-MOVER. One of several. The others are in the Army, the Navy, and the Marines.

SEXTON. I've met your father, boy. I've been to his yard on errands for the Pastor, but why couldn't he have taken the house to pieces where it stood instead of dragging it through the streets to the junkyard?

HOUSE-MOVER. Mr. Urge bought the house to live in.

SEXTON. *Live* in? Has your father lost *his* wits too, boy? (*To the* HOUSE-MOVER) The house is cursed, besides being filthy. A quarter of a century of lonely men and woebegone women have slinked in and out of it, in search of peace and pathetic privacy. No wonder no one bought the house all these years!

HOUSE-MOVER. Mr. Urge and his boy here have gone to a great
deal of trouble to sweep out the house, and my brother and
I have gone through the house with them and found it clean
and tight. It *is* old, and no doubt it *has* been visited by
unhappy people from time to time, but the house itself, apart
from local folk-lore, is still sound enough to be restored and
happily occupied by decent people, such as Mr. Urge, his
wife, and his children. The house will lose its fame when it
reaches Sundown Slums. Having been built where vanity was
all, the people could not help rejoicing in its fall and failure;
but when the house settles down where vanity is nothing,
they will not hate it—or themselves for rejoicing in the disgrace of that which they envy. The house will no longer be
Sam Ego's house and will no longer signify to the people the
fearful end to which things pass. It will be the home of a
plain family and the emblem of humble honor. My brother
and I have talked at great length about all this, in the midst
of our eating and reading, after work in the evenings.

SEXTON. (*A little confused*) Oh. (*Pause, wanting to be right, or
at any rate to seem to be*) I did not mention the awful ghosts
that haunt the house. What about them?

HOUSE-MOVER. I'll not say there are no ghosts, and I'll not say
ghosts have never haunted *this* house, but if there are ghosts
and if some of them *have* haunted this house, I'm satisfied
they'll never care to do it in the light of Sundown Slums, or
in the presence of people so reasonable as the members of
the Urge family.

A PAPER-CARRIER comes by with his loaded sacks and hands
the SEXTON a paper, glances at the house, and goes along.

SEXTON. The Pastor's Sunday paper, to help him prepare his
sermon. I'll put it on his desk. (*Suddenly*) What's this?
(*Reading the headline*) Noted Lunatic Escapes. (*He looks
meaningfully at the house, at the* HOUSE-MOVER *and at the
boy* EASY) The noted lunatic is Sam Ego of course, though
he was never noted as a lunatic but as a lawyer. (*He glances
at the paper and reads another line*) Sam Ego At Large

Three Days. Poor Sam, he's no more at large than any of us, he's simply wandered away from the Asylum, as any of us would do. I'd say he'd got his wits back at last, to do that. He was never mad anyway, he just couldn't stop laughing, and the Good Lord knows he had every reason not to stop. Now, if he'd cried, I suppose they'd have decided he was perfectly all right. (*He reads some more from the paper*) Seventy-five-year-old former leading citizen of Angels Aghast, Sam Ego, for the past twenty-five years hopelessly insane, sometime last Wednesday night escaped from the County Lunatic Asylum where he has always been a model inmate, and is still at large. Mr. Ego's affliction is characterized by trembling of the body as he apparently laughs to himself. He wears a fleecy white beard not unlike the one seen in photographs of the great poet of the people, Walt Whitman. Mr. Ego, although heretofore harmless, may now be dangerous, authorities at the Asylum declared last night in making formal announcement of his escape. Search for the lunatic has been secret and fruitless so far, but a city-wide search on the part of the entire police force, the fire department, and all troops of the Boy Scouts will begin early Sunday morning. Authorities at the Asylum are not sure the lunatic did not go off with a box of stolen matches with which to set fire to the city. When questioned whether the lunatic had ever before used matches to set fire to any of the buildings of the Asylum, the authorities replied that he hadn't, but that there was no telling what he might do. Mr. Ego's famous house in Sunup Heights was recently sold at public auction at an undisclosed figure to an undisclosed buyer who was willing to comply with the terms of purchase established by Mr. Ego while he was still sane. Named Ego's Rest by the lunatic when the house was built at the turn of the century, the house was renamed Eagle's Nest by the people in 1919 when the lunatic's son, just back from France in World War I, was killed in an automobile accident, Mr. Ego's wife committed suicide, and his daughter died in childbirth, all of which unbalanced Mr. Ego's mind. The famous building is now en route from Rich Angel Street in Sunup

Heights where it has stood forty-five years to Poor Angel Street in Sundown Slums where it is to be occupied by a family of seven. The choice land on which the house has stood for so long is presently to be sold as a site for a moving picture theatre. Citizens of Angels Aghast have watched the moving of the house with curious interest, and may now find it not far from the First Presbyterian Church on Old Angel Street.

HOUSE-MOVER. They shouldn't have said that. My brother and I don't like a lot of people hanging around when we're working because they always excite the horses.

SEXTON. The Pastor isn't going to like it, either. The whole Sabbath is going to be shot to hell with police, firemen, Boy Scouts, and you and your brother. Well, where *is* the man with the horses? Get the house down the street to the next corner *at least,* before the whole city turns up.

ADMINISTRATOR. (*Running up, panting for breath*) I'm an early riser, and I've read the paper. Where's Mr. Urge?

HOUSE-MOVER. This is his son.

ADMINISTRATOR. They'll fall on the house and tear it to pieces looking for the lunatic. I've got to have a talk with your father. Where is he?

EASY URGE. He said he would be here around six.

ADMINISTRATOR. Thank God for that. We've got to act and act quick! (*The* AUCTIONEER *shows up, running and out of breath*) I'm sorry I had to get you out of bed, but thank God you're here!

AUCTIONEER. Has anyone seen him?

ADMINISTRATOR. He's on his way here.

AUCTIONEER. You haven't seen him?

ADMINISTRATOR. No, but this is his boy.

AUCTIONEER. Whose boy?

ADMINISTRATOR. The *junkman's* of course.

AUCTIONEER. Has anyone seen the *lunatic?*

ADMINISTRATOR. Not yet, but we'll be searching the house as soon as the junkman arrives. (*He turns to* EASY) You understand, boy, that we'll be doing it in order to protect your father's property from the mob when it arrives. They'll want to go through the house pretending to be looking for the lunatic but actually they'll be doing it for the devil of it. And while they're at it they'll tear the house down. Is that clear, boy? Now, if we search the house *before* the mob arrives, we will be in a position to assure the police and the firemen and the Boy Scouts that the lunatic is *not* in the house, and thereby restrain them from destroying your father's property. Have I made myself clear?

EASY. I *guess* so.

ADMINISTRATOR. You've been *in* the house with your father, I hope. You've *explored* the rooms and the halls and the closets and every edge and corner in which a man *might* hide, and you'll be able to lead us about in our search for the lunatic?

HOUSE-MOVER. The boy and his father know the house well, having given it a thorough cleaning from top to bottom.

ADMINISTRATOR. Good. But we'll need all the strength we have if the lunatic's in the house.

SEXTON. If poor Sam's in the house, you'll need nothing but a little humanity in your heart. Sam Ego made his fame as a lawyer defending the accused from the state. If he was mistaken in his sentiments about the guilt or innocence of lawbreakers or about the responsibility of the state not to commit crimes against *them*, he was certainly never guilty of anything more foolish than soft-heartedness, and a respectable amount of vanity. Have you brought a rope with which to tie the poor man? He's been laughing since 1919. Perhaps if you saw yourself and the rest of the people of Angels Aghast as he probably does, you'd laugh too.

ADMINISTRATOR. That may very well be, but the paper says the man has matches and is dangerous.

SEXTON. The paper says he *may* have matches and *may* be dangerous. For a penny any man in the world may buy a box of matches, and no man—not even the Pastor himself—is *not* dangerous. It's the bouncing Boy Scouts I'm scared to death of, not Sam Ego!

BROTHER. (*Arrives in his coveralls with a toothpick in his mouth*) I've got the horses out front if you're ready to give the new system of ropes and pulleys a try.

ADMINISTRATOR. Horses!? You're not thinking of trying to move the house *now*, in face of the lunatic being at large and possibly in the house?

BROTHER. What lunatic?

HOUSE-MOVER. The man who built the house, Sam Ego. He's run away from the Lunatic Asylum.

BROTHER. (*To the* ADMINISTRATOR) My brother and I are paying good money to the stables for the use of the horses, and I think my brother will agree with me that it is no affair of ours who's at large or in the house. We've got to move the house and we've got to move it quick if we're not going to come out of this thing hungry and in debt.

ADMINISTRATOR. Quite right, no doubt. Let me ask—you've spent quite a bit of the two hundred and fifty dollars?

HOUSE-MOVER. Eighty dollars of it, and we haven't moved the house much more than a mile. We're glad to be doing the work of course, but we hadn't figured on not using the horses when we're paying for them.

ADMINISTRATOR. Fair's fair, and what you say is fair, but a lunatic at large with the whole city likely to turn out after him, like hounds after the hare, and all of them headed in the direction of this house—what does that mean in terms of simple arithmetic? Excitement, riot, and in all probability wreckage.

HOUSE-MOVER. Wreckage?

ADMINISTRATOR. Precisely. The precise point I've wanted to make—wreckage—the whole house a shambles. As administrator of the estate I have a very important announcement to make. (*Slowly and over-emphatically*) The house must not be destroyed. If the house *is* destroyed, by whatever means, whether accident, act of God, vandalism, fire, or whatever, my annual fee is forfeit, along with all commissions from the sale of the choice land in Sunup Heights from which the house has been removed, for which I have received a very attractive offer, as well as all fees from miscellaneous and sundry other properties belonging to the estate, and so on and so forth.

HOUSE-MOVER. Oh.

ADMINISTRATOR. Let me put it this way. The house must safely reach Sundown Slums and be occupied by Mr. Urge and his family. That is the basic requirement of the estate, by which I am employed.

BROTHER. Which is exactly what my brother and I hope to do, with the help of the horses.

AUCTIONEER. Not to mention that this boy's father is entitled to have the property he has bought at public auction and now owns protected from the mob.

ADMINISTRATOR. And as soon as his father arrives, we shall conduct our search of the house, declare it out of bounds, obtain adequate police protection for the house, whereupon you and your brother may proceed to move it to Sundown Slums.

SEXTON. Why don't you stop your jabbering and go on into the house, get the search over with, and let the brothers start moving it away? The Pastor isn't going to like a demonstration during his sermon.

ADMINISTRATOR. If the lunatic is found, he will be returned to the County Asylum. If he is not found, I myself will obtain the necessary police and other protection from the Mayor himself, with whom I have already had a preliminary discussion by telephone.

A speeding fire-engine is heard, its bell ringing and its siren wailing. The sound draws closer, skidding is heard, and THREE FIREMEN in uniform and helmets, each of them carrying crowbars and axes, come running. The terrified crying of horses is heard, and the stamping of hooves.

FIRST FIREMAN. Break the door down!

BROTHER. The horses! For God's sake, the horses! (*He jackrabbits around the house, followed by the* HOUSE-MOVER.)

ADMINISTRATOR. (*Screaming*) Stop! There's no need to break the door down. The house is not on fire!

SECOND FIREMAN. (*At the back door*) Who says it ain't?

ADMINISTRATOR. I, the administrator of the estate.

EASY. Anyhow, the door's not locked.

THIRD FIREMAN. Then let's go in and put out the fire. (*They disappear inside the house.*)

AUCTIONEER. (*Stunned*) Boogie boogie boogie!

UTMOST comes along. EASY runs to him, pointing to the house, and they hurry to the ADMINISTRATOR, the AUCTIONEER and the SEXTON. Axes chopping into wood are now heard, and the creaking of boards giving way to crowbars.

ADMINISTRATOR. (*Screaming*) Quick, Mr. Urge, go into the house and stop them! It's the fire department chopping the house down.

URGE. The fire department? What for?

THREE BOY SCOUTS arrive at a trot, look around, and run into the house.

AUCTIONEER. Boogie boogie boogie!

The church bell begins to toll crazily, like a public alarm.

SEXTON. Now who the hell's ding-donging the God-damn bell? (*He rushes into the church.*)

HOUSE-MOVER. (*Running around the house, followed by a bewildered* BOY SCOUT *who looks around, runs up the back steps, runs down, and then around the house*) The horses have run away! My brother's gone to bring them back! We tried our best to stop them, but they're scared to death! A crowd of people's gathered out front! The fire department's broken down the front door, and the people are running in with the firemen, the police, and the Boy Scouts!

AUCTIONEER. (*Disgusted*) Boogie boogie boogie!

ADMINISTRATOR. We've got to think fast! We've got to stop them!

HOUSE-MOVER. I'm awfully sorry they're wrecking your house, Mr. Urge.

UTMOST. What are they wrecking it for? I planned to paint the living room this morning.

HOUSE-MOVER. You'll find no more living room in *that* house, I'm afraid.

ADMINISTRATOR. (*Taking* UTMOST *by the arm*) Fast, fast, fast! Come with me to the police! You own the house and you have the right to insist on having them protect it!

AUCTIONEER. Boogie boogie boogie! (*Five more* BOY SCOUTS *arrive and rush into the house, as the* AUCTIONEER *winces at the sight of their eager faces and busy, small, uniformed bodies*) Good God Almighty, protect us! (*The* ADMINISTRA- TOR, *the* AUCTIONEER, *the* HOUSE-MOVER *and* UTMOST URGE *hurry around the house*) If it's not the boogie boogie, it's the brave Boy Scouts! (*The* GROUP *is met by* FOUR *more of them*) Oh, Jesus, have mercy on us!

They disappear. The FOUR BOY SCOUTS run about in silence, bumping into one another, while EASY watches them. Finally they disappear into the house, one of them suddenly blow- ing on a police whistle as they go. The SEXTON stumbles out of the back door of the church, shaking with silent laughter at what he has seen. The BOY SCOUT with the whistle appears at the second floor window, blowing the whistle with all his might. He sees the SEXTON shaking with laughter and takes the whistle out of his mouth.

BOY SCOUT WITH WHISTLE. There he is, men! I've found the lunatic! He's shaking with laughter, just like the paper said! Go get him, men! (*The stunned* SEXTON *looks up at the window, dives back into the church, locks the door behind him, as the* BOY SCOUTS *come out of the house and charge the door*) I've found the lunatic! He's in the church!

EASY. That's not the lunatic. The lunatic's got a white beard.

BOY SCOUT WITH WHISTLE. (*Screaming*) The lunatic's shaved off his beard! I've found the lunatic! He's in the church!

The BOY SCOUTS beat on the door, as the SEXTON appears at the window of the MINISTER's study, terrified, but unable to stop shaking. One of the SCOUTS sees him in the window.

SCOUT. There he is, men! Break the door down! Capture the lunatic! (*The* SEXTON *disappears.*)
EASY. That's the church janitor.

The SCOUTS break the door open and rush into the church, as more SCOUTS arrive and follow them. Churchbells, fire-engine bells, police whistles, police sirens, axe blows, crowbar creakings blend together into a kind of ridiculous and terrifying celebration of heroic imbecility. The SEXTON rushes out of the church, but is tackled by a HALF DOZEN BOY SCOUTS, who put him down and hold him, as POLICE and FIREMEN come running.

POLICE. We've captured the lunatic! (*He blows his whistle.*)
EASY. That's not the lunatic, that's the church janitor.

The SEXTON struggles to get free and more people, including GIRLS and WOMEN, come running to help capture the lunatic.

Scene II

Five hours later order has been restored, and the church-bell tolls peacefully and properly.

A line has been established and a crowd of PEOPLE, including the ANGELS, now wearier than ever, is standing behind a rope, patrolled by THREE BOY SCOUTS.

The SEXTON is sitting on a chair in the sunlight, still stunned and still shaking with what is certainly not laughter. The SEXTON's forehead is bandaged, his coat removed, his sleeves rolled, and his arms smeared with iodine.

The PASTOR is trying to control himself, to look reverent, and to give the SEXTON his full moral support all at the same time, along with an occasional half-smile and half-nod to someone behind the rope he thinks has noticed him and nodded.

A very small but efficient BOY SCOUT is swiftly putting a bandage on the SEXTON's left hand and arm up to the

elbow. The SEXTON is trying his best to sit still, but the
sight of the little BOY disgusts him. The worst of it is, the
BOY knows what he is doing. Even so, every now and then
the SEXTON slaps at him with his free hand, and once
knocks scissors out of his hand.

UTMOST and his son EASY are painting the house white,
beginning with that part of the side wall which is within
easy reach.

They work peacefully and thoughtfully, as if they were
at home, and alone. The PASTOR occasionally glances toward them and sighs ever so slightly, not approving of
their working on the Sabbath and yet more or less forgiv-
ing them. They work quietly, though, and the PASTOR's
thankful for that.

The HOUSE-MOVER is under the house working out a
problem. Every now and then he does a little hammering,
as little, it would seem, as possible, and as quietly as possible, whereupon the SEXTON gets to his feet and shakes
and mumbles to himself, while the PASTOR looks upward
and just barely tries to clear the inside of his head of something or other by pressing his hands against the outside.
And then gently urges the SEXTON to sit down again.

The Sunday birds in the church trees are busy warbling
now, and the PASTOR accepts full responsibility for them
each time they do so, his face brightening charitably—they
are only unreasoning birds. He smiles and bows to somebody behind the line after a bird negotiates a rather com-
plicated melody with almost perfect success. Presbyterian,
the PASTOR's manner implies.

The church organ begins to play just as the HOUSE-MOVER
and his BROTHER begin to ask and answer questions, shouting.

HOUSE-MOVER. Take up the slack as far as you can! Got it?
BROTHER. Got it!
HOUSE-MOVER. Start the horses very slowly! Don't let them
  hurry! Got it?
BROTHER. Got it! Giddap!

HOUSE-MOVER. Easy, now! Easy! Easy! Slower! Slower! Stop the horses, stop the horses!

BROTHER. Whoa!—whoa!—hold on there!

HOUSE-MOVER. No! We're not ready yet! Be a minute or two more. Stay where you are! Got it?

BROTHER. Got it! (*The* HOUSE-MOVER *begins to hammer just as the choir breaks into song.*)

PASTOR. (*Holding his hand out toward the* HOUSE-MOVER) Please, men! The opening hymn!

The HOUSE-MOVER hammers louder than ever, as the whole congregation joins the choir in singing the opening hymn. Little by little the HOUSE-MOVER's hammering wears the choir and congregation down, the singing falters, then stops, and only the usual brave, hysterical soprano goes on alone a bar or two. When she stops, the PASTOR is in despair, and the SEXTON is in such a rage he has to be bodily restrained by the PASTOR from charging under the house after the HOUSE-MOVER.

The CHOIR LEADER, a lady of sixty or so, obviously maiden, comes out of the church in tears, angry and hurt, and beseeches the PASTOR to do something. The PASTOR comforts her, walking her up and down. The hammering stops, and the PASTOR sends the CHOIR LEADER back into the church.

HOUSE-MOVER. (*Shouting*) All set here now! Ready out there? (*The organ begins to play again.*)

BROTHER. Ready here!

HOUSE-MOVER. Drive the horses just a bit to the right, but easy! Slowly! All right now, take up the slack! Slower, now! (*Groanings and creakings are heard*) That's it! That's just right now! (*The choir begins to sing. The* HOUSE-MOVER *shouts at the top of his voice*) Hold on a bit! Hold on, now! No! No! Stop the horses! Can you hear me?

The congregation joins the choir and this time they are ready for battle and the volume of sound is so great that the

HOUSE-MOVER can barely be heard, as the PASTOR smiles, holds his head on one side a moment, listens, lifts it heavenward, and then smiles and nods to a BOY SCOUT with pimples all over his face.

UTMOST and EASY listen to the HOUSE-MOVER and his BROTHER, and when it seems as if the man under the house is not being heard by the man in charge of the horses EASY runs around to the front of the house, and UTMOST goes to look after the man under it. After a moment the URGES return to their paint and brushes and go on with their work.

The PASTOR takes the notes for his sermon out of his pocket and examines them, his face filling with lines of thought. He strides into the church, to go to work and earn his poor living. The singing stops and all is relatively silent.

The BOY SCOUT finishes his first-aid work on the SEXTON, stands at attention before him, holding the Scout salute.

SEXTON. (*Disgusted, infuriated and ready for murder*) What do you want?

SCOUT. To serve my country, help maintain the peace, be a credit to my parents, and turn in more than my quota of salvage and waste fats. (*The* SCOUT *finishes the salute.*)

SEXTON. Ah, you make me sick! (*He threatens the* SCOUT *with lifted arm, but the* SCOUT *stands firm and fearless*) By God, if it's more trouble you're looking for—you and your brave little friends in your neat little uniforms—I'll give you all you want, old, wounded and trampled-on as I am! Get away from me, the lot of you!

The SCOUT begins to back away, while the THREE OTHER SCOUTS watch with apprehension, drawing up to help. One of them puts a whistle to his mouth.

SEXTON. Blow that whistle, so much as *breathe* on it, and I'll make you eat it! You've won the war, now get out of here!

(*The* scouts *go into a huddle*) No, no! No council! Just pick up your little bodies and go. I'm not going to have any more of you.

The huddle fails, and the scouts begin to be more or less normal, more or less themselves, little boys full of doubt about themselves instead of charging heroes in a campaign whose righteousness is unquestionable—little boys facing the wrath of an angry old man, who somehow, alone and unorganized, is more right and mightier than their whole group, or any group, drilled, trained, organized, always together, and always safe but silly in their togetherness. He tugs at the bandage on his left arm, tears it off and uses it as a weapon with which to start the rout of the enemy.

sexton. Get away! Run for your lives! The Pastor's not here to stop me, you know! Run home and ask your parents to be your parents instead of the imbeciles they are to let you run amuck in the parenthood of a mob! You'll never be men together. It's one by one or not at all! (*He takes down the rope behind which the* people *are standing and throws it among the* scouts, *who bolt and run as normal boys almost caught stealing apples do*) That's right! You've made a beginning at last! You may still turn out to be men! (*He turns with scorn on the* people *who have been standing behind the rope*) And what the devil do you mean standing there like cattle? Go on, get away from here with your sheep's faces, grown men and women of a free nation bullied every minute, and glad to be! (*The* people *turn and go, excepting the* angels, *who obviously cannot be seen. They fall down to sleep, exhausted*) It's your children who make fools of you and themselves. Go home and think about it.

The people are gone now. The sexton surveys the scene, watches the urges applying paint to the house, bends to see what the house-mover is doing under the house, listens a moment to the organ, takes up his broom and begins to sweep, as if he wanted to sweep away the harrowing experience he has been through. A new BOY SCOUT, a late riser, walking alone, calm and unexcited and dreaming peacefully, comes by to have a look at the house. The SEXTON lifts his broom and swings at the SCOUT, who leaps like a startled deer and takes to the woods, with the SEXTON chasing after him part of the way. The SEXTON stands still a long time, apparently thinking terrible thoughts, then takes to sweeping again. The PASTOR appears at the open window of his study just as the organ begins the offeratory solo: a very sweet and touching piece, somehow intended to serve as the accompaniment to the passing of the collection plate and the dropping of small coins onto it. The PASTOR hists at the SEXTON, who stops sweeping and looks up.

PASTOR. I shall preach now. Please ask the house-movers to be silent, and I shall oblige them by giving a very short sermon. The attendance is very poor, scarcely more than two dozen. The ushers are taking the collection now. I'm deeply distressed, for I have prepared a magnificent sermon, which I'm afraid I must save for next Sunday, as it would be a pity to waste it. Instead, I'll quote at random from the Good Book, and send the people home to Sunday dinner. (*He lifts his head, thinking, then recites*) Hearken unto this, O man: stand still, and consider the wondrous works of God. Job, thirty-seven, fourteen. There is much to ponder in that glorious line. (*He ponders some of it, then tries it again*) Hearken unto this, O man: stand still, and consider the wondrous works of God!

The URGES stop work to listen, and the HOUSE-MOVER comes around the house.

HOUSE-MOVER. Did somebody call me?
SEXTON. No. The Pastor's rehearsing his sermon.
HOUSE-MOVER. Oh, that!

He is about to return to his work when the PASTOR gives his rehearsing everything he's got, almost.

PASTOR. God thundereth marvelously with his voice! Great things doeth He, which we cannot comprehend. (*The* HOUSE-MOVER *stops, turns and decides to listen a little*) God saith to the snow, Be thou on the earth! Likewise to the small rain, and to the great rain. (*The* BROTHER *appears, holding a stolid, half-asleep horse*) Out of the south cometh the whirlwind; and cold out of the north.

BROTHER. I believe this horse is sick of fear.

HOUSE-MOVER. The Pastor's rehearsing his sermon! (*The organ solo ends.*)

PASTOR. (*Plunging headlong into his work*) Dost thou know when God caused the light of His cloud to shine? Dost thou know the balancings of the clouds, and the sky, which is like a looking-glass? Though men see not the bright light which is in the clouds, *His* wind blows upon them, and fair weather cometh out of the west.

BROTHER. (*Softly*) Out of the *north*, the north!

SEXTON. (*Whispering*) Be still, man! North or west, can't you see the Pastor's gathering his thoughts?

PASTOR. Wherefore, I pray thee, hearken unto my words. Behold, now I have opened my mouth. My tongue hath spoken in my mouth. My words are of the rightness of my heart. My lips utter truth clearly. The spirit of God made me. The breath of God gave *me* breath.

The CHOIR LEADER stands behind the PASTOR fretfully, wanting to tell him the congregation is waiting for him to give his sermon, but afraid to interrupt him. She shakes her hands before her with exasperation, as if she were a little girl.

PASTOR. Behold, I am formed out of the clay. In a dream, in a vision of the night, when deep sleep falleth upon men, in slumberings upon the bed, he openeth the ears of men, and giveth instruction, that men may learn the truth of themselves, that they are only men, but good things, none greater than the other, nor smaller, but all great and small, and full of eyes.

SEXTON. To the pulpit now, Pastor! Not *here!* To the pulpit! They're waiting for you in the church!

PASTOR. (*Alas, the* PASTOR *is off to the races, much aided by a failing memory*) Knowest thou the time when the wild goats of the rock bring forth? They bow themselves, they bring forth their young, they cast out their sorrows. Their young are good looking, they grow up, they go forth, and return not. Wilt thou trust him whose strength is great? The glory of his nostrils is terrible. He paweth in the valley, he rejoiceth on the hill. He mocketh at fear. He swalloweth the ground with fierceness and rage: neither believeth he the sound of the trumpets. He saith among the trumpeters, Ha, ha! Doth the eagle fly by wisdom to make her nest on high? She dwelleth on the rock, upon the crag, in the strong place.

An USHER holding a collection plate with a half dozen small coins on it comes out and stands near the HOUSE-MOVERS. He is followed by another USHER, and one by one by all of the PEOPLE in the church who are men, women, walking children, and babes in arms come out and stand in the yard.

PASTOR. Hearken unto me, O man: hold thy peace, and I will speak. Let us know among ourselves what is good, and who is virtuous. Let us know who drinketh up scorn like water. And who goeth in company with the workers in iniquity, and walketh with wicked men. Therefore hearken unto me, men of understanding: far be it from God, that he should do wickedness. And from the Almighty, that he should commit iniquity. The work of a man he shall tell him, and cause every man to find his way. God will not do wickedly, who hath given men charge over the earth, but if men dispose of it, cast down the whole world, deny his spirit and breath, all flesh shall perish together, and men shall turn again into dust. If now thou hast understanding, hear this: Shall he that hateth right govern? Is it fit to say to a king, Thou art wicked? To a prince, Thou art ungodly? God accepteth not the persons of princes, nor regardeth the rich more than the poor, for they are all the work of his hands.

In a moment they shall die, and the people shall be troubled
at midnight, and the mighty shall be taken away without
hand. (*The* house-mover *nods to his* brother *and each of
them drops a small coin onto each of the collection plates*)
His eyes are on the way of men, and he *seeth* all doings.
There is no place where the workers of iniquity may hide
themselves. He *knoweth* their works, and he overturneth
them in the night, so that they are destroyed. He striketh
wicked men in the open sight of others, because *they* send
the cry of the poor unto him, and the moan of the afflicted.
When *he* giveth quietness, who then can make trouble,
whether it be a whole nation, or one man alone? (*A tired
little* girl *is lifted gently by the* house-mover *and seated on
the horse, and his* brother *lifts a little* boy *and seats him beside the* girl, *as if the back of the horse were a bench*) Behold, God is mighty, yet despiseth no man, but if *thou* art
wicked, thy wickedness will hurt the man *thou* art. If thou
art *righteous*, thy righteousness will profit *thy* son. He giveth
songs in the night, and all things the beasts of the earth have
not, and maketh us wiser than the fowls of heaven. He will
not hear vanity. Hearken unto me, O man: say to thyself, If
I have walked with vanity, then let *me* sow, and let *another*
eat. If I have lifted my hand against the fatherless, when I
saw my help in the gate, then let my arm fall from my shoulder and be broken from the bone. If I have made gold my
hope, or have said to gold, Thou art my power, let thistles
grow instead of wheat, and cockles instead of barley. Gird up
thy loins like a man, saith the Lord. Clothe thyself with
majesty. Array thyself with glory. Cast abroad the rage of
thy wrath.

sam ego appears at the window of the house, but is noticed
only by easy, who has been watching the window as if he
believed the pastor were making his sermon to the man
hiding in the house, and as if he were afraid the man might
come to the window. easy tries to motion sam ego back out
of sight, but sam ego shakes his head, and easy very quietly,
as if the whole yard were church, makes his way unobtru-
sively to the back porch, and then into the house.

PASTOR. Hearken unto this, O man: stand still, and consider the wondrous works of God.

The PASTOR stops a moment to think, and EASY is seen in the second-floor window of the house, trying to get SAM EGO to move out of sight.

SEXTON. (*Quickly to help restore order*) Amen! And now, back into the church for the closing hymn and benediction! The sermon's over!

The PASTOR comes out of his trance, looks down with kindness upon the PEOPLE who, unlike himself, cannot preach the gospel, and gently motions them back into the church, as if his doing so were a benediction. The PEOPLE dutifully file back into the church, the SEXTON brings up the rear, the HOUSE-MOVERS go back to work, taking the horse with them, and soon the organ is heard, and the choir and congregation singing. EASY comes out of the house with SAM EGO. They go to UTMOST.

EASY. This is my father.

SAM EGO. (*Extending his hand*) Permit me to shake the hand of the father of this boy. My name is Sam Ego. Yes, I *am* the man. (*Pause*) Well, as I told your son upstairs, I'll be going back now.

UTMOST. But *why?* I have a home where you can stay. You needn't go *back*, and you needn't *hide*. You've no affliction I can see. Stay in my home, and when this house reaches Sundown Slums, live in it, for it *is* your house.

SAM EGO. Oh, I *am* afflicted, there's no doubt about that.

UTMOST. No doubt, but certainly no more than any of the rest of us. All living's the same affliction, is it not? Come with us to Sundown Slums. All my sons are at war, except this boy, and we can work *together* restoring the house.

SAM EGO. No, it wouldn't do, though I must confess I *am* tempted, for I hoped to see a wondrous flourishing of life within this house, and my own— (*He shakes his head swiftly several times*) No, no, mine are all gone, and yours are only coming along. It would not do, though as I say I'm tempted, tempted—is it vanity to be tempted? Was it pride that built this house and gave me hope to see a wondrous flourishing of life in it? I never believed it was pride, but now I've been so long among the caretakers of the mind, I don't know. Now there is so very little I know. An hour ago if you were to have asked my name, I would not have known what to say, or would have said Eagle's Son, or Sam Going, or something else thus tangled and blurred in the fading sound of things. I've been cluttered by the caretakers, as you can imagine, and made feeble by the clawing of the eagle at my heart. I know my wit if not lunatic is surely light, but I think I remember that it was *not* pride that instructed me to build this house, nor vanity, nor being above anybody I ever knew. I swear to God, it was love! (*He shakes his head very slowly*) Do you understand?

UTMOST. I understand as well as I'm permitted to, and that is why I ask you to come with us to Sundown Slums, for there we may easily learn the way to be who we are.

SAM EGO. Oh, I'm tempted enough, the Lord knows that, and filled with fighting, the one side saying it's proper to accept the good last chance you offer, the other side saying it would be wicked to name your charity my chance—and you must know—I must tell you—already I am filled with fretting for your sons. My only son came home from war and perished in the foolish streets, drunk from rejoicing, heedless with love —and killed for it in a fool's accident. No, no, no! The clutter, or the better wisdom I have learned from it, tells me that to *fret* is to *compel*, and already I fret for your sons! To *fear* the worst is to *create* the worst. Worse still, to hope for the best is to soften the heart until fearing and fretting create and compel the whole *multitude* of dirty dyings that are in things! Oh, I *am* cluttered, and would wish to be at your mercy, knowing that you would decide for *me*, but no, no, no, I must decide, and my decision must be to let you be! I'll be going along now.

UTMOST. (*Taking him by the arm and leading him around the house*) This is the way.

A POLICE and TWO MEN come along, but do not see UTMOST and SAM EGO go into the house, as the SEXTON and the PASTOR come out of the church and meet the POLICE and the TWO MEN.

POLICE. These men are from the Asylum. They want to search the house.

SEXTON. Oh, they do? Well, the whole town's already searched it, and knocked it to pieces. There's no one hiding in the house. (*To the* MEN) If you want the lunatic, I think you'll find him in the people of Angels Aghast, and in yourselves.

ONE OF THE MEN FROM THE COUNTY HOME. If you're the owner of the house, we've come to ask permission to search it, although we have the necessary authority to proceed *without* permission.

SEXTON. I am *not* the owner of the house! I'm the sexton of the First Presbyterian Church of Angels Aghast, as I've been thirty years! The description of Sam Ego you gave the paper last night rang the bell in the belfry at six this morning, and had me assaulted by twenty small boys who if they *didn't* kill me, tried their best. You've had Sam Ego twenty-five years. Must you have him longer still, if he's not dead somewhere?

MAN. He's a patient and needs proper care.

SEXTON. And if *he* doesn't *want* your care, as he's clearly indicated, I suppose he's got to have it, anyway!

MAN. He may be dangerous—to *himself* if not to others. He's not balanced.

SEXTON. (*Furious*) Where the hell have you been except in the Lunatic Asylum all these years? Do you know of somebody somewhere in the world who *is* balanced? *Yourself*, perhaps?

The HOUSE-MOVERS come around the house to see what all the shouting's about.

OTHER MAN. (*To* PASTOR) Who *is* this man? Who is responsible for him?

PASTOR. (*Swiftly, scared to death of the long arm of the local*

Lunacy Board taking away his old friend) I am responsible for him.

SEXTON. *(Blowing up)* Nobody's responsible for me! Do you take me for a child? You've both been Boy Scouts, I'm sure!

PASTOR. *(Swiftly)* He's had a wretched ordeal! He's all right! I'm responsible for him! He's served me well for thirty years!

SEXTON. *I* don't need to be protected from these blithering idiots from the Lunatic Asylum!

MAN. *(Nodding knowingly to the* POLICE, *then speaking to the* SEXTON) I want to ask you a few simple questions.

PASTOR. *(Taking the* SEXTON *by the arm and trying to go off with him)* It won't be necessary, I assure you! He's quite all right!

MAN. *(Stopping the* PASTOR, *who is now absolutely terrified, while the* SEXTON *is ready to fight)* It *will* be necessary. *(He nods to the* OFFICER, *who gets ready for trouble. The* MAN *looks up into the sky as he speaks)* Now, then. What is your name?

SEXTON. *(Clenching his fist)* This is what my name is!

He swings at the MAN, catches him on the side of the head, knocks him down, and takes to his heels with the POLICE running after him, the PASTOR hanging onto the coattails of the POLICE with all his might.

PASTOR. He's all right, gentlemen! I'm responsible! He's had an ordeal!

The POLICE blows his whistle. UTMOST and EASY quietly paint on the wall of the house, the HOUSE-MOVER stands over the MAN knocked down, while his BROTHER wrestles with the OTHER MAN from the Asylum.

HOUSE-MOVER. *(To the felled* MAN) My brother and I don't like to see children or old men teased.

BROTHER. *(Putting his* MAN *down while the* HOUSE-MOVER *helps his* MAN *up)* It's like teasing the Holy Ghost, and it's not nice, because it makes fools out of all of us!

ACT THREE

Scene *I*

UTMOST and EASY URGE are on the roof of SAM EGO's house, which is now on an unimportant and empty side street in the heart of Angels Aghast, looking toward Sundown Slums. The roof is shingled and steep, but there is a flat area in front of a rather large attic window and it is from here that the URGES climb onto the roof and work. A good many old shingles have been removed from the roof and are lying on the attic porch, and a few bad spots in the roof have already been patched with new shingles. UTMOST is lying on the roof putting nails into the last shingle of a small patch of new shingles. EASY is standing on the attic porch, helping him.

Only the heads of the ANGELS are visible over the top of the roof.

It is a peaceful, summer morning with a deep blue sky. Only a handful of lazy, indefinite clouds are about, and these few are going nowhere. Except for the roof and the sky, little else is open to view, although very far away the land and streets and houses of Sundown Slums are visible. The city itself, however, is *felt* to be all around, and near.

The occasional bark of an automobile horn is heard.

UTMOST finishes his work, hands EASY the hammer he has been using, slides down onto the porch and studies the work he's done.

UTMOST. Well, it isn't much, but it's finished, so if you're as hungry as I am, and if you *like* the idea—bring up the lunch and we'll have it here on the roof.

EASY. I'm hungry all right. (*He slips through the open attic window to the attic.*)

UTMOST. And of course ask Mr. Ego to join us.

EASY disappears, and UTMOST refreshes himself, stretching and yawning slowly and easily. He tidies up the attic porch a bit, scuffling old shingles into a pile, getting his tools in order, and putting a box up lengthwise for a chair. EASY and SAM EGO appear in the attic, and EASY slips up through the window and onto the porch with the lunchbox, while SAM EGO smiles and waves to UTMOST. There is little uncontrollable shaking in SAM EGO now, and he seems untroubled and at ease. He is wearing a suit of UTMOST's clothes.

SAM EGO. I'm just as starved as I can be, and I need the air and light! There's a sky to remember a minute or two! Are you sure it's all right for me to appear on the roof?

UTMOST. (*Helping him through the window and onto the porch*) Of course it's all right. In any case, if you'll sit here, you'll not be seen. But if you are, that will not change a thing. You're free.

SAM EGO. (*Sitting on the box*) I am free, isn't that the truth? If you could only know the free sleep I sleep in this new life! What luck it was for me that you bought my house, sir.

The lunchbox has been passed around and they ALL have sandwiches.

UTMOST. I scarcely bought the house. I accepted it as a gift, for the auctioneer and the administrator of the estate wanted it off the land and away.

SAM EGO. A wicked, haunted house that no one wanted to buy, the house I built so long ago! But even at that, you might have thought twice before buying it or accepting it as a gift, as you say. The house is loathed by everyone, in which I put the fairest hopes of living. You might have thought twice. Why didn't you?

UTMOST. I wanted the house. A great deal can be done with any house, let alone a house so well-made, if anybody wants to bother, and as I'll never see the house I dreamed I'd one day have—well, here I am with another dream and *this* house. Still, dreams go on, fitting themselves to whatever they must, and the difference is never so great as to make the dreamer lose his sleep. Here's house enough for my rest and sleep, and new design and repair to my old dream. *Dying* fills me with the only hate I know, so I *like* to start things out again, which is in the line of my business, dealing as I do in things that others feel are finished. Among the junk of the yard I run in Sundown Slums, I've had the time it takes to learn that *nothing* ends. People or things neither die nor finish but change and reach another order of being, and as I find great beauty in change, my work, though full of what appears to be debris, to me is full of beauty and surprise.

SAM EGO. Isn't that the truth? Isn't that the truth, right here next to the sky, free and at peace, eating our lunches?

UTMOST. Old and new are bound together and part of the same thing, which is change, and why we breathe at all, go and come, hang on, fall to pieces, or steal away. The broken jug of clay is not death; it is the child's shovel or the world he must mend and manage. (*He places his hand on his son's head*) The weight of this Easy head balances heaven and earth. (*He looks out at the sky*) You see what a sky does to a man who hates dying. Still, I say there's no such thing.

SAM EGO. Ah, you speak to heal me, and your healing lets me speak. Isn't that the truth? You bought this house to give me back my own, I know. What luck to be here with you on the attic porch of my own house, free, easy, and a closer neighbor to the sky than I have ever been. These eight or nine days that we've been in this one place have been the freest days of my life. Is it any wonder that I almost wish the journey would never end? Has it been nine days or nine hundred? I forget.

UTMOST. We've been here nine days if we've come to Tuesday, as I believe we have. (*To* EASY) What are the facts, my son?

EASY. The day is Tuesday the 14th, the month August, the year 1945, and it is seven minutes before noon.

SAM EGO. Isn't that the truth? Go on, my boy.

EASY. The house has been here, in the middle of Merry Angel Street, near the Center of Angels Aghast, several hours more than nine days. The house-movers abandoned the horses at that time and hired a tractor, which also failed to move the house. They then discovered that their rollers had sunk into the tar of the street, made soft by the hottest summer since 1919. They also discovered certain flaws in the system they had devised, and went to work correcting the flaws. (*Pause.*)

SAM EGO. Yes, my boy. Please go on.

EASY. Well, the *Angels' Herald* has published daily accounts of the progress of the house, an editorial demanding that the house be destroyed as a public nuisance, a cartoon showing the house blocking traffic, and the opinions of three dozen leading citizens, all in favor of destroying the house, except one.

SAM EGO. And who was that?

EASY. Judge Zodiac.

SAM EGO. Now, isn't that just like a man I always thought was a charlatan to be the *only* man in town who's not? Isn't that the truth? And how will it all end, I wonder?

EASY. The matter is being considered by the city government, and it's the main topic of conversation throughout the city. The *Angels' Herald* has charged that Utmost Urge is hiding Sam Ego either in his home in Sundown Slums or in the Eagle's Nest itself, or knows where Sam Ego is. (*Sudden noise*) And I think something's happened! (*The whistles of the city begin to scream one by one*) I think the War's over! (*He looks at his father and at* SAM EGO *and speaks very quietly*) The War's over!

UTMOST. I *believed* it would be one day. Well, that's fine.

UTMOST helps SAM EGO to the edge of the porch where UTMOST points to the celebrating people. The TWO MEN and EASY stand in silence and listen to the shouting of the people: "The War's over, the War's over!" They are excited but unable to do anything but watch and listen. Steam whistles and automobile horns of all kinds and in all kinds of musical patterns cover up for the celebrating people their hysteria, or impel them into it deeper. The piping of a steam calliope weaves in and out of the high-pitched uproar, busy with popular songs and old favorites. MEMBERS OF A BAND appear to gather spontaneously, and begin marching through Angels Aghast, playing marches and dances. The band sounds as if it has about three big drums and three big horns too many. Every now and then a pistol or rifle shot is heard, and occasionally someone fires three shots in quick succession. Little by little the clang and boom and roar, the hum and buzz and cry of the whole sorrowful hullabaloo weaves itself together into something with the quality of an elegy or funeral march trying very hard to be a sentimental waltz.

DANCEY URGE, a girl of fourteen or so who has been running swiftly for a long distance, appears at the attic window, climbs out, throws herself into her father's arms, and helplessly stares with inexpressible joy at him, and SAM EGO, and EASY.

UTMOST. (Shouting) My daughter Dancey. (To the GIRL) Darling, this is Mr. Ego. (DANCEY just barely curtsies, and SAM EGO makes a deep bow. UTMOST shouts to everybody) No use trying to talk!

SAM EGO. (Shouting) Isn't that the truth? I'll go to my room and lie down now! I'm glad the war's over!

EASY slips through the window to the attic, his father helps SAM EGO through, and EASY helps from the other side. SAM EGO bows to DANCEY, nods to UTMOST, then disappears into the house with EASY. EASY soon reappears at the window and slips out. He goes to the edge of the porch to watch the people some more. UTMOST climbs onto the roof to return to work, while EASY and DANCEY stare down at the celebrators. When EASY hears his father hammering on the roof, he goes to help him, and after a moment or two DANCEY begins to dance to the music of the elegy.

Scene II

The HOUSE-MOVER and his BROTHER are under a forward edge of SAM EGO's house during the End-of-War revelries of the people in Merry Angel Street. Where they are is seen as if the eye were a yard or two behind them, and what the HOUSE-MOVERS see is all that is open to view. They see the lower half of what appears to be hundreds of people, and what they hear is not the elegy-waltz that SAM EGO and UTMOST and EASY heard, and DANCEY danced to. The HOUSE-MOVERS hear feet. They also hear voices of all kinds, screaming of all kinds, cries of all kinds. They also hear music, but it is not at all like the music that was heard from the roof. They are too close to the celebration to hear it well. They are sitting on what appears to be tar-paving, almost facing each other, but looking out to the street and the swarming half-bodies there. They are BOTH calm, and surely alive in the life of the mind.

The ANGELS sit nearby and listen.

HOUSE-MOVER. Well, the War's over, and the money's all gone. (*He turns his wallet upside down.*)

BROTHER. And it's *still* three miles to Sundown Slums! (*He holds out three fingers.*)

HOUSE-MOVER. It's these interruptions slowing us down all the time.

BROTHER. First, the Boy Scouts, and now the End of the War.

HOUSE-MOVER. I'd get married if I could find a girl who could cook, sew, sing, and carry on a decent conversation.

BROTHER. I don't believe I heard you that time.

HOUSE-MOVER. I say now that the War's over I'd get married if I could find a girl who could cook, sew, sing, play the piano, carry on a decent conversation, and have children.

BROTHER. Cook, sew, sing and *what?*

HOUSE-MOVER. (*Shouting*) Have children! Have children!

BROTHER. Yes. I'd like a good wife myself.

HOUSE-MOVER. A pretty girl who knew her way about in a kitchen.

BROTHER. I'd like her to bake bread.

HOUSE-MOVER. Nothing nicer-smelling than fresh home-made bread.

BROTHER. Yes. I'd like a girl like that very much.

HOUSE-MOVER. Haven't smelled fresh bread since the War began.

BROTHER. And here it is all over with.

HOUSE-MOVER. We might have moved the house a little this afternoon except for all the people in the way.

BROTHER. I never thought the War would end this *afternoon*.

HOUSE-MOVER. It did, though.

BROTHER. For awhile there I thought it was never going to end.

HOUSE-MOVER. Next thing you know, some afternoon we'll be moving a house and *another* War will start.

BROTHER. And we'll have to crawl under the house to get out of the way of the excited people.

HOUSE-MOVER. It started out to be a nice afternoon, but now I'm half-ashamed of being a human being.

They sit in silence a moment, listening to the noise and watching the half-bodies. A heavy YOUNG WOMAN in loose clothing sticks her head into the line of vision, to look under the house.

YOUNG WOMAN. Yippee! The War's over! (*She gets down on her hands and knees*) Come on, girls, let's crawl under old Sam Ego's house!

The HOUSE-MOVERS look around in alarm. A half-dozen GIRLS and WOMEN of assorted sizes, all in summer dresses, all hysterical, get on their hands and knees and crawl under the house, headed straight for the HOUSE-MOVERS. The GIRLS scream and giggle as they charge. "Yahoo! Wahoo! Whoopee! Wow! The War's over! We won the War! Oh, Nagasaki!" And so on. The HOUSE-MOVERS squirm around on their hands and knees and start scuttling for cover or concealment, but the wild WOMEN are too fast for them, and the MEN are leaped upon, hugged, kissed, tickled, goosed, and generally driven far afield from the life of the mind.

WOMAN WITH HEADLOCK ON HOUSE-MOVER. Oh, Hiroshima!
WOMAN PIGGY-BACK ON HOUSE-MOVER'S BROTHER. Oh, Nagasaki!

Scene III

It is almost three months later, a pleasant afternoon in late October, and for some time now SAM EGO's house has been on Poor Angel Street in Sundown Slums, restored and repaired inside and out, the home of UTMOST URGE and his family, and their permanent guest, SAM EGO.

A triangular edge of the front porch, including steps and front door, is out into the line of vision, overlooking the URGE place of business, which is a spacious yard containing junk of all kinds so neatly arranged as to make a pleasant picture. Included among the junk are old-fashioned wood-burning stoves, framed circles and squares of stained glass from old houses, doors of various kinds, copper kettles highly polished, kerosene lamps, dinnerware, silverware, jugs, bottles, beds, tables, chairs, pipes, faucets, wash-basins, bathtubs, books, framed pictures, and all sorts of other objects.

The ANGELS are not in sight.

The porch and yard have been hung with decorations, to mark the home-coming of the three URGE boys, who are of course the Angels.

DANCEY is sweeping the steps and dancing to the music of an old record on an old phonograph which EASY is winding. The phonograph has an enormous horn painted red.

UTMOST and SAM EGO are standing in the yard, looking toward the street. MRS. URGE steps out onto the front porch, waves to her husband and SAM EGO that all is ready, and goes back into the house, leaving the front door open.

The HOUSE-MOVERS come along, each with a WOMAN on his arm, selected from among the assortment which fell upon them under SAM EGO's house the afternoon the War ended.

HOUSE-MOVER. You wanted to see us, Mr. Ego?

SAM EGO. Yes, and thank you both for coming.

BROTHER. Is anything the matter with the way we put the house in place, Mr. Urge?

MR. URGE. There it is, as it's been for almost two months now. It looks to me as if it's quite at home.

HOUSE-MOVER. It certainly looks the way it *ought* to look, Mr. Ego.

BROTHER. It always was a handsome house, Mr. Urge. Oh, excuse me. This is my wife.

HOUSE-MOVER. We both got married the day after we finished moving this house. (UTMOST *and* MR. EGO *smile and nod to the* WOMEN) The only thing we've *moved* since that time, though, has been a small barn that was no problem at all.

BROTHER. We did it for nothing for my wife's father.

SAM EGO. I sent for you because until yesterday I was not in a position to thank you for your work as I had hoped to do.

HOUSE-MOVER'S WIFE. We read all about you in this morning's paper, Mr. Ego. It must have been an awful experience to be hunted down that way, and taken back that way, and examined by all those people that way, and asked all those silly questions that way! (HOUSE-MOVER *stares at her with anger*) Well, *I* wouldn't like to be treated that way, teased and tormented the way they did to Mr. Ego, to keep him from getting back his own rights and belongings! I wouldn't like it one bit!

SAM EGO. Thank you very much for—

OTHER WIFE. They had their nerve trying to pull a dirty trick like that on you, Mr. Ego. (BROTHER *stares at her with amazement and despair*) A lot of tin-horn crooks and politicians trying to make a fool out of a man whose shoestrings they don't deserve to tie, so they can put him out of the way and grab his fortune for themselves.

SAM EGO. Thank you both for your kind sympathy.

HOUSE-MOVER. And shut up for a minute!

HOUSE-MOVER'S WIFE. I'm glad you're safe and sound at last, Mr. Ego!

HOUSE-MOVER. Stop it, will you?

OTHER WIFE. And healthy and wealthy!

BROTHER. Stop it, now!

The TWO WOMEN look at one another with outraged pride, then at SAM EGO, who nods with understanding and sympathy, permitting them to feel that they have not talked out of turn and are just as nice and pretty and intelligent as ever, in spite of the rudeness of their husbands.

UTMOST. And very soon my three sons are coming home, and we want you to stay to dinner and help us welcome them.

HOUSE-MOVER'S WIFE. Oh, how nice! Where have they been?

UTMOST. One's been in the Navy, in the Atlantic and in the Pacific. One's been in the Army, first in Greenland, then in Africa, and finally in Europe. And one's been in the Marine Corps, first in Australia, then in the Philippines, and finally in China and Japan.

OTHER WIFE. Oh, they've been everywhere, and now they're coming home to dear old Angels Aghast!

HOUSE-MOVER'S WIFE. Home from the War to peaceful Sundown Slums!

OTHER WIFE. How proud you'll feel, Mr. Urge, when you see them in their uniforms marching up Poor Angel Street to the door of their handsome home!

HOUSE-MOVER'S WIFE. How proud Mrs. Urge must feel of her hero sons who volunteered to fight for our civilization and save our way of life!

MR. URGE. I'm sure she's going to be glad to see them after so long, but they didn't volunteer. They were drafted.

OTHER WIFE. (*Let down a little*) Oh. (*Pause*) Well, anyway, how proud we all are of our brave boys!

UTMOST. Oh, I suppose they've been brave enough in many ways. They were certainly brave enough to try to get deferments from their Draft Board, but of course the deferments weren't granted.

HOUSE-MOVER'S WIFE. How wonderful to have them home again at last, safe and sound anyway!

UTMOST. Yes, it will be wonderful, though they may not be as sound as they once were, for I believe they've all been to the hospital many times.

OTHER WIFE. Weary and wounded and sick of battle!

UTMOST. No, I believe the boy in the Navy got drunk and fell out of a taxi in Liverpool and broke his leg. The boy in the Marines was cut up in a fight in a saloon in Manila, and the boy in the Army had a nervous breakdown in Paris.

HOUSE-MOVER'S WIFE. (*Almost disgusted*) A nervous breakdown?

OTHER WIFE. (*Trying to be helpful*) Battle fatigue, the Army calls it.

UTMOST. No, I don't believe it was that. My boy was a clerk in the Army. He sat at a desk all through the War.

BOTH WIVES. Oh.

UTMOST. And of course they've had their share of the common illnesses that plague us all, but Mrs. Urge and their younger brother and sister are going to be glad to see them, and so am I. If you'd like to join Mrs. Urge in the house while your husbands wait with us out here, I'm sure she'll be delighted.

BOTH MEN eagerly disengage themselves from their WIVES, who go off in silence into the house, just as EASY puts another record on the phonograph. From the sound of it the record is as old as the phonograph. SAM EGO hands each of the HOUSE-MOVERS a sealed envelope, which they put in their pockets, and the FOUR MEN stroll about the yard, looking at the handsome junk. After a moment EASY stops the phonograph, takes off the record, examines what is written on its label, and puts it back on the stack of old records.

SEXTON. (*Comes into the yard. Almost shouting*) I've come this Sabbath afternoon for two reasons. To shake the hand of Sam Ego, and to buy a pole for the Pastor—a flagpole of course—to replace the one that was broken by the Boy Scouts. (*He takes* SAM EGO's *hand*) Sam, it's good to see you, though we were neighbors not long ago when this house stopped beside the church I serve as sexton.

SAM EGO. (*Delighted, trying to make out who the* SEXTON *is*) Please don't tell me! I remember, only it's been so long.

SEXTON. Yes, it has been a long time, Sam.

SAM EGO. Ah, of course, of course! Al Fable! I knew you the moment I saw you! For a time we were thrown together quite a bit at school. I'm delighted to see you, Al. You know Mr. Urge.

SEXTON. (*He smiles and nods to* UTMOST) Of course I know him.

SAM EGO. Well, we're waiting for three boys who'll soon be coming home after an absence of almost half a dozen years. Stay and help us welcome them. Have you met the house-movers?

SEXTON. (*Waving to the* HOUSE-MOVERS) Know them well! They saved my life one day. (*Almost shouting*) Have you found the wives you told me you hoped to find?

HOUSE-MOVER. They're in the house with Mrs. Urge.

BROTHER. (*He looks as disgusted as he can be*) They're both in there.

SEXTON. Now, about the pole for the Parson, Mr. Urge. Do you have a pole?

UTMOST. (*To* EASY) Do we have a pole put away somewhere for Mr. Fable to take to the Parson?

EASY. I don't think so. I think we sold the last pole we had to that new group that calls itself Patriots First, Last and Always, Incorporated, but I'll look around. (*He goes off to examine what's in the yard.*)

SEXTON. Imbeciles First, Last and Always is what they are! They're always the first to put a flag on a pole and threaten everybody with it.

EASY. They asked me to join their club and give them the pole for nothing. They said it would be unpatriotic to make them pay seventy-five cents for the pole, but I made them pay for it just the same. (*Pause*) No, we haven't got another pole.

The ANGELS, now in ill-fitting civilian clothes, appear and stand nearby, watching.

SEXTON. Well, no matter. (*He suddenly discovers the house*) Sam, I saw that house built at the turn of this fierce and fateful century, but it never looked as real and right as it looks this minute. I must confess I never believed it was worth fooling with, but there it is, looking as neat and sharp as a brand-new apple on a tree you never thought would have anything but worms, and here I am glad to my boots to have been so mistaken. (*To* UTMOST) Now, how the devil did you do it? You didn't call in the Boy Scouts, did you? Lord help us when *they're* called in. I'm stunned by the beauty of it. (*A small* WESTERN UNION MESSENGER *arrives by bicycle in the yard and hops off. The* SEXTON *leaps for cover*) Good God, is that a Boy Scout?

EASY. No, that's a messenger.

MESSENGER. Telegram for you, Mr. Urge. It's from the boys. It says, Ought to be home around four but don't make a fuss. Signed, Inner, Outer and Ample. But I see you're all set to make a fuss. Want the telegram as a souvenir, Mr. Urge? (*He hands the sealed telegram to* UTMOST *and walks to* EASY) Have you got a good pair of handlebars for my bike, Easy?

The THREE YOUNG MEN stroll into the yard easily, just barely exchanging greetings with EVERYBODY, as people do who don't know one another but aren't required to introduce themselves.

FIRST YOUNG MAN. I'd like a nice comfortable chair if you've got one.

UTMOST. Well, we've got several kinds of chairs that are comfortable. Have a look at them and maybe you'll find one you like.

SECOND YOUNG MAN. Is it all right if I look around for a nice old-fashioned bed?

UTMOST. Go ahead. You'll find the beds over there.

THIRD YOUNG MAN. I haven't decided what I'm looking for, so if you don't mind, I'll just wander around awhile.

MRS. URGE. (*On the porch*) Where are they, for Heaven's sake?

UTMOST. Toby just brought a telegram saying they ought to be here around four but not to make a fuss. It's half-past four now.

MRS. URGE. Well, let's not make a fuss, then. I'm going to sit here on the porch and rock. (*She takes the rocker and rocks.*)

FIRST YOUNG MAN. (*Sitting in a chair*) Now this is a good chair. I think I like this chair, but I'll just sit in it awhile and make sure.

SECOND YOUNG MAN. (*Stretching out on the wire spring of an old-fashioned bed*) I think I'm going to like this bed.

THIRD YOUNG MAN. Damned if I know what I'm going to like. (*He wanders around, picking things up and putting them down.*)

SAM EGO sets a chair down beside the FIRST YOUNG MAN's chair, and sits down as if to chat with him. A steam calliope is heard as it moves along a nearby street. The WIVES of the HOUSE-MOVERS come tearing out of the house onto the porch.

HOUSE-MOVER'S WIFE. Is it them?
OTHER WIFE. Of course it is!

The TWO WOMEN run off toward the music. The HOUSE-MOVERS take long strides in the hope of catching up with their WIVES and stopping them from making fools of themselves. The SEXTON wanders around the yard with the THIRD YOUNG MAN, looking at the junk with him. UTMOST stands over the YOUNG MAN lying on the bed and looks at him a long time.

UTMOST. I'm afraid you'll have to tell me which one you are.
EASY. (*Showing* MESSENGER *a pair of handlebars*) He's Ample.
UTMOST. Well, that's fine.

MRS. URGE comes down the steps with DANCEY skipping after her, and they wander around the yard, looking at the THREE YOUNG MEN as they go.

SAM EGO. (*To the* FIRST YOUNG MAN) If you're wondering who this feeble old fellow with the whiskers is, and what he's doing here, he's something like a friend of the family or a distant relative, and he's boarding here.

UTMOST. (*To the* FIRST YOUNG MAN) You're Outer, I know, although you've changed a lot. Well, that's fine.

SEXTON. (*To the* THIRD YOUNG MAN) Now, a book might be what you're looking for. How about this one for size? (*He hands the* YOUNG MAN *what appears to be the telephone directory of a large city.*)

THIRD YOUNG MAN. (*Opening the directory*) It's a little big, but I think it's just the thing I am looking for.

UTMOST. (*To* MRS. URGE) Well, it certainly is a beautiful day. I think I'd like to sit down and eat a lot of roast beef, and then a lot of apple pie, and then drink a lot of coffee.

MRS. URGE. Well, the roast beef's ready, the pies are baked, and the coffee's waiting to boil. You let me know, and I'll fix your place at the table.

SECOND YOUNG MAN. (*Sitting up on the bed*) I think I'd like a place, too, if it's all right. (*To the* FIRST YOUNG MAN) How about you?

FIRST YOUNG MAN. I'm hungry all right, and I'd certainly like to see the inside of that fine house. (*To the* THIRD YOUNG MAN) You feel like a little food with these nice people, you with the book over there?

THIRD YOUNG MAN. Yes, I believe I do.

UTMOST. Well, no hurry, but I think I'll go in and sit down. (*To* EASY *and* MESSENGER) You coming, boys?

MESSENGER. Thanks a lot, Mr. Urge. I'll sit down a minute, but I've already had my Sunday dinner.

EASY and MESSENGER follow UTMOST into the house.

FIRST YOUNG MAN. (*Getting up and taking* SAM EGO *by the arm*) Well, no use putting off a nice Sunday dinner any longer.

He and SAM EGO go into the house.

THIRD YOUNG MAN. (*Taking the* SEXTON *by the arm*) I'm just as hungry as I can be, and I hope you are, too. ·

They go into the house. The SECOND YOUNG MAN gets off the bed and yawns long and easily as he looks the whole place over. While he's yawning the music of the calliope fades away, and the HOUSE-MOVERS come back with their WIVES on their arms.

SECOND YOUNG MAN. They've gone inside to have Sunday dinner.

HOUSE-MOVER'S WIFE. Aren't they going to wait till the heroes get home?

The HOUSE-MOVER gives her a sad look and just barely shakes his head with despair.

OTHER WIFE. I never heard of such a thing! Three heroes coming home after years of fighting, and nobody wants to give them a decent welcome!

MRS. URGE. (*On the porch*) Dinner's on the table, everybody! Won't you please come in?

HOUSE-MOVER'S WIFE. Aren't you going to wait till the heroes get here?

HOUSE-MOVER. (*Whispering*) Ah, shut up!

The HOUSE-MOVERS escort their WIVES into the house. The SECOND YOUNG MAN comes up on the porch, looks at MRS. URGE a long time, then gives her a hug, and escorts her into the house.

A DECENT BIRTH,
A HAPPY FUNERAL

A Play in Three Acts
and Six Scenes

PREFACE

It MUST have been sometime during the year 1941 that I was impelled to write this play which is about superstition. Only the superstitious are able to regard superstition as nonsense, for it is superstition to feel that it is necessary to discredit superstition. It is not necessary at all. What's more, science itself (or the careful and unbiased examination of evidence) long ago came to the conclusion that there is a measurable element of reality, meaning and value in all of the thinking and believing which had for so long come under the heading of superstition.

My grandmother Lucy believed it was dangerous as well as a waste of money to call in a doctor when a member of her family was ill, for wasn't he a stranger who did not know anything about the family and therefore could not possibly know how to relieve one of them of pain? Hot lemonade with rakki was her medicine for colds, fevers and respiratory illnesses; singing for upset children; spankings for the mischievous; praying for those in pain, though from the way she prayed one always knew the act of praying and not help from above was her medicine, for she set up a vocal clamor of poetic language that was certainly distracting. She cursed imaginary enemies, mocked the neighbors, and claimed that God and she had never failed one another, and certainly wouldn't now after so many years.

If she dropped a fork, she said visitors were on their way to our house, but when the visitors turned out to be my brother and myself, home from selling papers, she insisted on treating us as guests, addressing each of us as Lord, and asking us how we had found conditions in Bagdad.

After coffee she turned her cup over onto the saucer and when the cup and saucer had become stuck together she separated them and studied the picture the pulverized grounds had made inside the cup, telling her own fortune.

At a picnic she carried an enormous watermelon to the bank of Kings River where she meant to place it in the water for cooling, but fell in and was fished out by a son, a son-in-law, two grandsons and a granddaughter, all of whom she rebuked for not having reminded her that in her reading of her fortune the previous night she had warned herself to stay away from water.

"I might have drowned," she said, and then more to herself than to anyone else she went on, "But what can you expect of Armenians?"

When a grandson said, "But you're an Armenian yourself," she replied, "I am a Saroyan, and that's nothing to be proud of, either."

She picked fights with everybody because, as she said, it was boring not to hear a little shouting in a house now and then, and she gave accurate but unkind names to everybody she knew to their faces.

She called a man who had grown pompous from having amassed a fortune of $500 Mr. Rockefeller, and was amazed that the man was flattered.

"I had no idea even he could be so stupid," she said.

She walked around the house barefooted, and preferred to eat with her fingers instead of with silverware because she claimed the food tasted better that way. She liked strawberry pop because it made her belch. She went to funerals because they made her happy, although she wept all the time, and she ate peaches without peeling them because she felt it was shameful to be fussy. She once served a grandson who had graduated from college a bunch of grapes on a plate and asked his pardon for not having peeled them and removed the seeds, for she felt that schooling was for fools, and that having graduated he must be one.

She believed in nothing except life, intelligence and humor, and suffered all her life from angry and proud melancholia. Just before she died at the age of ninety or so she said, "When I get on my feet again I know who the two people are that I am going to see," for she believed that she was sick in bed, in a hospital in a small town, because she had not been loved enough by two people. But an hour later she dropped it all—the superstition and all the rest of it—and said, "I can no more," and died.

She was superstitious all right, but is there anyone who is not? Is it possible to live and not be guided by a personal code of living based on instinct or hunch?

Sometime during 1941 I went to a Hungarian restaurant somewhere in New York with Jed Harris and a number of other friends, and after dinner a fortune-telling girl visited our table and with a deck of fortune-telling cards told our fortunes. The cards were old and worn, but I wanted a deck of them to examine carefully, so the girl took my name and address saying that she would obtain a deck and send it along to me. When the cards didn't arrive after a month, I presumed that the girl had lost my name and address, and only occasionally remembered that I felt it was important for me to examine a deck of fortune-telling cards carefully as soon as possible. Two or three months later the deck of cards arrived at last with a note from the fortune-telling girl in which she explained that it had been necessary to send to Europe for them. I immediately dropped everything else and carefully studied each card in the deck.

The next thing I knew I was writing this play.

Now, the theory is that each of us knows his fortune and therefore doesn't need to have it told. We are born, we survive for awhile, we die. That is the broad form of everybody's fortune. What we want to know, though, is how we are going to survive, and everybody tells his own fortune of survival every day: tells it or endures it: wishes or works for the improvement of it, or just waits, accepting without care or protest the unvarying pattern of it, or being resigned to its probable insignificance or inadequacy.

The fortune-telling girl at the Hungarian restaurant appears in the play in the manner in which she impressed me. Her telling of our fortunes was entertainment, not revelation. Each of our fortunes was good. None of us was warned against boredom, anger, pride, avarice, jealousy, or any of the other enemies of grace and health; we were all pleased and cherished one another and believed that we were secure because we were good.

None of us selected the card of death, for instance, and this accident made us laugh and drink and think well of ourselves.

Having been so pleased about the three cards that I had selected made me wonder how I would have felt had they been cards of disorder or disaster. The good cards had made me feel pleased. Had they been bad would I have felt that my having picked them was meaningless? If so, why hadn't I felt that picking three good ones had *not* been meaningless?

These thoughts were responsible for my wanting to own a deck of the cards, and by means of them to look into the whole matter of superstition, for while I knew I had been superstitious all my life, I had never looked into the matter carefully.

But the play is not about superstition alone. There is more to everything than any of us has time to know; a very great deal more. We live by means of shortcuts, for it is impossible to get everything straight, and long before the very simplest thing has been reasonably understood, the thing is taken for granted, and we are well involved in other things, equally incomplete in meaning to us.

The daily risk and danger of living, the absence of accurate information as to how much time we have, and the fear that we may be swindled or left by the wayside if we don't keep moving, impel us into techniques of survival based on speed and hunch.

A man who lives right, according to gamblers, can do no wrong, i.e., cannot have a wrong hunch. And the man whose hunches have been wrong feels that he has not been living right.

The play is also about birth, death and marriage. Birth is always an accident, for even when a man and a woman plan to have a child, they cannot know whether it will be a boy or a girl, and they cannot control the kind of boy or girl it turns out to be. Death is also an accident, for no man knows when it is apt to happen, how or why. But marriage can frequently be an event that is more or less unaccidental. Broadly, then, the play is about birth, death, marriage, the accidental, the non-accidental, and superstition, including the Christian super-

stition of the heavy drinker, Pál Szent-Gyorgyi, which is also a
purely personal superstition since the man has not been trained
in the church and is not a professional man of religion. Being
an amateur, being a Christian by accident and a heavy drinker
by choice or necessity, the form and variety of his personal
superstition is very nearly the fullest: the lore of the man himself, the lore of Christ, and the magic of alcohol.

Joseph, August and Ernest Hughman are so named because
these three men are meant to represent three common kinds
of men: the unconscious man, who as we see, may frequently
rise to the rank of Colonel; the introspective conscious man
who may be anything; and the extroverted-introspective conscious man who is often an artist in one form or another; hence,
a show-off.

Joseph Hughman, in other words, is a man who is now old
but was once young; who is beginning to suspect that he never
did an important thing in his life by conscious choice.

August Hughman is a much younger man who has brooded
all his life, trying to get things straight, and had little luck at it.

And finally Ernest Hughman is a professional actor who has
guessed about things and long since decided to show-off because
it's fun to do so.

They meet by accident and seek out a woman apiece, each
for his own reasons. The men and women have food and drink
together and wonder about one another.

The brooding man marries his girl; the show-off says good-
bye to his; and the unconscious man asks his girl a lot of silly
questions.

At the happy funeral in the play there is some fooling around
on the part of three burlesque comics; and the usual sort of
emotional confusion as to what is going on whenever the living
are gathered together to acknowledge that one of them is no
longer one of them. The brooding man, whose responsibility it
is to see that the funeral is a happy one, is preoccupied with the
colossal responsibility of impending fatherhood. The arrival of
mixed news ends the play: a son is born to the brooding man,
and it is learned that the show-off was not killed, as previously
reported, but was lost in Army production of a play.

The tone of the play being reasonable rather than emotional, I felt justified in permitting the show-off not to have been killed, for he is the artist, and art goes on forever. I felt justified in not having the mother die in childbirth. And I felt justified in not having the child die, or be sickly, or crippled. I know that a man who is said to be dead is more often than not dead. I know that mothers frequently die in childbirth, and that infants are frequently born dead, ill or crippled. In short, I know exasperating, surprising and terrible things do happen, but I chose not to make anything of this in this play.

All the same I suspect that the play *hints* at more authentic tragedy than a good many plays that are supposed to be tragic do; and the play is comic, for reason and intelligence are always comic. It is impossible for the tragic act to be intelligent. The tragic act is always performed by someone who is sick, stupid, or grand in the sense that he believes himself to be important and his experience unheard of heretofore, and when all is said and done a bigger bore than a salesman of life insurance.

And yet the hold of the tragic in art upon all of us remains tight and terrible. Love of the tragic in art is backwardness. We love trouble, disorder, passionate imbecility, grand violence and death in art because these things are both comfortable and comforting there, and it is rather nice to be reminded now and then of the sort of creatures all of us *could* be—almost under any circumstances at all, for the tragic is inherent in *all* circumstances and only needs someone who is a nut to make the most of it—and to be reminded of the kind of behavior we are lucky enough, lazy enough, or bright enough not to need to indulge in.

If any part of living is tragic, all of it is tragic; and it is therefore backwardness to pick and choose, and to make more of sick emotionalism and pathologic violence than of ordinary patience, commonplace politeness, universal resignation, unashamed intelligence, decent superstition.

In a sensible world playwrights would find it impossible to pretend to be capable of writing a tragic play; they would be ashamed of trying to do so.

There is a popular theory among playwrights and drama

critics that plays about monstrous human beings are more important and more real than plays about human beings who are not monstrous. According to this theory such plays are important because they expose such people and warn us against them. The theory is baloney.

The truth of the matter is simply this: that it is easier to give an impression of having written a great play if the play deals with sick and stubborn people who insist on getting into grand trouble than it is to give an impression of having written a great play if the play deals with reasonable and not ungiving people who prefer to avoid getting into grand trouble. In short, the Royalist playwright (choosing the equivalent of nutty kings, queens, princes and princesses for his characters) has an advantage over the Democratic playwright whose characters are just about anybody at all; and if the purpose of drama is to give people the kind of good time my grandmother used to have at funerals, weeping all the time but actually laughing her head off because it wasn't her funeral, then of course there is a strong case for the tragic drama, though I never saw one yet that didn't seem to me bogus. The only noise on a stage that I am able not to regard as offensive is the noise which is inevitable when people are having fun: music, singing, laughing, dancing, playing.

In short, staying alive is what's tragic; hurting, killing, being hurt or committing suicide are esthetic sensationalism and backwardness. Can there be, then, an exciting and powerful drama in which all behavior is reasonable or tries to be, and no one is spiritually tortured or physically annihilated? Yes, there most certainly can be such a drama, but it is not easy to achieve.

All people begin by having a decent birth, but few end by having a happy funeral. Mr. George Bernard Shaw appears to be the only famous man whose disappearance at last will constitute a quiet (and profoundly tragic) triumph; a disappearance that no one may be able to refer to as death; for which a new word will have to be created; the only man in our memory and time whose *ceasing* at last will be the occasion for international joyous celebration; the first man apparently to live all his life;

the first man to make a complete monkey out of death and out of the theory of dying in general; the only man ever to achieve immortality in his own lifetime by the simple expedient of hurting everybody's feelings but never hurting anybody's little finger; by honorably engaging in his profession every day; by trying all his life to think clearly; by daring to turn clear thinking upon the most popular misconceptions and false theories; the only small man who ever succeeded in establishing the enormity of smallness and thereby annihilating and exposing the impertinence of the theory of individual greatness; virtually the sole citizen of the world.

Well, when Georgie Porgie vanishes, it will be a happy time, not because he has gone at last but because he was here at all and made so much of it, so much that is henceforth anybody's. Every country in the world should appoint an ambassador to Mr. Shaw for the rest of his life, and his funeral should take place as a festival in every city of the Western world, and be an annual event: Georgie Porgie Day.

On that day every year everybody would be encouraged to wink and be intelligent.

THE CHARACTERS

COLONEL JOSEPH HUGHMAN

ERNEST HUGHMAN

AUGUST HUGHMAN

STELLA

BECKY

ELINORE

PÁL SZENT-GYORGYI

VIOLINIST

WOMAN

GYPSY GIRL

WAITER

KOCHANEK

1ST BURLESQUE COMIC

2D BURLESQUE COMIC

3D BURLESQUE COMIC

TELEGRAPH MESSENGER

THE SETTING

ACT ONE
  SCENE I. The Colonel's office.
  SCENE II. A Hungarian Restaurant.

ACT TWO
  SCENE I. A Sutton Place apartment.
  SCENE II. The Hungarian Restaurant.
  SCENE III. The same.

ACT THREE. The Hungarian Restaurant six months later.

ACT ONE

Scene I

An elderly, absent-minded and very small COLONEL of the Army is seated at a desk, looking over two medical examination reports. On a bench are two serious MEN who are waiting patiently, in anxious silence. The COLONEL studies one report, then the other, glancing at the TWO MEN, and whistling softly. When the TWO MEN begin to whistle softly too, the COLONEL speaks.

COLONEL. Ernest Hughman.

BOTH MEN get up. They look at one another, shake hands. The ELDER of the two steps to the desk.

ERNEST. (*At the desk*) At your service.
COLONEL. (*Surprised*) Are you Ernest Hughman?
ERNEST. I am.
COLONEL. This report says you are in perfect physical condition.
ERNEST. That is a good thing to know.
COLONEL. (*Absently*) Yes, it is. (*Cheerfully*) It isn't often that a man of your age—and profession—is in such excellent health. (*Pause*) I wonder if you can suggest the reason for that.
ERNEST. I'm afraid not, for being an actor I have always enjoyed a casual life, so to speak. On the other hand, acting is like having a hundred lives to live, instead of one. By the time a disease reaches one of the lives, the actor is off to another, and the disease is deserted. Perhaps that is why my health is good. (*Laughing*) I'm only guessing of course.
COLONEL. Of course. And yet there seems to be something to

what you say. I notice you have been in the theatre a good
many years.

ERNEST. Since I was twenty-two.

COLONEL. Your age is forty-four. (*Figuring*) Hence you've been
in the theatre exactly twenty-two years. (*Pause*) I have been
in the Military the greater part of my life. How did you
happen to choose the theatre as your profession?

ERNEST. (*Amused*) I entered the theatre because I am a show-
off. I hope to enter the Army for the same reason.

COLONEL. And your brother on the bench, how does it happen
that he—?

ERNEST. The man on the bench is not my brother. Except of
course figuratively. It's true we have the same family name,
but that is only a coincidence. To make the coincidence still
more baffling the given names of his father and mother are
the same as the given names of mine. That is, Joseph and
Mary—but of course those are common Christian names.
We are both Catholics, we were both born in New York
City, we come from practically the same class: the proud
poor. His given name is August, mine Ernest. His age thirty-
three, mine forty-four. His profession law, mine acting. We
are brothers of course, as all men are.

COLONEL. Yes. (*Smiling*) One of those things. You even *look*
alike.

ERNEST. What's more, he is a single child, and I am a single
child. He is a bachelor, and I am a bachelor. Yet except for
this War, it is not very likely we would ever have met. He is
an orphan from his third year, brought up in a Catholic
orphanage, and I am an orphan from my seventh year,
brought up in a Catholic orphanage. The same orphanage,
I might point out: St. Dominic's, on East 97th Street. I ran
away from the orphanage to go on the stage before he was
installed there. We met an hour ago when we came here
to enlist. Being ten years his senior, and a man who has lived
a careless life, I was afraid we might be separated after meet-
ing at last. Now, I feel easier.

COLONEL. I'm afraid you are going to be separated. (AUGUST

HUGHMAN *stands*) Yes. I regret very much, August Hughman, that your application for enlistment must be rejected.

AUGUST. I don't understand. I'm in perfect health.

COLONEL. Yes, I believe you are, except for one thing.

AUGUST. And what is that?

COLONEL. Your right ear is deaf. And the eardrum is punctured. Place your left hand over your left ear and it is unlikely that you will be able to hear anything.

AUGUST. (*Placing his left hand over his left ear*) I don't believe it. Will you speak, please, so that I may listen with my right ear?

COLONEL. If you do not hear, you must not *pretend* that you do. Can you hear? (*Pause*) I say, can you hear?

AUGUST. (*Brings his hand down from his left ear*) I had no idea the ear was *totally* deaf. (*Cheerfully*) But surely one good ear is as good as two. Surely you are not going to turn me away simply because my right ear is deaf.

COLONEL. *Punctured*, and deaf. Unfortunately, your *left* ear is partially deaf, too. There is no telling when it will become totally deaf. (*Pause, earnestly*) How did you happen to choose law as your profession? You see, I'm curious about such things. I have never been able to understand exactly how or why *I* entered the Military. It is not my field at all. When you decided to become a lawyer, did you know what you were doing?

AUGUST. Not at all. A man has little choice. My friend entered the theatre because he wanted to show-off. He is now enlisting in the Army in order to go on showing-off. Whereas I do not know why I chose law as my career, or why I am eager to enlist in the Army *now*. I would like to *believe*, however, that my reasons are sensible and perhaps unselfish. The truth is, I am sorry to say, I do not know *why* I want to be in the Army, except that I am tired of law, tired of being on the outside of such an enormous thing as the War, and a little tired of *myself*. Yes, that's the truth. I gave up my practice two weeks ago. I have no intention of returning to it. I have more money to spend on a comfortable life than I could ever manage to spend in thirty years. I am a little bored with the whole business of law and—yes, of life. And that is not a good thing. I believe I look for this experience of War to give my life purpose and meaning, and to restore me to a joyous feeling about mankind and myself. I even look forward to the worst: I do not mean that I *want* to be dead. On the contrary, I want to be alive. I have only once wanted to be dead, and that was when I was three years old—when I was installed in the orphanage. But as death is a difficult thing to achieve—the most difficult of all, I suppose—I want it to be achieved—if need be—for me—by the world, by circumstances over which I have no control—by inevitable accident, in other words. It simplifies everything for me in a way that I believe I can honestly feel is satisfactory—not an evasion of responsibility to myself exactly, but at the same time not too personal an event either, as death would be if I died in bed from disease or while standing in line at a movie from boredom. I do not like the idea of going back— one ear totally deaf, the other half-deaf—to try to achieve a decent life, with no help from the world or the circumstances of it. I don't know how to get out of it, that's all. Surely you can find a place for me in the Army? (*The* COLONEL *shakes his head several times slowly*) I could stay beside my friend. He could listen for me. (*To* ERNEST) You wouldn't mind very much, would you?

ERNEST. (*To the* COLONEL) I promise to listen for him.

COLONEL. I know, and I wish I could let the defect pass unnoticed, but I can't. It might result in some unexpected disaster. (*To* ERNEST) You might, for instance, be killed, and it might be very important for *his* hearing to be sharp and sound—and then what? Suppose the destiny of a whole squad depended on his hearing? Or a whole company? Or perhaps even a battalion or a regiment? No, we cannot afford to risk so many lives on one man's hearing. I cannot tell you how sorry I am.

AUGUST. (*Eagerly, almost desperately. Kneeling*) Then accept me as an office worker. I have no taste for private life any longer. Unless I am permitted to enter the Army, in one capacity or another, my life is ended. I have no fancy for cities, or for

the goings on in them. I want War. I dislike melodramatics,
even though I am a lawyer and have pleaded many cases in
a melodramatic style of speech, but *I* ask you on my knees
to let me enter the Army. It is a matter of life and death
with me.

COLONEL. I'm sorry I cannot satisfy your request. (*Pause*) When
you decided to become a lawyer, didn't you believe you
might like to be something else, *too*, perhaps? I am extremely
curious about such things. Didn't you think you might like
to be a doctor, too, for instance?

AUGUST. (*Getting off his knees*) No, sir. I have never wanted to
be a doctor. As a matter of fact, I dislike doctors—all of
them. This is a ridiculous way to feel about them, but it is
the way I feel. I think of them as murderers, although they
spend their time trying to save lives. (*Earnestly, suddenly
going to his knees again*) Please forget that I am deaf in one
ear. Let me go into the Army with my friend.

COLONEL. It is no use. Regulations are regulations, no matter
how unjust or unreasonable they may seem. In this case, I
myself would say they are a little too general—a little too cut
and dried—as I believe you are the kind of man to make a
good soldier. You are intelligent and have no romantic no-
tions about the War, and as far as I can tell you have no
desire to save civilization. But unfortunately there is nothing
I can do. Absolutely nothing. Your right ear is deaf. (*Eagerly*)
How did that ear go deaf?

AUGUST. (*Getting off his knees*) It was boxed by a Sister at the
orphanage the day I was taken there. It's been out of com-
mission ever since.

COLONEL. Why did the Sister box your ear?

AUGUST. I'm not sure, but it was probably because she was irri-
tated with herself. Of course I was no help to her at all. I
do not imagine that I charmed her with a cheerful person-
ality or a contagious joyousness. I was bewildered and unhappy, and wanted to be dead. That is to say, I *believed* I
wanted to be dead. I didn't understand anything, and when
a man doesn't understand anything, he sometimes imagines
he wants to be dead. That is, if he's three years old. If he's

thirty-three, he can see the absurdity of such an impulse, but at the same time he can also see the still greater absurdity of just dragging along with himself. Which is the way it is with me now. I hoped being in the Army would simplify the dragging. (*Pause, beginning to go to his knees*) Then, I'm not wanted?

COLONEL. I'm sorry.

ERNEST. (*Lifting* AUGUST *to his feet*) You needn't be so down in the mouth about it. *I'm* going, and I'll keep in touch with you. It's not as if *both* of us were turned down—or accepted. (*To the* COLONEL) Now, what about me?

COLONEL. Everything is in order. As you are a man of the theatre—and as the Army is in need of entertainment for the maintenance of morale—as Chief Classification Officer, I recommend that you continue in the field of the theatre.

ERNEST. I beg your pardon?

COLONEL. We try as far as possible to assign every man to the field for which he is most fitted. You are an actor. Naturally, we like to feel that you will continue as an actor.

ERNEST. Don't worry, I shall act all right. But not on any such trifling stage as that of a theatre. If you don't mind, let me have a uniform, a gun, and the Army Regulations, the same as anybody else.

COLONEL. You mean you wish to go into the Infantry?

ERNEST. Yes. I wish to be a soldier. A *foot* soldier. I am quite flattered that my health is so good. I would like to test it with some sound, regulated living, as against the vagrant, unregulated living which I have enjoyed so far.

COLONEL. Are you *sure* you would not rather continue as an actor? We shall not be making any concession to your past life. It is simply that we need more actors than soldiers.

ERNEST. I am quite sure that I would rather be a plain soldier.

COLONEL. Then it shall be so. (*Sincerely*) But can you tell me the reason for your decision? I am endlessly curious about how men make the decisions they make.

ERNEST. I have always wanted the biggest part in any play. The biggest part in this play is the soldier. The anonymous man. The one among the many. The unknown man. If killed, he is sometimes called The Unknown Soldier. A moment ago you wished to know why I chose acting as my career. I believe I can answer that question more fully now. I chose acting as my career in order to enlist in the Army at the age of forty-four as a common soldier. (*Pause*) This is one of the proudest, one of the happiest moments of my life. I am at last to act for the only audience worth bothering about: myself and God. I know one half of that audience approves of me, my half, and in all probability the other half will soon approve of me, too.

COLONEL. Such a casual and wholesome attitude toward soldiering should not be allowed to go to waste in a performance directed to so limited an audience.

ERNEST. Limited? (*Pause*) Well, perhaps. But I think you will agree it is not *too* limited.

COLONEL. I will tell you honestly, sir, that I am tempted to *draft* your talent into the theatre of the Armed Forces, because it is so needed. We have sickened our men with lies. No soldier in the field has time to think about what he is doing. He has a job to do, he tries to do it to the best of his ability at the time and under the circumstances. He knows it is a dangerous job and he knows he may be *stopped* at any moment. And that is where we have failed him. We have tried to tell him that if he *is* stopped it will not have been in vain.

ERNEST. Men live in vain. There is no other way for them to die.

COLONEL. Precisely. If you were to go before soldiers in a play made out of the way you feel, I know it would do them more good than the kindnesses which a confused propaganda and public forces on them. The men do not believe the lies. It is time somebody told them the truth in a decent way— as you *feel* the truth for yourself. Before I grant your wish to enter the Army as a foot soldier, may I appeal to you as an actor—not as a patriot, not as anything but an honest actor—to abandon your wish to be *entertained* by the circumstance of war, and to adopt a policy of being *both* entertained and entertaining to others? I will not say that you

owe it to your country, because you have already offered your
person to your country, for your own reasons—but I believe
I can say that you owe it to your profession, which I never
knew until now was such a proud and sensible one.

ERNEST. I'm tempted, sir, but I must remain as I am and have
always been: that is irresponsible—a man with no serious
purpose. To seek to entertain the endangered, other than
myself, is too much for me. I am sorry that I cannot with a
cheerful heart accept your offer.

COLONEL. I understand. I will not urge you any further. The
Infantry, then.

ERNEST. Thank you, sir.

COLONEL. It's been pleasant chatting with you. (*To* AUGUST)
And with you, sir. I am sorry you are not to go with your
friend.

AUGUST. I can't understand what difference it can possibly make
that my right ear is deaf. What is there to hear, anyway?

COLONEL. Nothing, for the most part, but a regulation is a
regulation. Good luck to both of you. I hope we shall all
survive the War. I hope we shall meet again. And I hope the
War shall soon be won—by *us*.

ERNEST. (*Shaking the* COLONEL's *hand*) It's won already. It is
not simply that we are Americans, but also, sir, that there is
art in us—and in spite of everything a certain amount of
purity, besides. It is not that we are more right than the
enemy, for every man is right in his heart—it is simply that
we have the best manners. The War is won, since we do not
hate anybody and want the enemy, *after* the War, to have
his modest share of what we shall have after the War. That
is to say, his modest share of nothing—or at least nothing
worth one man's murder. And if I may, sir, the War is won
because I, an actor, as irresponsible a member of society as
ever breathed, have been found in body, at the age of forty-
four, sound and undamaged by a careless, casual life; because
I have been accepted into the Infantry; and because I am
proud of it all, without believing for a moment that any of
it means anything. But I am an actor, and I love the stage.
(*To* AUGUST) Let us at least have supper together, and if you

like—and if I may—let us each enjoy the company of an actress.

AUGUST. The company of an actress?

ERNEST. Yes. There is nothing more confusing—or more refreshing.

COLONEL. Excuse me. My wife passed on quite a number of years ago, and—

ERNEST. By all means. I know just the actress. You will be delighted. She is ripe, but there is still much pretending of greenness in her.

COLONEL. I would like to ask her simply how it happened that she became an actress.

ERNEST. I know, and I know the incredible answer she will give. You will be most impressed.

AUGUST. (Softly) I can hear every word you say.

ERNEST. Come along. What's better than the three of us having a whole night ahead, and an actress apiece? (To the COLONEL) Your name, sir?

COLONEL. It is Hughman, too, the same as yours. (To AUGUST) And yours, sir. (Smiling) It never occurred to me that I might be the father of one or another of you, or both. I am hardly a man of imagination. My given name is Joseph.

AUGUST. Joseph Hughman? Then, sir, as you have the name of my own father, who died as a young man when I was three, forget the regulations of the Army, and let me go with my brother into the Infantry, so that tonight we may enjoy the world as equals and good members of the same family, with women of the stage to fascinate or confuse us. (Pause, with great sincerity, getting on his knees) I beg of you, sir—forget the regulations.

COLONEL. How unfortunate that I am unable to satisfy your wish. When I began the military life I believed I would be killed before I was thirty, and here I am going on sixty, with nothing better understood than at twenty, or even ten. I cannot help you, sir. I ask you to forgive me.

AUGUST. (Getting up. To ERNEST) Then I had better say goodbye, and go home. The actress will bring me no enjoyment. I would only bore her, and she would only bore me.

ERNEST. Not the actress I have in mind for you. She is a queen.

AUGUST. A queen?

ERNEST. Of the only true family of queens: burlesque. If she bores you, brother, you deserve to be bored. Besides, she has read a book and will speak to you of various meanings, with pleasant parts of her body in every meaning.

AUGUST. Even so, I don't want a woman for the architecture of her, or for the reading she's done, but for the foolishness of it. What good will her parts be to me if my own parts will not be moved by joyous absurdity to hers? I do not like to discuss ideas with bodies. Therefore, if we are to enjoy the night, let me be rid *here* of all ideas. Let me be a body, and then let the body go out and eat and drink, enjoy its weight and warmth with the weight and warmth of the body made by God to go with it. (*To the* COLONEL) I am embarrassed that I must keep appealing to you, but I am a dead man if I am not allowed to become, with all other men, only a body. I beg of you, sir.

COLONEL. If it were up to me as a person, your wish would have been granted long ago, but in the Military you must understand that I am not a person, I am a piece of machinery which performs routine work, according to regulations. I do not know why I ever went into the Military. It is not my field at all. I have never before realized what a terrible mistake I made, now that I am unable to let you live as you wish to live.

AUGUST. (*Shaking the* COLONEL's *hand*) I shall appeal to you no more. If I were my own lawyer, pleading my own case, and my *client* too, I should not know, as client, whether it were the case that was hopeless or the lawyer. In the courts of New York I have done better. Murderers have been transformed into saints by my pleading; thieving corporations have become benefactors of the poor; cheap lies have been turned into noble truths, but for myself I am no lawyer at all. (*To* ERNEST) Good-bye. It will be best for me to begin at the beginning again, for I have a whole life to live over. (*He shakes* ERNEST's *hand*) Good luck. (*He turns to go.*)

ERNEST. Wait. This is too sad. There is not this much sadness in the whole body of things, let alone in *this* small circumstance. I am sorry that I have had the better ear, and therefore go my way, as I wish. Even if it were unkind and rude to ask you once again, come along with us tonight.

AUGUST. (*Tapping his right ear*) My ear is deaf.

ERNEST. It's nothing. When the left ear is deaf with the right, thank God for the silence. In the meantime, you are my brother, and he is our father. We are without wives. I am of the theatre and a number of my friends are women of the stage. There is no tribe more suitable for us, and no night more suitable for the fun of them. Come along, brother. (*To the* COLONEL) Come along, father.

COLONEL. Thank you, my boy. I am an old man, bred in the Military, and fed up. Dull, dull, and no excuse for it, after all.

Scene II

ERNEST and AUGUST HUGHMAN, and the old COLONEL (JOSEPH HUGHMAN) are at a large table in a Hungarian Restaurant on 87th Street in New York. With them are THREE ACTRESSES: BECKY, very young and beautiful for AUGUST, since he is the youngest of the men; STELLA, not quite so young or beautiful, for ERNEST; and ELINORE, who is probably in her early fifties, for the COLONEL. At a nearby table is another COUPLE. There is a middle-aged WAITER. There is also a GYPSY TRIO: piano, fiddle and cimbalom. The music is going, and the WAITER is singing in Hungarian. There is a YOUNG WOMAN, dark and a little lonely-looking, who is wearing a gypsy fortune-teller's costume. She is standing by, waiting for somebody to have his fortune told. When the music ends, ERNEST gets to his feet, applauding, and then speaks.

ERNEST. My friends: a toast to the War. (*He lifts his glass.* EVERYBODY *at his table stands. He looks toward the other* COUPLE *at the nearby table*) In the name of Love, let us

drink a toast to the War. (*They stand. The* MAN *cries,* "Pál!
Pál Szent-Gyorgyi!") You do not like the War?

PÁL. Hate war!

ERNEST. Why?

PÁL. War kill!

ERNEST. Waiter, fill his glass. (*To* PÁL) Drink a toast, my friend.
(*The* WAITER *fills* PÁL'S *glass*) Why are you unhappy?

PÁL. Tirty year ago I come from Hon-gary.

ERNEST. Ah, you weep for the years gone by. A toast to the good
man's lost years. What is your name, my friend?

PÁL. Pál. Pál Szent-Gyorgyi, same as my fodder.

ERNEST. A toast to Pál Szent-Gyorgyi, and to his fodder Pál
Szent-Gyorgyi—and to my fodder, Pál Szent-Gyorgyi. (*Swiftly;
to* PÁL) It was my own father's name, too. Pál! Pál Szent-
Gyorgyi. A toast, ladies and gentlemen—to the thirty years
of Pál Szent-Gyorgyi. Everybody drink. (EVERYBODY *drinks.*)

PÁL. Pál Szent-Gyorgyi—that's me! You bet. Tirty years, come
from Hon-gary. (*Laughing*) Tirty years more, I go back. (*He
begins to weep. He looks at* ERNEST) Anoder toast to Pál
Szent-Gyorgyi—you bet. Big fellow, fight like Christian man,
kill tree Turks one hand. (*Shows his broad shoulders and
powerful arms*) Pál—you bet. Szent-Gyorgyi, from Hon-gary.
Drink champagne. Everybody drink to good Christian man.
(EVERYBODY *drinks*) Hofe! Hofe! (*He sits down.*)

ERNEST. Orchestra! Play a song for Pál! (*To* PÁL) What song will
it be, Pál?

PÁL. Pragnienie, Pragnienie!

VIOLINIST. Pragnienie, Pragnienie.

He begins to fiddle, and the other MUSICIANS join him in
lively sorrowful song. While it is playing PÁL gets up drunkenly and begins to dance.

PÁL. (*Dancing*) Pragnienie! You know? Homesick. (*To* WAITER)
Myslonky, myslonky. (*Tapping his forehead*) Tinking—tirty
years tinking.

ERNEST. What do you think, Pál?

PÁL. I tink zlodziej! Robber! Zlodziej come and steal— Take my fodder, take my modder, take my brodder, take my sister. Zlodziej! Zlodziej!

AUGUST. He calls Death, whom he does not love, and yet he calls as though Death were a woman.

BECKY. (*Leaning over and kissing him*) You're sweet.

AUGUST. Sweet?

BECKY. You're sweet to say what you said. It's wonderful to be able to say things like that. Am *I* wonderful, too?

AUGUST. You *are!*

PÁL. Zlodziej, zlodziej! Smierc, smierc!

AUGUST. Do you hear him? Listen, listen.

PÁL. Zlodziej! Smierc! (*He smiles, comes to the table, and speaks to* ERNEST) You know smierc?

ERNEST. Only in English, I'm afraid.

PÁL. In English, same ting, smierc!

AUGUST. (*To* ELINORE) He means Death. I can tell from the smile.

ELINORE. Death? Why would he smile about Death?

AUGUST. He's told us. He's a Christian man.

BECKY. (*A little drunkenly*) You're sweet.

PÁL. (*Nodding wisely, looking about, gesturing at everything*) Smierc. You know?

ERNEST. Yes, I believe I do.

PÁL. You know black horse? Night-time? (*Smiling*) No rider? Come in night for rider? Come for Pál—you bet. Pál Szent-Gyorgyi, Christian man. Smierc come like black horse for good rider. Pál, Pál. (*He sighs drunkenly*) I doan know. Hofe, hofe. Pragnienie! Homesick. (*He staggers over to his table, kisses his* WOMAN *on the lips, sits down, buries his head on his arms.*)

AUGUST. He is a man of decent sorrows.

BECKY. You're sweet.

AUGUST. (*To* ERNEST) You said she had read a book. She keeps telling me I'm sweet. Of what book is that the message?

ERNEST. Becky, be intelligent for my friend.

BECKY. He's sweet.

AUGUST. You see? I've heard her say nothing else. I have never before been told that I am sweet.

BECKY. But you are—you are! You're sweeter than anybody.

AUGUST. (*To* ERNEST) What does she mean?

ERNEST. We'll go soon, Becky. We'll go when they close. (*To the* COLONEL *and his* WOMAN) We'll all go.

COLONEL. Yes, my son. I don't know why I ever went into the Military. (*To his woman,* ELINORE) It's not my field at all, you know. And now it's too late to do anything about it. You see, I didn't know. I was too young. I thought I would be killed before I got to be thirty, but I wasn't. There was a little skirmish in Honduras—two natives stole pigs—and I had to go after them with a squad of men. We had to wade after them through swamps. One of the men turned and shouted at us. He called us names. I did not know what the names were, but I did not like his calling them. It does a man no good to be called a name. There was nothing else to do. I gave the order. Ready—aim—fire! Twelve men fired as one. Twelve men—but he got away. We never did catch him. I never knew his name, or his friend's name, or what he called us. When we got back we were tired and muddy, and some native women came and asked if we wished to be refreshed. Yes, that's exactly how they put it—great big women, with big faces. They knew we had waded through the swamps, in the heat. They knew we were tired. It's not my field at all. I have never before known people like yourself, and these other two young women. And the man who came from Hungary thirty years ago.

ELINORE. You *look* like a military man.

COLONEL. I'm not at all, though. Not at all. It was a boyish escapade, nothing more. We chased them five miles through the swamps. When we got back the native women came and asked if we wished to be refreshed.

ELINORE. What were they selling?

COLONEL. Oranges. It was only that we'd been away from home so long. Otherwise we wouldn't have *talked* to them, even. They speak very little English anyway, and we wouldn't have talked to them.

ELINORE. I see nothing wrong in selling oranges. (*Suddenly*) Ernest, I can't believe you're going off to be a soldier. I think it's most mysterious. And look at poor Stella, speechless and broken-hearted about the whole thing. Absolutely speechless.

STELLA. I'm drunk. A cup of coffee and I'll be as bright as ever.

ELINORE. But you *are* broken-hearted about Ernest, aren't you? I know *I* am.

STELLA. Ernest? Who's Ernest? (*Looking around, finding* ERNEST's *face*) Oh, yes. Good Lord, why should I be broken-hearted about *him*? He's only showing-off. He'll be no soldier. It's nothing more than another part for him to act.

AUGUST. I can hear every word. And they say I'm half-deaf. I can hear everything everybody says.

BECKY. You're sweet.

STELLA. Why should I be broken-hearted about Ernest going off to be a soldier? He'll only come back with a scratch on his nose, prettier than ever. Won't you, darling?

COLONEL. Excuse me, dear girl, he's not going out to a little skirmish. It is not going to be the way it was in Honduras with nothing more than two pig-thieves to chase. This is a real War. You may as well know he may be killed at any moment—any moment, dear girl.

STELLA. I don't believe it. I simply don't believe *anything* can kill Ernest. It's simply out of the question.

AUGUST. I can hear everything you say. It's all nonsense. (*To* STELLA) Excuse me. I hope you are right.

STELLA. Oh, I'm right all right. I know Ernest. I know him better than anybody here. He will not be killed. He simply will not be killed. Why, who would want to kill a man like that, who has nothing but comical thoughts for everybody? I have never known anybody to dislike him, except for a moment—and then only women, and *only* for a moment. Who in the world would want to kill Ernest?

AUGUST. I hear every word you say. I'm sure nobody in the world would *want* to kill him—nobody.

STELLA. Now, Ernest, would *you* want to kill anybody? Anybody at all?

ERNEST. No. Not even accidentally.

STELLA. You see? He is not going to be a soldier at all.

AUGUST. I hear every word. With only one ear, and that ear half-deaf, I hear everything.

BECKY. You're sweet.

AUGUST. I speak poorly, but there is no *sweetness* in it. (*To* STELLA) If he is killed, he will not know who kills him. If *he* kills, he will not know who it is he has killed.

BECKY. You're very sweet to say that.

AUGUST. (*To the* COLONEL) You have made a mistake to put him in the Infantry and leave me out. It ought to be the other way around.

COLONEL. My dear boy, a regulation is a regulation.

AUGUST. (*With anger*) It's nonsense.

BECKY. You're sweet.

AUGUST. Just a moment, Becky. (*To the* COLONEL) If I can hear as well as anyone, what difference does it make if I hear with only one ear, instead of two? I hear everything. I have been listening all night. I heard everything. I heard things you did not hear, sir, and things *he* did not hear, either. Do you remember when Pál Szent-Gyorgyi was dancing? Well, did you hear the woman at his table? Did you hear *her*, any of you? No, you didn't. Your ears are not deaf, but you did not hear her, and *I* heard her. She said to herself saying three times —yes, exactly three times—Pál, Pál, Pál!

COLONEL. Well, of course. What else would the poor woman say? He is her husband or lover, and he is unhappy, in spite of her, *so* unhappy that he must get up and dance in public. Well, then, what else would she say? You did not *hear* her, my boy. You *saw* her. You *knew* what she was saying. You did not hear it, I assure you. You scarcely hear anything I am saying. You see it. You know the nature of it from the expression of my face and the tone of my voice. Well, noises —military noises—have neither expressions nor tones. You might be killed.

AUGUST. I suppose he *mightn't* just because he's *not* deaf.

COLONEL. He *might*, too.

ELINORE. Poor, poor Ernest.

STELLA. Don't be silly. He's not going to be killed.

AUGUST. But suppose he is? What then?

COLONEL. What *then*? Why, nothing.

AUGUST. Nothing! Every man must have a *funeral*, and it ought to be a decent one, Christian or otherwise.

ERNEST. I *would* like a nice funeral all right.

AUGUST. That is the least any man is entitled to. Mourners, appropriate music, ashes to ashes, and all the rest of it. What about his funeral?

COLONEL. Every effort is made to give every man a decent burial, but of course there is scarcely time for anything elaborate, or even *whole-hearted*. If there is time, someone says a prayer, and everybody gets a grave.

ERNEST. Oh, that'll never do for *me*, sir. I am an actor. I would expect a *theatrical* funeral. Everything traditional to begin with, and after the routine things, then a good many more, according to my own inclinations.

AUGUST. What would you prefer, after the traditional rites?

ERNEST. Well, naturally I would like a good deal of weeping—of any kind, by anybody. I would like the kind of weeping we had tonight from Pál Szent-Gyorgyi. Yes, I would like *him* to be at my funeral. He should be paid to mourn. He may not remember me. If so, he should be paid. If he *does* remember me, and is sincerely grieved, then of course he will not *wish* to be paid. I would like others to mourn—any who have a talent for it.

AUGUST. I will look for Pál, in the event—

ERNEST. Then, too, I would like Becky to work.

AUGUST. Work?

ERNEST. Yes, of course. Her best costume, her best routine, and the proper lighting.

AUGUST. I'm afraid I don't understand. I'm not of the theatre.

ERNEST. I would like Becky to dance at my funeral.

BECKY. (*To* ERNEST) *You're* sweet, too.

ERNEST. You'll do it, won't you, Becky?

BECKY. I'll do it *now!* (*She gets up*) I'm tired of so much clothes. (*She turns to the* VIOLINIST) Orchestra, *Melancholy Baby!*

ERNEST. Not now, Becky. At my *funeral.*

BECKY. Clothes make me sweat. I stink when I sweat. I'll work now. Orchestra, *Melancholy Baby!* Lower those lights! I want to work!

ERNEST. Not now, darling.

BECKY. I'm tired of clothes. I look lousy in clothes. People never know what I really look like in clothes. They think I'm any-body—and I'm *not*. (*She takes off her coat and reveals that she's not.*)

ERNEST. (*Helping her back into her chair*) Of course you're not.

BECKY. You're sweet. You're almost as sweet as *him*.

ERNEST. Now, what else do I want? Well, I want a funeral march. Then I want plenty of food and drinks for everybody. Some low comedy. Becky can get three of the boys from the Gayety.

STELLA. (*Scoffing*) Stop showing-off!

COLONEL. He may *not* be killed. Only a certain number are killed, and you may not be among the unlucky ones.

STELLA. Of course he won't be killed. Why, who in the world would want to kill Ernest?

ERNEST. I'll call the fortune-teller. She'll tell us if I'm to be killed. (*He stands*) Gypsy Girl!

GYPSY GIRL. You want me?

ERNEST. Please. (*The* GYPSY GIRL *comes over to the table*) Sit down, Miss. (*She sits down*) Now. Tell my fortune.

GYPSY GIRL. (*Shuffling a deck of cards*) These are fortune-telling cards. They tell the truth. I will shuffle them carefully. Then I will cut them seven times—to the lucky card, or the un-lucky card, whichever is the truth. Then let him whose for-tune is to be told shut his eyes. Let him hold his eyes shut, and let him think about his life. (ERNEST *has shut his eyes*) Now. Here are the cards. Take one and place it face down on the table. (ERNEST *takes a card and places it face down on the table*) Now, that is your first card. There will be three. But the first card—that is your card. The card of your life. I hope it is good, for the cards tell the truth. In my family the cards have told the truth for three hundred years—for my mother, for *her* mother, and for many more of our mothers. They have always told the truth. You must not be afraid of the truth, whatever it is. For whatever it is, it is the truth. If it is bad, then fill your glass and drink. (*She puts a finger on the card*) That is your card—your life. I will turn it over. Let your eyes be clear and unafraid upon it, whatever it is. Do not be proud if it is good. Do not be afraid if it is bad. Whatever it is, that is what it is, for you have taken it from the many cards with your own hand and with your own eyes closed. Now, I will turn the card over. It will tell the truth. Do not let your eyes blink. (*She turns the card over.* EVERYBODY *looks at the card.*)

AUGUST. (*Excited*) What card is it? I cannot see. I can *hear* everything, but I cannot see.

GYPSY GIRL. (*Holding the card aloft*) This is the card. From thirty-two cards, this is the card you have taken with your own hand, with your own eyes closed. Do not be afraid.

AUGUST. But what card *is* it? What does it mean?

GYPSY GIRL. There were thirty-one other cards to take. Some good, some bad, but every one of them true. Joy, Sadness, Marriage, Misfortune, Letter, Children, Hope, Money, Sickness, Longing, Falsity, News, Jealousy, Ideas, Enemy—and so on. But this is your card.

AUGUST. Yes, but what card *is* it? Tell us. What does the card mean?

GYPSY GIRL. This is the card of Death. See? There is Death in its white robe. Death—or, as Pál says, Smierc. It is the same in any language. It is the same no matter what the word is. Death or Halal or Tod or Morte or Muerte or Smierc or Smrt—it is the same, and it is the truth. This is your card, selected with your own hand, with your own eyes closed. Do not be angry, it is no use. Do not laugh at the cards, for they tell the truth. Now, take another card. (ERNEST *takes a card*) Now, one more. That is all. Three altogether. (ERNEST *takes another card. The* GYPSY *turns over one of the cards*) This card is Gayety. That is a very strange card to go with Death, but it is the truth. The cards do not deceive us. Two cards: Death and Gayety. Now, the third card. (*She turns the card over*) Yes, it is the truth. There they are. The third card is

the Priest. There he is in his robe, in the church. That is all.
Death, Gayety, and the Priest. Do you understand?

ERNEST. Yes, I believe I do.

GYPSY GIRL. You are not angry?

ERNEST. (*Drinking*) Not the least. The cards have told me what
I know.

GYPSY. You have known you shall die?

ERNEST. I have known it all my life.

GYPSY GIRL. Have you known it shall be soon?

ERNEST. I am celebrating tonight the acceptance of my enlistment into the Army, in the Infantry.

GYPSY GIRL. You wish to die?

ERNEST. Not at all, but at the same time I do not particularly
wish *not* to die. I am forty-four years old. I have been an
actor twenty-two years. I have appeared in every kind of play
ever written, and now I have found it impossible to resist
appearing in *this* play.

GYPSY GIRL. You look upon the War as a play?

ERNEST. Yes, I do.

GYPSY GIRL. This card—Gayety. I do not understand it well. Can
you tell me what it means?

ERNEST. You are a poor fortune-teller.

GYPSY GIRL. It is not often that I tell the fortune of one like
you. My fee is fifty cents, but for you it is nothing. I will not
take any money. Only a sip of wine, to drink to you. What
is the meaning of this card—Gayety?

ERNEST. I am not a fortune-teller, but I believe it means that
I shall have a happy funeral. (*To the* WAITER) A glass, please,
for the Gypsy Girl.

A glass is placed on the table. ERNEST pours champagne into
it. The GYPSY GIRL looks at him seriously and lifts the glass.

GYPSY GIRL. I drink to you—happy man! (*She drinks and throws
the empty glass suddenly to the floor, breaking it*) What I
shall tell you now is not in the cards, but it is the truth, as
I am a fortune-teller, and my mother was a fortune-teller
before me, and her mother before her—three hundred years.

When you die, as you shall, and soon—well, you shall not die. It is not in the cards, but it is the truth. I do not know *how* it is the truth, but there is no fear in you, and if there is no fear in a man, how can he die? It is impossible.

ERNEST. It *is*? Well, thank you.

GYPSY GIRL. You will not die. I do not *ask* people if they want their fortunes told. I am going now, but if any of you wants to know the truth, then look at me, and I will understand. (*She waits a moment,* EVERYBODY *looks down, except* BECKY, *who looks at her in a drunken, sweet stupor*) You are looking at me, but you do not need to have your fortune told. It is all very clear. You are a beautiful girl.

BECKY. You're sweet. (*The* GYPSY GIRL *goes.*)

AUGUST. I heard every word, every whisper.

PÁL. (*Sitting up suddenly and looking around, speaking softly*) Smierc, smierc!

ERNEST. Orchestra, play a song for Pál Szent-Gyorgyi!

PÁL. (*Shouting gaily*) Pragniene, Pragniene! (*The orchestra begins to play.*)

ERNEST. (*Lifting his glass*) Here's to my funeral.

Scene I

It is early nightfall of a day three months later. AUGUST is standing in darkness at the window of his Sutton Place apartment, looking down at the river. A key in the door is heard. AUGUST does not stir. BECKY comes in. AUGUST turns. BECKY goes to him and kisses him.

AUGUST. What have you done to your hair?

BECKY. (*Removing her hat*) Combed it down, that's all! I got a letter from a man who said my hair should be combed down, because I am Esther. You know. Esther, of the Bible. Is he right? Do you like my hair down?

AUGUST. Who is the man?

BECKY. He didn't sign his name. He just said I ought to comb it down. (*Opening her handbag*) Here's the letter. Do you want to read it?

AUGUST. You read it.

BECKY. Well, it's very sweet. (*Reading*) Miss Becky, Gayety Theatre, New York. Dear Miss Becky: Last night I saw you take off your clothes at the Gayety. You are very beautiful, but there was something wrong when all your clothes were off. I didn't know what it was, but I have been thinking about it, and now I know. As your hair is very black, and your body very white, your hair should not be combed up on your head. It should fall straight down on your shoulders. You are Esther, of the Bible. Comb your hair down, Miss Becky, so that everyone who sees you will know who you are. I am a Christian and once preached the Gospel, but now I am too old, and come to the Gayety to worship. I am almost ninety and very unhappy about the War. Over and over again

202

I told them from the pulpit to watch out, but they would not listen to me. I have written letters to everybody, just as Paul of the New Testament did, but nobody answers my letters. I am from the Bible, too, and my letters are part of it, but nobody answers them. I don't know how Paul got his letters into the Bible. I have written letters to the Jews telling them how to live, but they do not answer me. I have also written letters to the Christians and to the Unbelievers. There are really no Unbelievers of course, because not believing is only another kind of believing. I am still in good health and pray every night for the mercy of God to reach the hearts of men. My great grandson, a boy of twenty named Philip, was killed in the War three months ago. I miss him very much because a boy of twenty to a man of ninety is like a baby, not a soldier, and now where is he? Well, Miss Becky, I thank you for being Esther, but I will not sign my name because I am an old man and do not want you for myself, as some old men do. I am glad you are so beautiful, though, because it is necessary for women to be beautiful if there is ever going to be any goodness in this evil old world. Yours truly, A Christian. (*Pause*) Is he crazy?

AUGUST. No man is crazy who lives to be almost ninety and then goes to the Gayety to worship.

BECKY. I didn't *think* he was crazy. (*Pause*) There were a lot of soldiers at the matinee. I threw kisses to them. They liked me very much. I kept looking for Ernest, but I didn't see him. Every time I see a soldier I think he might be Ernest.

AUGUST. He'll be here soon.

BECKY. (*After a pause*) What?

AUGUST. Yes. I've been waiting for him since six o'clock. He wired that he would be here between six and eight.

BECKY. I can't believe we haven't seen him since the night we all went to the Hungarian Restaurant. (*Pause*) I was pretty drunk that night. Did I do anything wrong?

AUGUST. No, you didn't. I don't think it's possible for you to do anything wrong.

BECKY. (*Removing clothes, as if she were working*) You aren't sorry you're in love with me, are you?

AUGUST. I'm not sorry—I'm amazed.

BECKY. I'm not sorry I'm in love with you, either, and I guess *I'm* amazed too. Three months ago if anybody told me a man like you would fall in love with a girl like me, and I would fall in love with him—well, I would have told him he was crazy. (*Continuing, after a pause*) What's the matter? Have I said something wrong again?

AUGUST. No—no. (*Pause, suddenly*) I want you to telephone the Gayety immediately.

BECKY. What for?

AUGUST. Well, Ernest is going to be here soon, and I thought we would spend the night together, the same as we did three months ago. We might even go to the Hungarian Restaurant.

BECKY. I've got two more shows. I won't be through till half-past eleven.

AUGUST. I want you to telephone the Gayety and tell them you're not going back.

BECKY. Why?

AUGUST. Well— (*Pause. He looks at her strangely*) I haven't asked you to give up your job—because— Well, I won't ask you now, either— Well, this is very awkward. If you'll be my wife, then I would like to ask you not to go back to the Gayety.

BECKY. You don't have to ask me to be your wife to ask me not to go back to the Gayety. You can just ask me not to go back to the Gayety. Maybe I won't go back, if you want to ask me.

AUGUST. No, I want you to be my wife.

BECKY. (*Almost all of her clothes removed*) But I've lived here three months, anyway. I got up the next day and *wanted* to go away, but you yourself told me to stay. If you asked me then not to go back to the Gayety, I wouldn't have gone back. You don't have to ask me to be your wife just to ask me not to go back to the Gayety.

AUGUST. I *want* you to be my wife. Do you want to be my wife?

BECKY. Yes.

AUGUST. (*Pause*) If you know, will you tell me why? Please try to tell me *exactly* why, no matter how foolish the reason may be.

BECKY. (*After a moment of eager and honest thinking, she shrugs her shoulders*) I guess I don't know why.

AUGUST. It is not impossible, then, that we were meant for each other.

BECKY. Am I supposed to know why I love you?

AUGUST. No. It is simply the custom to pretend that people who love one another love *only* one another. It is seldom suggested that a man's love for a woman is actually a celebration of his love for *all* things.

BECKY. Like the Fourth of July?

AUGUST. Or Christmas.

BECKY. (*Sincerely*) Well, I don't care. (*Long pause*) I love you.

AUGUST. What do you mean?

BECKY. I love you. (*Pause*.)

AUGUST. (*Looking at her curiously*) What are you trying to tell me?

BECKY. I wasn't going to— But if we're going to be together for good—well— (*Long pause.*)

AUGUST. Are you sure? *I* haven't learned to live, how shall I instruct another?

BECKY. I was afraid you'd be angry, but I don't care. There are better things than knowing how to do them— (*Pause*) Well, I mean—

AUGUST. (*Swiftly*) I know what you mean. (*He looks at her, smiling faintly*) This is most ridiculous—and awe-inspiring. But why haven't you told me?

BECKY. I wasn't sure, but now I am, and I'm going to have my fun.

AUGUST. Fun? But it's written of woman: In *sorrow* shall you bring forth.

BECKY. I don't care what's written. If you knew what I know, or feel what I feel, you'd know that *that* sorrow for me is fun. (*Pause*) —If you're not angry.

AUGUST. A good father is never angry at his infant's closest parent, or critical of his infant's first home, since it is the only home provided in the beginning. My infant's found as sweet a place to start as any infant ever found. (*He holds*

her by the shoulders, at arm's length) Now, whether I like
it or not—and perhaps I *shall* like it—I am turned from the
end of things to the beginning of them. You have turned me
around sooner than I deserve, for I have not yet learned anything about the end of things—but one thing's sure: A man
should have a decent birth, a happy funeral, and in between
a life both pleasant and honorable.

BECKY. I don't know how a man can have a happy funeral when
he's dead, or a decent birth when he's too little to know the
difference.

AUGUST. One thing's sure— (*Pause, suddenly*) What did you say?

BECKY. I said how can you have a decent birth when you're too
little to know the difference? How can you have a happy
funeral when you're dead?

AUGUST. (*Almost amazed*) Yes, that's what I *thought* you said.

BECKY. I'll go telephone the Gayety. (*She goes.*)

AUGUST spends a few minutes at the piano, tapping one key
many times, and then another. The door-chime sounds. BECKY
runs to the door, which is not seen. The door is heard to
open. BECKY and ERNEST come in together, arms around one
another. ERNEST is in the uniform of a private.

AUGUST. (*Happily*) How are you?

ERNEST. I've lost ten pounds. I've forgotten most of art. But, by
God, I *feel* all right—a little doggy, as boys turned loose from
Reform School must feel. I want a woman. I want a good
table. I want good drink. I want *everything*—quick! (*Pause*)
That's how I feel. (*He kisses* BECKY's *cheek. He turns to*
AUGUST) What's this girl doing here?.

AUGUST. Well— (*Almost embarrassed*) We're to be— (*Noticing*
ERNEST's *closeness to* BECKY) We're married.

ERNEST. (*Pushing* BECKY *away pleasantly*) Away from me, then!
I've told you how I feel. (*To* AUGUST) Good boy! I'm glad
I brought you together.

AUGUST. And I'm *grateful* that you did. You have no idea what's
happened to me.

ERNEST. (*Glances at* BECKY) I can imagine. Becky! One last kiss. (*To* AUGUST) I never saw a wife for myself in any girl until another did. Becky *might* have been mine, you know. (*He kisses her*) This is the end. (*He looks at* BOTH *of them, delighted*) You go well together. I would never have believed it, but you do. (*To* BECKY) Have you learned a good deal from this man? How is your way of speech now? Has it improved? Say something, so I may judge.

BECKY. You're sweet.

ERNEST. (*Happily*) She's the same, thank God. It's good to see you both, and better still to see you together. (*He sits down, a little weary, looks at the floor. After a moment he speaks softly*) I'm tired.

AUGUST. (*Pouring a drink*) Well, have a drink.

ERNEST. Yes—thanks. (*Suddenly*) Now, for God's sake, don't be just a husband and wife with me, will you? (*He takes the drink from* AUGUST; *gulps a good deal of it*) Let's say it's the night it was three months ago, and take it from there.

AUGUST. Yes, of course. I was hoping we'd get the others, too, and go to the Hungarian Restaurant— (ERNEST *looks at* AUGUST *curiously, as if he were remembering the restaurant but not too pleasantly*) We haven't been there since that night, waiting for you to return.

ERNEST. (*Smiling again, standing*) Now I feel fine. Yes, that's what we'll do. I wish to God we could change clothes for awhile, though.

AUGUST. Clothes?

ERNEST. Yes—this stuff's too heavy for an actor. It's not cloth, it's iron.

AUGUST. Iron?

ERNEST. On my word, after one day of it the body is locked, and then all the rest of it is locked, too. Locked in iron. (*Pleasantly*) Shall we go? We can telephone the others from the restaurant.

BECKY. I can't go now.

AUGUST. Why?

BECKY. I telephoned the Gayety, and they begged me to do the last two shows, too. If it wasn't Saturday, it would be all

right, but it's Saturday. They begged me to do the last two
shows and I couldn't refuse. (*Pause*) Could I?

AUGUST. No, of course not. But get in a cab after the last show
and come to the Hungarian Restaurant.

BECKY. (*She kisses* AUGUST) I thought you'd be angry.

AUGUST. (*Gently*) I am angry, but not at you.

BECKY. I'll see you at the Hungarian Restaurant. (BECKY goes.
ERNEST *turns to* AUGUST.)

ERNEST. What are you angry about?

AUGUST. I have no right to be happier than you, or in different
clothes.

ERNEST. But you're *not* happier than I.

He sits at the piano, suddenly tired again. AUGUST watches
him curiously, moving toward the window. After a moment,
ERNEST begins to make little sounds with the piano, while
AUGUST listens.

ERNEST. I'll tell you what I've learned. It isn't much, and I'm
sure it isn't going to be useful to anybody, but I think I'd
better tell you just the same. Death begins with help'ssness,
and it's impossible to joke about. In the Army everybody is
helpless and grim. Death is a lousy idea from which there is
no escape. The idea is made out of imprisonment and weari-
ness. It is impossible for any man to joke about Death while
he is imprisoned and weary, for he is Death itself, or life
desperately in need of rest and refreshment. It is horrible to
need refreshment and not to get it. The idea of Death is no
fun at all to me because I'm too tired to see straight, and
cannot know when I shall be able to rest again. If I were
refreshed the idea of Death would be refreshing and I could
no more fear it than I could fear kissing a beautiful girl.
As it is, I'm scared to death of it. It's not funny at all, and
I can't wait for the War to end, so I can learn to love Death
again, if I live that long. (*Slight pause*) That is what I've
learned.

Scene II

The Hungarian Restaurant, a little before midnight. Everything is exactly as it had been three months ago, including the presence of PÁL SZENT-GYORGYI and his WOMAN.
The GYPSY TRIO is playing the same song, the PEOPLE are
all the same, everything is the same—except that BECKY
is not there yet. When the music ends, once again ERNEST
gets to his feet, applauding.

ERNEST. (*Happily*) My friends—a toast. Let us drink to the War
no more. Let us drink instead to the Peace. (*He lifts his drink.*
EVERYBODY *at his table stands:* COLONEL HUGHMAN, *his woman*
ELINORE, ERNEST'S *woman* STELLA, *and* AUGUST. ERNEST *speaks*
to PÁL SZENT-GYORGYI *at the nearby table, who is again drunk*)
My friend, in the name of Love, let us stand. (PÁL *and his*
WOMAN *stand, holding their glasses. Suddenly, the same as*
last time, PÁL *shouts with grief*) Ho! Saint George! Do you
still weep? Save it, I beg of you, for my funeral! Do not cry
now, Pál. This is not the time for it.

PÁL. Smierc—smierc.

The GYPSY GIRL comes to the table and looks at ERNEST curiously.

ERNEST. You have not forgotten, have you? Poor Pál has forgotten. While I am still alive, he forgets. How will he remember when I am dead?

PÁL. Pál no forget. Pál remember—ha ha! Smierc. Ho ha—ha
ha! Ho ha—ha ha ha! Smierc. Smierc!

GYPSY GIRL. The cards do not lie, and yet—

ERNEST. Oh, I shall die, but please don't hurry me.

GYPSY GIRL. No, no—the cards tell the truth.

ERNEST. Don't fret. I shall not embarrass the cards.

GYPSY GIRL. (*A little excited*) No, no. You did not take the card
of Death. The cards do not lie. You did not take it. Someone

else took it. It was taken with your own hand, with your own eyes closed—but it was not for you, for I know these things, and my mother before me knew them.

ERNEST. Of course I took the card. It was no other. I am satisfied, and there is no place in fortune-telling for courtesy. Smierc it was, and Smierc it remains. Now, our toast—to the Peace. (*They* ALL *drink, including the* GYPSY GIRL.)

GYPSY GIRL. I drink with you to the Peace, but I know these things, and I do not speak from courtesy. You did not take the card.

AUGUST. Who took it?

ERNEST. (*To* AUGUST, *objecting*) Sit down, sit down. If you want your fortune told, sit down and take your card.

AUGUST. (*Sitting down*) I want my fortune told.

GYPSY GIRL. (*Sits down and shuffles the deck of cards*) The cards tell the truth. I shuffle them carefully, and cut them seven times—to the lucky card, or to the one which is *not* lucky, whichever is the truth. Then let him whose fortune is to be told shut his eyes. (AUGUST *shuts his eyes*) Let him think about his life. (*She holds out the deck of cards to* AUGUST) Now, here are the cards. Take one and place it down on the table. (AUGUST *takes a card and places it face down on the table*) Now, that is your card. There will be two more, but that is the card of your life, and the truth. Now, open your eyes. (AUGUST *opens his eyes*) I will turn the card over. It will tell the truth. (*She turns the card over, and* EVERYBODY *looks at it.*)

ERNEST. What card is it?

GYPSY GIRL. (*Holding the card aloft*) This is the card. It is the card of Gayety. It is not the best card of all, but it is *almost* the best. Take another card. (AUGUST *takes another card*) Now, one more, and that is all. (AUGUST *takes a third card. The* GYPSY GIRL *turns over the second card*) This is your second card. It is good, also. This is the card of the Priest, but as Gayety is your first card, the Priest following Gayety is for marriage or baptism. Now, this is your third card. (*She turns over the third card*) This is the card of Death, but as it is in its proper place, you will live well and long. In the end all men die, but it is better to die in the end than in the beginning, and you will die in the end, after living. First a happy life, marriage and children and baptisms, and then, when the time comes, a pleasant death. That is your fortune, sir. My fee is fifty cents.

AUGUST. (*Handing her a coin*) Now! Are you sure *I* took the cards?

GYPSY GIRL. Of course. I saw you with my own eyes, and everyone here saw you.

AUGUST. And the three cards are the same three which *he* took three months ago, drawing them from the deck in a different order? Is that right? Do you remember?

GYPSY GIRL. (*Thinking*) Yes. Yes, they are the same cards. The order of his taking was Death, then Gayety, then the Priest, but *that* order is not the same as *this* order. That order means Death at the beginning—heedlessly, with no care, with Gayety —then the Priest for burial. Three in numbers is not many, but in combinations, three is *all*—but first *one* is all, and then three tells *how* one shall become all. It is always Death, but three tells how it shall be.

AUGUST. I understand. I understand. Now. (*Simply*) I did not take the cards.

GYPSY GIRL. Of course you took them.

AUGUST. No. (*Of* ERNEST) *He* took them, and three months ago *I* took the cards, and *he* did not.

GYPSY GIRL. You are brothers perhaps. A brother does not like to see his brother die. The cards tell the truth, and do not know brothers.

AUGUST. Of course the cards tell the truth. Everything tells the truth. Lies tell the truth. (*He points*) Pál tells the truth. The violin tells the truth. There are no lies to tell.

PÁL. (*Shouting*) Pál Szent-Gyorgyi! (*He gestures in a circle at everything.*)

AUGUST. Pál, what is the truth?

PÁL. Ha—ha! What is the *truth?* Ho ha—ha ha! You know. You do not need to ask Pál.

AUGUST. Tell us, Pál. What is the truth?

PÁL. (*Almost sobbing again*) I do not like the truth. The truth is bad. The truth is robber. (*He sits down*) Dirty robber!

AUGUST. (*Anxiously, worried, suddenly impatiently*) For God's sake, what's happened to her? It's after twelve. Where is she? (*The* GYPSY GIRL *goes back to her place.*)

ERNEST. She'll be here. (*Pause*) Orchestra! A song for my friend, my brother. A happy song for a happy man.

PÁL. Pragnienie, Pragnienie!

ERNEST. Yes, Pragnienie—that's it! Thank you, Pál. You live a steady life. Smierc, zlodziej, and Pragnienie—you have a fine group of three. (*The orchestra begins to play the song*) That's it, that's it! (*To* AUGUST) She'll be here. Why are you so fretful? She's been alone in this city all her life. She was not lost and not in danger when you did not even know she lived. What is it?

AUGUST. (*Excited*) I must tell you. I have been wanting to tell you all night. I don't know how to feel.

ERNEST. What is it, man?

AUGUST. She is with child. Can you believe such a thing? Yes. (*He gets up suddenly*) I am going out to look for her. Something's happened.

ERNEST. (*Grabbing him by the shoulders*) Sit down, man. Nothing's happened, but something *will* happen if you go looking for her. She'll be here. (AUGUST *sits down*) Now, fill your glass and drink.

AUGUST. (*Almost furious*) I tell you she's with child. It's not the same when that's how it is. It's altogether different. (*He drinks untidily, excited*) It's the most awe-inspiring thing that's ever happened to me. I'm stunned every minute. I've got to see her. After tonight I'll not let her out of my sight. Every man's entitled to a decent birth. How do I know where she is? The infant's with *her*—not with me. What time is it now?

ERNEST. (*Laughing*) It's seventeen minutes after twelve. (*He stands*) My friends, another toast. Let us stand proudly and drink the best toast of all. (EVERYBODY *stands*) Let us drink to—the Infant! (*They* ALL *drink,* AUGUST *spilling some of his drink*) Let us drink to the Infant again! (*They* ALL *drink.*)

PÁL. Baby?

ERNEST. Baby is the word for a certain kind of young woman. We drink to the *Infant!*

PÁL. Ho ha—ha ha! Ho ha—ha ha ha! Baby, O Baby, Baby! (*He kisses his* WOMAN. EVERYBODY *sits down.*)

AUGUST. Let me go out into the *street* at least. Let me at least be there to welcome her.

ERNEST. You're excited. You might slip and fall, or knock somebody down who is innocent and does not know what's happened. Sit down. She'll be here.

Music and dancing. PÁL and his WOMAN. The swinging door swings open and a BURLESQUE COMIC, in baggy pants, stands in the doorway.

AUGUST. Who's that? Where is she?

Two more BURLESQUE COMICS come in, and with them is BECKY.

ERNEST. (*With relief*) There she is, man. For God's sake, you had me frightened.

AUGUST gets up and walks toward BECKY.

Scene III

It is a little after two in the morning and everything is still the same, except that everybody has had more to drink. The GYPSY VIOLINIST is putting his violin back into its case. The PIANIST is yawning sleepily. The PLAYER OF THE CIMBALOM is covering the instrument. PÁL is asleep on his folded arms. His WOMAN is standing over him. Every now and then she taps him gently on the shoulder. The WAITER is standing politely in a corner. The GYPSY GIRL is the least changed. She appears to be still troubled about ERNEST and the three cards he selected three months ago: Death,

Gayety and the Priest. ERNEST is smiling vacantly, while his woman, STELLA, looks at him sleepily. AUGUST and BECKY have their arms around one another. COLONEL HUGHMAN is holding the hand of his woman, ELINORE. The THREE BURLESQUE COMICS sit quietly. The THREE GYPSY MUSICIANS put on their hats and coats, and, bowing, leave the restaurant.

PÁL'S WOMAN. (Whispering) Pál, Pál!

He does not answer. She taps him gently on the shoulder. The WAITER takes off his white coat and puts on his street coat and his hat. He turns off several of the strong lights.

ERNEST. What's this? What's this?

WAITER. (Politely) It's closing time, sir.

ERNEST. Closing time? But we are all so peaceful at last. Surely you're not asking us to go?

WAITER. Oh, no, sir. You may stay as long as you like, but the restaurant is closed. The door is locked. We cannot serve anything more to drink, but there is food.

ERNEST. Thank you, sir.

WAITER. The lights I will put up again if you wish, although it is the custom to dim them when we are closed.

ERNEST. We will abide by the custom.

WAITER. The watchman is in the kitchen, and will stay all night. He is a simple man, by name Kochanek, and a good cook.

ERNEST. Kochanek?

WAITER. He will come when you call. He will let you out when you wish to go. (Pause, smiling) May I say goodnight, sir? I thank you for remembering our humble place, and I wish you good fortune.

ERNEST. I thank you, sir. Goodnight.

WAITER. (Bowing) Goodnight. (To the OTHERS, bowing) Goodnight.

EVERYBODY bows, and one of the BURLESQUE COMICS gets to his feet to make a real bow, his face very serious and sad.

The WAITER goes to PÁL, and without a moment's hesitation, almost shouts at him, shaking him.

WAITER. (*Speaking in Hungarian*) Pál, the place to sleep is home! Get up, get up now! (PÁL *looks up, in a stupor. The* WAITER *very kindly slaps him awake*) Awake, now—awake, Pál Szent-Gyorgyi! (PÁL *smiles*) That's it—that's it! (*The* WAITER *turns to the* OTHER, *and speaks in English*) Excuse me. We are friends from boyhood, from the same town in Hungary—almost brothers. His wife is my sister. Every night it is like this. He sits and drinks, then goes to sleep. I wake him up and together we go home.

PÁL. (*Listens, smiling*) You bet—Pál Szent-Gyorgyi! That's me! Christian man. (*He gets up proudly and spreads himself out. He is almost a giant*) Ho ha—ha! ha! Ho ha—ha ha ha! You bet. (*He stretches*) Pál— (*He spreads his arms out, and embraces his* WOMAN *and the* WAITER *in one big embrace, and kisses them* BOTH) Hey—my girl, my girl! My brother, my brother! Ho ha—ha ha! I love you! (*He squeezes his* WOMAN *and his friend*) Ho ha—Szent-Gyorgyi, Christian man—! (*He releases the* WOMAN *and the* WAITER.)

WAITER. (*The* WAITER *turns to the* OTHERS) He is the strongest man I know.

PÁL. (*Putting on his overcoat*) You bet. (*He comes over to* ERNEST; *looks at him strangely, smiling*) You soldier now. (*He kisses* ERNEST *on the forehead*) Good-bye, my friend!

ERNEST. Good-bye, Pál.

PÁL puts his arms around his WOMAN and the WAITER, and together they go.

PÁL. Soldier die quick, soldier die good! Ho ha—ha ha! Soldier die best, ha, ha, ha, ha!

There is a strange silence now, for a moment. ERNEST watches the GYPSY GIRL, who is standing in her place, as if the evening were just beginning.

ERNEST. (*Calling*) Kochanek—Kochanek!

KOCHANEK. (*An old man comes out of the kitchen to the table. He is smiling pleasantly*) I am Kochanek. (*He bows.*)

ERNEST. (*Standing*) I called only to see who Kochanek is, and to have Kochanek see who we are. I am Ernest Hughman. (KOCHANEK *nods*) These others are friends. Thank you for coming. (*He sits down, after bowing.* KOCHANEK *bows, smiling, and returns to the kitchen.* ERNEST *looks again at the* GYPSY GIRL. *At last he speaks to her*) What is it?

GYPSY GIRL. (*Eagerly*) Thank you, sir. I could not speak until spoken to, as that is the rule of my family, but I have been waiting for your permission, and I would have waited all night.

ERNEST. (*Pleasantly*) But what is it? You should be home now asleep. It is no pleasure to stand so long.

GYPSY GIRL. I do not live for pleasure. I live for the truth. (*She moves to the table, with her cards in her hands*) I'm sorry I've displeased you.

ERNEST. I'm *not* displeased. Please sit down.

GYPSY GIRL. Thank you. I'll stand. It is no good to doubt the cards. It is wrong to challenge their truth, but I cannot help it. (*Pause*) Will you take your card again?

ERNEST. Of course, of course, if you wish.

GYPSY GIRL. But you must not believe the cards are foolish. They are old and wise, but they are not foolish. It is not right for me to ask you to take your card twice, for no man lives twice, or dies twice. He is born once, and that is the truth of it. He dies once, and that is the end of it. But I am troubled. I am even frightened of what I am doing. I would be humiliated if the truth were told twice. But I *do* doubt the truth told you by the cards. I do not believe it was *you* who took the card of Death. I do not know who it was, but I do not believe it was you. Now, even if I am to be humiliated will you take your card again? I have warned myself—but I do not warn you, as this taking is for *me* only— that if you take the card of Death again, if the truth *has been* the truth—well, then I shall not know what to do, as I have

lived by the truth of the cards all my life, and hope to die
by it.

ERNEST. Do not be uneasy. I do not scoff at any faith, least of
all yours, but surely it will be impossible for me to take the
same card out of thirty-two *twice.*

GYPSY GIRL. For *you,* I hope it will be impossible, no matter
how I shall be humiliated. I hope you do not take the card of
Death again.

ERNEST. I don't see *how* I can. It is one of thirty-two.

GYPSY GIRL. Here. (*She places all of the cards face-up on the
table*) Here they are. All of them. Thirty-two cards, each with
its own name and picture. Only one of them is the card of
Death. Here it is. (*She holds it up*) I will put it among the
others, and shuffle them all. (*She shuffles the cards*) Now, I
will cut them seven times. (*She cuts the cards*) Now, this
time do not close your eyes. Look at the cards, and then take
one. There will be only one—the first. I do not care about
the other two. Only one—the truth. (*Almost frightened*) Take
one, when you are ready.

ERNEST. (*Looks at the cards, smiling. He reaches out and draws
one out a little, then changes his mind*) No, not that one.
(*He draws another out*) Nor this one. (*He touches a card, and
draws it out swiftly, hitting it down face-up on the table*)
This is the one!

EVERYBODY looks at the card. The GYPSY GIRL gets up. She
looks at ERNEST curiously, and then at each of the OTHERS.

GYPSY GIRL. (*Softly*) I'm sorry. Please forgive me. I'll go home
now. (*She turns to go, moving awkwardly.*)

ERNEST. (*Gently*) You've left your cards.

GYPSY GIRL. I do not want them any more. They tell the truth,
they tell it well, but I do not want them. (*Softly*) I'm sorry.
Please forgive me. I had no right. (*She goes.*)

EVERYBODY sits quietly. One of the BURLESQUE COMICS lifts
the card and looks at it. He speaks seriously.

COMIC. We used to do a sketch with a gypsy girl, and three comics asking to have their fortunes told. Of course what they wanted to know about was life, not death. Would they have a beautiful woman? Would they have money? Would they go on a journey? And so on. We used a regular deck of fortune-telling cards. Something like this deck. It didn't matter what card we took. It was only part of the business of the act, to make the people laugh. We each drew one card. At first it didn't make any difference what card it happened to be, but after six or seven performances we got to asking each other what card we had drawn, and then on the last day we got to *watching* each other's cards. In twenty-one performances I didn't draw the card of Death once—not once. I even *wanted* to draw it, after awhile. I just wanted to see if I *could* draw it, but I never did, even though, in the act, I was always the first to take a card. I just couldn't draw the card of Death. The three of us were Will Jackson, Sad Joe Hill, and myself. I drew first, Will Jackson second, and Sad Joe Hill third. By the time we got around to watching each other's cards there were three performances to go. Sad Joe Hill, drawing third, drew the card of Death three times in a row. He wasn't an old man. He was about forty-five, ten years younger than I am, now. He died three days later. That's the truth, and none of us believe his dying had anything to do with the fortune-telling act, but all the same we never used the act again. I remember the pictures on the cards. They were a good deal like the pictures on these cards, and the picture on the card of Death was *exactly* like the picture on this card. It was one of those things, but we never used the act again. (*To* ERNEST) I'd like to tear this card up. Do you mind?

ERNEST. (*Pleasantly*) Thank you for asking. I'd like to keep the card, for I drew it from the deck twice. (*Happily*) Wake up, wake up! You are all too pleased with one another, too happy, or too unhappy! (EVERYBODY comes to life, as if from a trance) Here! We've still a bottle or two. It's still night, and this is still living. Now—this card—look at it. (*He shows it around*) Do you see? It is my card. (*He puts the card in his pocket*) I am not given to the cult of unhappiness, I am not a bitter man, I do not speak in double tongues, I tell you honestly and plainly—I am *proud* of my card. It's meaning is that I shall die. I shall. If I shall die soon or late is no matter, for I shall not know how soon it was or how late. I leave the city this morning. When it is light again, I shall be among the weary warriors again. After that, I do not know. (*Of* AUGUST) My friend here, my brother, happy at last and soon to be a father—for which I thank God—will be informed of my death—by telegram, I suppose. We are all tired of this night, and want our beds. Before we get up and go, I ask a favor of you. No, I *charge* you with this: to give me a funeral, and a happy one. I will not have any sorrow among you, but if it pleases our friend Pál Szent-Gyorgyi to weep for me, then let him, for he is a strong man, a Christian, and a man with a gift for weeping. (*Pause*) Do you understand?

AUGUST. How can we have a funeral for you—any kind of a funeral—when you will not be at the funeral?

ERNEST. I do not ask a funeral for my *body*. I ask a funeral for me—Ernest Hughman—actor. Myself, but not my body. I charge you with this. You cannot refuse.

AUGUST. But what shall be buried if the body is not there?

ERNEST. Bury the casket, and see that it is a handsome one.

AUGUST. Are you drunker than I am? Are you as drunk as *that*?

ERNEST. I am not drunk at all. But here! Let's you and I and the Colonel have another glass. (*He pours*) Let us stand and solemnly swear that if I am killed, you will provide me with a happy funeral. Now, let us drink on it. (*They touch glasses and drink*) I am deeply grateful to you. (*Of the* COMICS) These good men, who make people laugh, will perform at my funeral.

AUGUST. But what will lie in the casket?

ERNEST. A living man—what else? It's to be a *happy* funeral. You are my brother, and we are of one size—when the telegram comes—make all arrangements immediately—and lie in the casket for me, in formal clothes. Sit up when you please, have a drink, instruct the mourners, the speech-makers or the players. I want music, food, drink, dancing, playing, speeches, mourning, and finally I want the casket to be buried—but of course not with you in it. With nothing in it. You must not humor me. You must swear that you will do it, and then you must do it—and just as I have said. (*To* AUGUST) Do you swear it?

AUGUST. (*Shaking his hand*) I do.

ERNEST. (*Filling his lungs proudly, looking around, smiling*) I thank you, and return now to the War. (*He calls out happily*) Kochanek—Kochanek! (KOCHANEK *appears*) We are ready to go, my friend.

KOCHANEK. Yes, sir—follow me.

EVERYBODY follows KOCHANEK and ERNEST, moving slowly. Suddenly the YOUNGEST BURLESQUE COMIC comes back to the table and looks at the cards. He lifts one, then the other, then a good many. Then he puts them all together, shuffles them, cuts them seven times, then very ceremoniously takes a card. He looks at it, is obviously pleased with it, and decides to take another. This card pleases him, too. He takes another. They are all wonderful. He puts his three cards back into the deck, puts the deck in his pocket and goes, but as he goes he allows himself to trip and fall in the burlesque comedy manner. He gets right up and goes on.

ACT THREE

It is six months later, and the happy funeral is taking place in the Hungarian Restaurant on a platform which has been built for the purpose. On the platform is a handsome casket, and one of the BURLESQUE COMICS, in the costume of a Priest. On a table are plates of food, bottles, glasses, bowls, and so on. Around the table and near it are many people: PÁL SZENT-GYORGYI, his WOMAN, COLONEL HUGH-MAN, his woman ELINORE, the other TWO BURLESQUE COMICS, in costume: one as Death, the other as Gayety—clown, or jester; the late ERNEST HUGHMAN'S woman STELLA; and AUGUST himself, in formal clothes, walking about nervously. The GYPSY TRIO is playing Pragnienie, Pragnienie. The GYPSY GIRL is standing by, in loneliness. The WAITER is serving everybody.

PRIEST-COMIC. (*Opening and closing a book, and rolling out a yo-yo*) My friends, I do not have to tell you the reason for this happy occasion. We have all read the telegram. Ernest Hughman is gone, and in accordance with his own wishes we are here to celebrate his exit. August Hughman, his friend—his brother almost—is here, and in his person, in the absence of the person of his brother, shall occupy the casket when the ceremony begins. Unfortunately August Hughman's wife Becky—whom we all know and love—is *not* here, having been called away last night three minutes after the arrival of the telegram. She was called away by one who is also not here in person, but shall be any minute now. I refer to a man (or woman) we do not know yet—one who is still unknown, in person, even to his own mother, and more so to his own father. It is fitting that as we celebrate the departure of a man we all know, and love, we also celebrate the arrival of one we do not yet know, but love just the same. We are out of touch with the friend who has gone, but we are not altogether out of touch with the friend who is coming in—or out, as the case may be. We do not know about these things and the man gone may be the one who is arriving, while the one coming in may be the one who is leaving. It is the custom on an occasion such as this for everybody to cry, even though—if the circumstance is a sorrowful one, and we are not sure that it is or is not—the man who should be most saddened by it is the one who is dead; but *he* cannot enjoy the sorrow, or whatever is right and fitting for him to enjoy, or not. Therefore, since the man himself is not here to be sorry, he has asked us, who are here, *not* to be sorry, and insofar as it is in our natures to be happily inclined we must be so inclined now, and if possible more *so* inclined than ever. The only two men who might tell us whether it is sad or joyous to leave here, or to arrive, are speechless, and yet they alone have departed and arrived— or will arrive soon. We respect their silence humbly, and do not urge them to try to break it, since if they *did* we might be confused. That is to say, if they broke their silence and told us what we do not know, we might be so pleased to have once arrived as to find leaving unbearable, or so *displeased* as to wish to leave immediately. But fortunately both of our friends are speechless, one permanently, the other temporarily, and we are grateful to them for it. If departure is an occasion for sorrow, then arrival is also an occasion for sorrow—but we have decided among ourselves—even though we are only a few of the people in the world—that this is *not* an occasion for sorrow, but an occasion for happiness, and therefore arrival is also an occasion for happiness. However, if there are any here who wish to weep—for any reason—their tears will be accepted with gratitude. It is not necessary for them to weep only for the man gone—they shall not be asked why they weep, and it will not matter if they do so because *he* has gone, and not they; or because they shall some day go; or because they enjoy weeping; or because it is all so confusing. Any kind of mourning will be gratefully accepted, as it is a kind of happiness for the mourner. Now, it is not my purpose to tire you with talk, but to set the stage, so to speak, for the ceremony itself. First, more food and drink for each of you—but with music. (*The* GYPSY TRIO *begins playing, and* EVERYBODY *eats and drinks happily. The music stops*) Next, the casket— The time has come for the casket to be occupied. (*Calling*) Mr. Hughman—the casket!

AUGUST (*Confused, worried*) The casket? It's there beside you.

PRIEST-COMIC. Yes, but the time has come for the casket to be occupied.

AUGUST. Occupied?

PRIEST-COMIC. Yes, you are to lie in the casket for everyone to see, and after that you are to sit up and watch the celebration, or to instruct the players and the speakers.

AUGUST. Is it time already? I don't know what's happened. Is she all right? Is the Infant all right?

PRIEST-COMIC. We are in touch, and shall be promptly informed. This is the immediate matter. Will you lie down in the casket, please, so that we may proceed?

AUGUST. (*Going onto the platform*) I must be informed promptly. I cannot just lie in the casket forever. (*He stands in the opening of the casket, then wiggles himself into it, and disappears. He sits up*) I must be told immediately.

PRIEST-COMIC. You shall be told. Now, please lie down, so that everyone may walk to the casket, look at you, and pass by.

AUGUST. I would like no dawdling, please, and no questions, if possible.

PRIEST-COMIC. You must be gracious, even though you are on the verge of becoming a father. It is not our intention to *tell* anyone *how* he shall enjoy this celebration. Please lie down.

AUGUST. It is very warm in here.

PRIEST-COMIC. It is furnished better than most homes. Lie down, please.

AUGUST. Very well. (*He lies down and disappears.*)

PRIEST-COMIC. Now, then. The time has come to look into the casket. We have all done so before, and we have always been shocked that what has been in it has been dead, not alive. Now, we shall not be shocked, for while the house is warm and narrow, the man who inhabits it is himself warmer and

a little narrower. He is wearing the proper costume for burial,
but sometime tonight he shall take it off—and perhaps a
bath. Now, then, one at a time, please—come up and look
into the casket. It is now occupied.

COLONEL. (*Goes up onto the platform to the casket, stands looking down into it*) You do not look as well as many I have
seen.

AUGUST. (*Sitting up*) Why should I look well? My wife is about
to become a mother. I am about to become a father. Between
the two of us, another is about to come along and breathe.
But *will* he breathe? That's the question. Will the Infant
breathe? All infants have done so. They have all waited until
the right moment and then they have breathed, but suppose
this one does not breathe? Suppose he changes his mind?
Suppose he refuses to take a breath? What then? Where am
I, then? Where is she? And where is the Infant?

COLONEL. Oh, he'll breathe all right. You needn't fret about
that. Why wouldn't he breathe?

AUGUST. I am a stubborn man, and once when I was angry I
did not eat for a week. I was seven years old, and refused to
eat. Suppose the Infant comes along angry and decides he
doesn't want any part of it? I'm a stubborn man, and he's
my son. Suppose he decides he would much rather stay put?
What then? Where am I?

COLONEL. My son, the Infant will breathe. He won't know any
better. He will burst into tears the moment he feels the cold
pressure of air upon his skin, and the swift rush of open space
upon his ear-drums. Once he starts bawling, he'll be breathing, and then it's all over—he's born, he's here, he's alive,
and God love him, he's human.

AUGUST. Suppose he chooses not to cry? Suppose he decides it's
all nonsense, not the least bit worthy of tears, and refuses
to bother? He *might*, you know. I'm a stubborn man and
never saw much sense to it—until now—and now the only
thing I want is for *him* to burst into tears, so I can burst into
tears, too—and be glad.

COLONEL. Lie down, lie down—he'll burst into tears all right.
I did and you did, and *who* wouldn't? Just lie down and rest.

He's not going to be the first man to enter the world. There have been other entrances. Lie down—you do not look well—but you are alive, I'll say that.

AUGUST lies down, the COLONEL moves away, and steps down from the platform. The late Ernest Hughman's woman, STELLA, now steps to the casket and looks down. She looks long and painfully, then begins to cry. AUGUST sits up.

AUGUST. Stella! What are you crying about? I'm the one who's troubled—Becky's the one who's in pain—the *Infant's* the one who's supposed to cry. What are you crying about?

STELLA. It is so beautiful, so beautiful!

AUGUST. Beautiful? What's beautiful about it? Have you ever been a mother? No. Have you ever been a father? No. Then how can you cry? How can you say it's beautiful?

STELLA. I don't know—but it is, it is. I have never seen anything so beautiful. You look beautiful.

AUGUST. *I* look beautiful.

STELLA. Yes, you look like Ernest, ten years ago. I remember him in Hamlet. You look exactly as he looked then. He was younger, and the best Hamlet of all—everybody said so. He was so beautiful and troubled—and he said his lines so clearly. Lie down again so I can see him as he was then, ten years younger, and full of Hamlet's brooding, just as you are. Please lie down again. (AUGUST *lies down and disappears.* STELLA *looks at him, and bursts into tears again, shaking her head from side to side*) It's so beautiful! I was twenty-three then, and he was thirty-three. (AUGUST *sits up and looks at her*) They said my Ophelia was the best ever, too. It was only ten years ago.

AUGUST. Stella, you're a woman! You understand such things. It's in your blood. How is she? Is she all right? Is she going to be able to make it all right?

STELLA. (*Weeping*) Everybody died in Hamlet, and now— (*She is overcome.*)

AUGUST. Stella, how is she? Is she going to be all right? (*Shout-*

ing to the PRIEST-COMIC) Has no word come? Is the Infant breathing?

PRIEST-COMIC. Be patient—be patient! A man is not made in a moment. His making takes as long as the making of a mountain of rock. He is not to be rushed, but will come along in his own time, dawdling and stopping to pick flowers. Be patient. We'll bring you the news when it comes.

AUGUST. Stella, you're a woman. How is she?

STELLA. Lie down and let me have one last look at Ernest in Hamlet. Farewell, farewell!

She almost forces AUGUST down. She looks at him tenderly, turns away, sobbing, moves along, and then steps down off the platform. The next to come to the casket is the BUR-LESQUE COMIC who represents Death. He is dressed in Death's white robe, but he acts like what he is: a burlesque comic.

DEATH-COMIC. What's this? A man? What happened, fellow—died?

AUGUST. (*Sitting up*) Not yet, but I've got a good start. Have you ever been a father?

DEATH-COMIC. I? A father. I've been Father and Mother, *both*.

AUGUST. (*Shouting*) Has no word come? Is there no message yet?

DEATH-COMIC. Message? (*He raps his knuckles on the casket*) There's your message, fellow. Listen. (*He raps*) Hear that? Wood—all wood, and good for ten years, if the man inside could count them.

AUGUST. I've got to know what's happened. Is he breathing yet? That's the question.

DEATH-COMIC. If it's breathing you want to hear, hear this. (*He breathes deeply, holds it, then exhales*) There's breathing for you. Inhale. (*He inhales*) Exhale. (*He exhales*) I've a cold in my lungs, but even so I still breathe.

AUGUST. Not you, the Infant, the Infant!

DEATH-COMIC. I *was* the Infant. I was the Infant in my day, and breathed, and having breathed breathe still. Listen. (*He breathes fast and furious*) Have you heard better breathing?

That is my best breathing, and it is still the Infant doing it.
Lie down now, fellow, lie down.

AUGUST lies down. The DEATH-COMIC passes by and steps
down off the platform. The next to come to the casket is
the COLONEL's woman, ELINORE. She nods to AUGUST politely.
He sits up.

AUGUST. Why do you greet me?

ELINORE. (*Cheerfully, as if it were a game at a pleasant party*)
Oh, I know you're not dead. I wasn't born yesterday, you
know.

AUGUST. I know, I know, and I wish the Infant *had* been.

ELINORE. Why, it's as plain as the nose on your face that you're
not dead. Who ever heard of a dead man sitting up and
talking?

AUGUST. Who said I was dead? I'm simply waiting for the Infant, that's all.

ELINORE. But it's all so simple, I don't see how you expect to
fool anyone. But why isn't Ernest here?

AUGUST. He couldn't come.

ELINORE. (*Laughing*) Oh, nonsense. Why isn't Ernest here?

AUGUST. (*Shouting*) Somebody tell the woman why Ernest isn't
here. What I want to know is why the *Infant* isn't here. Tell
her, somebody.

PRIEST-COMIC. Ernest isn't here, Ma'am, because he's there.

ELINORE. Where?

PRIEST-COMIC. Wherever they go when they go, and where that
is *I* don't know.

ELINORE. He was a soldier, I know, but they give them fur-
loughs, don't they?

PRIEST-COMIC. If they find them, and if there's time, they do.

ELINORE. Is Ernest lost?

PRIEST-COMIC. The telegram doesn't say. It only says he's dead.

ELINORE. *Dead?* What do you mean?

PRIEST-COMIC. He's dead, and I don't know *what* I mean.

ELINORE. Why, what in the world are you talking about?

PRIEST-COMIC. I don't know, Ma'am.

ELINORE. (*Gaily, delighted*) This is such fun, and so original. But you're not dead!

AUGUST. (*Bitterly*) How do you know?

ELINORE. (*Laughing*) I know, I know. One can tell. Anybody could get into a casket— I could myself—you're not dead.

AUGUST. Have you ever been a mother?

ELINORE. (*Laughing gaily*) That would be telling, wouldn't it? Ask me no questions—(*She laughs gaily*)—and I'll tell you no lies. (*Seriously, in her own fine way*) But I do wish Ernest would stop his hiding and come and enjoy the fun. (*To the* PRIEST-COMIC) Where is the boy?

PRIEST-COMIC. It is not a question of where, Ma'am, but what. And the answer to that is not worth giving.

ELINORE. What is he? What is Ernest? Why, everyone knows he's an actor.

PRIEST-COMIC. And where does he act?

ELINORE. Ernest has appeared in New York, Boston, Philadelphia, Baltimore, Chicago, San Francisco, and dozens of other cities. He acts where his play is, or goes.

PRIEST-COMIC. And where is his play? Where has it gone?

ELINORE. He left the theatre for a moment, to enlist in the Army.

COLONEL. (*Seriously*) My dear, Ernest was killed. This is his funeral, as he wished it to be—a happy funeral.

ELINORE. (*Laughing, then stopping*) I don't understand.

AUGUST. (*To the* PRIEST-COMIC) Show her the telegram. (*The* PRIEST-COMIC *goes to* ELINORE *quickly with the telegram.*)

ELINORE. (*Holding the telegram but not reading it*) What does this mean?

PRIEST-COMIC. This—this piece of paper—is the Official Announcement of the man's death. Official—and final! There. Read the words.—Killed in action.

ELINORE. Killed in action? What sort of action?

PRIEST-COMIC. Soldier action, I suppose, although, as he was an actor, it might have been the action of acting. He might have been bowing at the time. The announcement does not give details. It simply says, in Biblical language, that he was killed in action three weeks ago.

ELINORE. Ernest?

PRIEST-COMIC. Ernest was his name alive, Ernest it is dead. (*He takes the telegram, goes and stands behind the pulpit with the book on it, the toy horn, the yo-yo, and the rubber ball, which every now and then he bounces.*)

ELINORE. (*Sincerely troubled*) I'm sure I enjoy the spirit of this pleasant party, but—(*Her voice cracks*)—I'm afraid you are not playing fair. You are withholding something from me. What is it?

AUGUST. (*Impatiently*) Ernest is dead. We are withholding nothing. You are withholding. He's dead, and unless I die of worry first, I am about to become a father.

ELINORE. (*Her lips trembling*) You mean Ernest is *actually* dead?

AUGUST. As actually as actually can be.

ELINORE. (*She looks around, tears in her eyes*) I think you're all horrid. I despise every one of you—to carry on in such a fashion. (*She begins to cry*) I'm ashamed of myself, laughing at a time like this. You've tricked me. I didn't know, I didn't know. (*Pathetically*) I'm going to faint.

PRIEST-COMIC. (*To* DEATH-COMIC) Catch the woman, as she faints.

The DEATH-COMIC rushes onto the platform and stands behind ELINORE, with his arms open, ready to catch her. She turns and gives him a dirty look.

ELINORE. (*With anger*) Go away, you silly thing! Don't stand behind me—with your arms open. You are from burlesque, but *I* am from the theatre. How dare you stand behind me?

DEATH-COMIC. What's this? I come to catch her as she falls. She turns and mocks my kind intention. (*Politely*) Will you faint, Madam?

ELINORE. I'll *box* your ears!—that's what I'll do if you try any of your low comic tricks on me. Your theatre and mine are as far apart as hell and heaven, and your play and mine are as different as sin and innocence. Now, go away—go away—don't tease me any more. (*To* AUGUST) I am ashamed of you—

ashamed! To sit in such a place when your own brother is dead. You are all disgusting, but you especially.

AUGUST. It was his own wish. He made me swear to give this funeral. I received the telegram last night. I didn't know he would be killed—I believed he wouldn't—and I didn't know when the telegram would come—but I *had* given my word. The telegram came exactly when the Infant began *his* coming. If I had known the two were to happen together, I would not have promised. How can I be happy—when I am here for *him*, not for myself, and should be where the Infant's coming in, and where its mother is allowing him—or, I hope—urging him to come in? (*To the* PRIEST-COMIC) No word yet?

PRIEST-COMIC. Soon, now, soon! I've told you. It takes time. (*To* ELINORE) Madam, you are holding up the parade. Look, and pass by, as the custom is.

ELINORE. I despise you all! (*Weeping, she goes*) Poor Ernest! Poor, poor sweet Ernest!

COLONEL. (*The* COLONEL *helps her down from the platform*) Now, now! You mustn't take it hard, for after all he died for you and me.

ELINORE. (*Bitterly*) I don't care! I don't care what he died for! You're all swine, and I'm going to faint. (*She faints into the* COLONEL'S *arms. He drags her away.*)

PRIEST-COMIC. (*Working the yo-yo*) All right, now, let's keep it moving. Let the next mourner move along. Hurry, now. (*To* AUGUST) And you, sir, lie down.

The next person to come up onto the platform is PÁL SZENT-GYORGYI. He looks into the casket at AUGUST, then stretches himself out, getting very big.

PÁL. Zlodziej, zlodziej! Ho ha—ha ha! Ho ha—ha ha ha! (*He becomes limp with sorrow, and grows almost small, looking into the casket, fascinated. He whispers*) Christian man—no die! (*Almost shouting*) Pál Szent-Gyorgyi lift him! (*He reaches into the casket and lifts* AUGUST *up*) Christian man no die. Pál lift him up!

AUGUST. No, no, Pál! I must stay here until the ceremony is over.

PÁL. No—no! Pál fight smierc. Nobody die if Pál fight. (*He tugs at* AUGUST.)

AUGUST. Take him away—take him away!

The THREE COMICS fall on PÁL, who struggles with them. His WOMAN hurries to him. He stops struggling to look at her.

PÁL'S WOMAN. (*Softly*) Pál! Pál!

PÁL nods several times sadly. The COMICS release him. He puts his arms around his WOMAN and the DEATH-COMIC. AUGUST lies down in the casket and disappears. PÁL moves with the other two closer to the casket, and looks down a good long time. Then he looks at his wife, then at the DEATH-COMIC, then back into the casket, then at his wife. He kisses her on the mouth, then looks at the DEATH-COMIC and kisses him on the forehead.

DEATH-COMIC. What's this? A kiss?

PÁL. (*Releasing his* WOMAN *and the* DEATH-COMIC, *turning to the* ORCHESTRA) Pragnienie, Pragnienie! (*The music begins immediately, and* PÁL *dances*) Ho ha—ha ha! Christian man no die! Ho ha—ha ha ha! (*He suddenly takes his* WOMAN *by the hand and they dance together. He then holds his free hand out to the* DEATH-COMIC, *who takes his hand and joins the dance*) Ho ha—ha ha! Pragnienie, Pragnienie! Woman—my friend! Smierc—my friend! Woman—I love! Smierc—I love! Ho ha—ha ha! (*The music stops. The dance ends. The* DEATH-COMIC *goes off with* PÁL'S WOMAN *for a drink.* PÁL *turns to* AUGUST) How you feel?

AUGUST. I'm worried, Pál! Nothing like this has ever happened to me before. I'd feel fine if I knew the Infant were breathing, and the Mother peacefully sleeping, but I don't know anything. They've sent no message. I don't know how I feel. I've never been a father before, and they won't tell me if I'm a father now.

PÁL. You gonna be fodder?

AUGUST. I *hope* to be. Everything is ordered for it, and the time has come, but the message hasn't.

PÁL. Why you sit in box?

AUGUST. To help make the funeral a happy one, as my brother wished it to be.

PÁL. Your *brother—who*?

AUGUST. Ernest Hughman—you remember, don't you?

PÁL. Soldier?

AUGUST. Yes, Pál.

PÁL. Soldier die?

AUGUST. Yes, Pál.

PÁL. Where soldier die?

AUGUST. The telegram does not say. It's a military secret, but he died somewhere in the War.

PÁL. (*Angry*) War got no secret. War no good. War murder baby. War murder young man. War kill Christian man. War murder Jesus. Pál no believe in War. Pál believe in baby—Jesus. Baby, baby, O little baby! Come to bad world and live for Pál. (*He makes a cross of his body, and his face becomes deeply pained*) Then baby—smiling baby—die for Pál! Baby come with love, but War murder baby, send him back. Hey hoh—baby, sweet baby! (*He turns away and steps down off the platform*) Hey hoh, hey hoh!

PRIEST-COMIC. (*Bounces tennis ball*) Come along, come along. Who's next?

AUGUST. Send the Gypsy Girl! Maybe she can tell me if the Infant breathes now.

PRIEST-COMIC. (*Blows the toy horn*) Gypsy Girl! To the casket, please. (*To* AUGUST) Lie down, now.

AUGUST lies down. The GYPSY GIRL goes to the casket and looks down at AUGUST. AUGUST sits up.

AUGUST. Is the Infant breathing? Where are your cards?

GYPSY GIRL. I have left them. They tell the truth, but I do not like their manner of telling it. The truth is always there for telling of one sort or another, but I do not like the way the cards tell the truth. I tell fortunes no more. I am waiting to learn if any sort of telling of the truth is good. I do not know. Perhaps it would be best to leave it all untold.

AUGUST. Whatever is best is no matter to me now. Only tell me is the Infant breathing, is the Mother sleeping peacefully?

GYPSY GIRL. Two things are most alike of all, and yet most unalike—that is why I have left the cards, and do not know if with them I should also leave the search for truth. Two things: coming and going. To come is to begin going, and therefore the same as going. I've left the cards. I cannot answer anything.

GAYETY-COMIC. (*Leaps onto the platform*) Here are the cards. I've kept them six months, but the card of Death is not among them, it is with the man whose death we celebrate, so take the cards—free now of Death—and tell the troubled man if the Infant breathes, the Mother sleeps. Here. Take the cards.

He thrusts the cards out to the GYPSY GIRL. She looks at them, somewhat angry with herself and angry at the cards, and yet somehow deeply tempted to take them back—without Death—to see if now their way of telling the truth may be better. The GAYETY-COMIC waits, watching her, then speaks.

GAYETY-COMIC. Take them! You are old friends, and want each other. I can see that you do, and that you need each other. So here they are. I've saved them for you. Take them, shuffle them, and ask the man to take his card. Death is not in them now. Death has served its purpose, and cannot serve it again. Tell the man what he wishes to know. Is the Infant breathing? Here. Take the cards. (*The* GYPSY GIRL *takes the cards*) That's right. You're a sensible Gypsy Girl, and pretty, too. I have never believed in Gypsies, or in telling any fortune but my own, but if you are a Gypsy, and not simply another pretty girl; and if you must tell the fortunes of other people, and leave your own untold, then take the cards and be what you prefer, and tell what you must. I believe in nothing more alarming than the kiss, and want no other fortune. Since this is so, and I have kept the cards for you, and restored them to you—no longer made impure by the presence of Death—then I deserve a confirmation of my own faith—or, in other words, a kiss!

GYPSY GIRL. You are a—

GAYETY-COMIC. Wait, wait! I do not want my fortune told, other than its greatest end, or beginning: a kiss with you. (*He thrusts out his head*) You will not refuse. It would be unholy. (*He pushes out a little more, his mouth almost touching the* GYPSY GIRL's *mouth*) You've very little distance to go. But if you make the journey, do not make it in poverty. Come down to my country with all the sweetness of your nation. And do not come for a tiny visit, but stay awhile.

The GYPSY GIRL makes the journey and stays a good long while. The GAYETY-COMIC lifts a foot backward slowly, relishing the wondrous flavor of wealth and good fortune, holds the foot suspended there as if it were holding the swift-passing delight, finally brings the foot down again, stirs a hand out in space, rises up slowly, and soon instead of being under the GYPSY GIRL he is over her. Then he puts his arms around her, and moves with the kiss from the realm of the allegorical to the realm of the real, or at any rate the realm of no fooling. The GYPSY GIRL struggles womanfully, but the GAYETY-COMIC has got her well—tricked or not tricked—and holds her until she struggles no more, but tightens herself about him, as he is tightened about her. Then the GAYETY-COMIC breaks it up, stands back, nods smartly, as if to say, O.K.

GAYETY-COMIC. Now, I would thee wed. Would thee wed me?

AUGUST. For God's sake, I am wed and nearly a father. Ask her later. (*He looks at the* GYPSY GIRL) She would thee wed—or *should*—but now, first, let her tell me the story of my fatherhood, if so it is. (*To the* GYPSY GIRL) Tell me, tell me! Am I a Father? Is the Infant here? Is he breathing? Is the Mother sleeping? Shall I step out of this box and be delighted with the joy of it all?

GAYETY-COMIC. You rush me, man! You've had your wedding, and your wife, give another clown a chance. We are all brothers, aren't we? I'd like to suffer fatherhood myself. (*To the* GYPSY GIRL) Wouldst suffer motherhood, whilst I suffer fatherhood?

GYPSY GIRL. (*Confused*) I don't know. (*Suddenly, after riffling the cards in her hands*) Take a card.

GAYETY-COMIC. Good God, I asked you, not the cards. I would not wed them, for their kiss is dry. I seek yours to carry me straight through next winter's snow.

AUGUST. (*Impatiently*) Take a card, take a card! It's sure to be a lucky one—or one she'll say is lucky—or lucky enough. Take any card. It'll do. At a time like hers, any card will be the holy one. Just take it, and let her tell my story, too. I'm dying, while you come to life.

GAYETY-COMIC. What can the cards tell me that I don't know? I want her through all winter, don't I? (*To the* GYPSY GIRL) Here. Give me the cards. I'll be the fortune-teller. You have your fortune told. It's time you did, a girl of nineteen years or so.

GYPSY GIRL. Twenty-one, which is a number not to take lightly.

GAYETY-COMIC. I'll take it heavily and lightly both, as you prefer. It *is* truly a number, and it's seldom given. Give me the cards and I'll tell your fortune. (*He almost takes the cards out of her hands. He fools with them, looks upon them with a smile, since he knows them all, front or back*) Close your eyes, now. Here. Take your choice! It's sure to be me!

He has pushed a card out beyond the others. The GYPSY GIRL takes this card, looks at it and smiles.

AUGUST. What card is it?

GAYETY-COMIC. Look at her. Are you blind?

AUGUST. No. Only half-dead. What card is it?

GAYETY-COMIC. It's my card. I don't have to look at the card. I know it's mine. (*To the* GYPSY GIRL) Tell him.

GYPSY GIRL. It *is*. The cards tell the truth, no matter who holds them. This is the card. Here. The Lover. In this corner, the red heart. Here, standing, the man with the sword. Here on the table beside him, the red rose. It is *his* card.

GAYETY-COMIC. (*Cockily*) Take another card. (*The* GYPSY GIRL *does so*) Tell him what the second card is.

GYPSY GIRL. (*Happily, amazed*) It is *my* card. The Loved One. The twin of his card. Here in this corner, the red heart again. Here, standing, the woman with the book of life in her hands. And there on the pedestal the monument of naked love, with the empty bow.

GAYETY-COMIC. There, you see? (*Swiftly*) Take another card. (*The* GYPSY GIRL *does so*) Now, tell him what the third card is.

GYPSY GIRL. (*Almost solemnly*) It is Marriage. Here, on their knees, holding hands, are the man and the woman of the first two cards, before the Priest. Behind the Priest is the pillar of the church, the cross, the window, and the burning candles.

AUGUST. (*Impatiently*) That's fine, but what about me?

GAYETY-COMIC. Take another card. Take them all, one at a time. They'll come out fine, in perfect order. My name is Joe.

GYPSY GIRL. No. Three is all. Three cards tell everything. My name is Mary.

AUGUST. (*Impatiently*) Mary, tell me is the Infant breathing?

GYPSY GIRL. It is.

GAYETY-COMIC. I, Joe, take thee, Mary. That's it. It's done now.

AUGUST. (*Excited*) Wait a minute, wait a minute! Have your marriage ceremony later! Mary, what did you say? Is the Infant breathing?

GYPSY GIRL. It is. It is now breathing.

AUGUST. How do you know? I didn't take a card.

GYPSY GIRL. I know. The message is on its way! You will see.

AUGUST. Are you sure? How did you find out? How do you know?

GYPSY GIRL. The Infant began to breathe when *I* stopped breathing in the kiss.

AUGUST. Did you stop breathing?

GAYETY-COMIC. She did, and so did I. We almost died.

AUGUST. Mary, is this true?

GYPSY GIRL. It is! The message is on its way. You will see.

AUGUST. And how is the Mother? Is she sleeping peacefully?

GYPSY GIRL. She is well and happy, deep in the living sleep.

AUGUST. And the Infant, is it man or woman?

GYPSY GIRL. It is man, but like himself from first of all, it is man, born of woman.

AUGUST. (*Almost delirious with relief*) I feel weak. (*He looks up*) I thank God. The Infant is here, the Mother sleeps, the Father— (*He falls back into the casket.*)

The GYPSY TRIO hurries to the casket, and look down at AUGUST, crowding one another.

VIOLINIST. He is a father now. Look at him. He's fainted.

GYPSY GIRL. It's nothing. He has gone to her in sleep, but will return soon. Let him stay with her a moment. He will sit up soon. Play a happy song.

The GYPSY TRIO go back to their places and begin playing Pragnienie, Pragnienie. There is singing, dancing, eating and drinking. In the midst of the gaiety, a TELEGRAPH MESSENGER comes in. He stands bewildered a moment, watching and listening. PÁL hands him a drink, which the YOUNG MAN swallows. PÁL takes his hand and drags the MESSENGER into the dance. EVERYBODY is happy. The music stops.

MESSENGER. (*Officially*) Telegram for August Hughman.

AUGUST. Where am I? (AUGUST *sits up in the coffin*) What's happened? Did somebody call out my name?

MESSENGER. Correction. Two telegrams for August Hughman.

AUGUST. (*Looking at the* MESSENGER) I am August Hughman, I believe.

MESSENGER. I have two telegrams for you.

He goes to AUGUST and hands him the two telegrams. AUGUST opens one with shaking hands.

PÁL. What is message?

AUGUST. *This* telegram says I am the father of a seven-pound man. I do not know what this one says.

GAYETY-COMIC. Read it, read it, and tell us.

AUGUST opens telegram and reads it. He falls back into the coffin, and the telegram drops to the floor. The GAYETY-COMIC picks it up and reads it.

PÁL. What's message? What's message?

GAYETY-COMIC. (*With importance*) My friends, I have a most happy message for you. The man whose funeral we are celebrating is not dead. He is alive.

PÁL. (*Shouting*) Christian man no die! Christian man no die! Pál Szent-Gyorgyi fight smierc, keep Christian man alive!

GAYETY-COMIC. (*Continuing*) The message says that he was lost, but has been found. He was found in a small part in an Army play. The message does not say where he is now, but wherever he is, he is alive. (*To the* GYPSY TRIO) Music, please.

AUGUST. (*Sits up*) Get me out of this terrible tomb. (PÁL *leaps to him and helps him out of the casket to his feet*) Music now, music! The funeral's over. It was a happy funeral. The Infant is born. It was a decent birth. Music, now—dancing and singing.